Joy, associated wit these two concepts, But modern stress is more complex than the familiar episodes of carnage that we see on the evening news. Stress influences our children at school. Stress also affects our performance as adults, influencing our work, our play, and our relationships. Even the lack of Stress can have a negative effect on the elderly.

As a medical doctor, Peter Hanson has seen how stress can affect over 90% of all illnesses, aches, and pains. He also sees a nation turning to drugs and other passive "cures". (One of the fastest growing prescriptions is the anti-depressant category, in pediatrics!) The same insights he gives his patients are here in his book.

When Dr. Hanson self-published ***"The Joy of Stress"*** in 1985, it exploded onto the world's best seller lists. It has sold over a million copies in more than twenty languages, proving the universality of the subject matter. This edition of ***"The Joy of Stress"*** is completely re-written by the author, using the latest input from his busy practice in family medicine and in sports medicine.

While stress is certainly timeless, it has morphed into a truly formidable challenge in the age of the internet. Dr. Hanson's vital perspective gives great action tips to help the reader avoid the pitfalls, and instead turn stress to a positive influence on our health and happiness.

An athlete cannot set a personal-best time on a training track; he or she needs the stress of top competition to achieve records. An actor gives his best performance when facing the stress of a live audience. In just the same way, you can learn Dr. Hanson's secrets to turn the stress in your life into a huge benefit, instead of a fatal detriment.

Dr. Peter G. Hanson has had more than his share of high stress levels, as a medical doctor, public speaker, author, and co-developer of the "FaceMaster" for Suzanne Somers.

His *"The Joy of Stress"* brings up-dated tools and insights to the reader, to help each person develop a unique strategy for their own stresses.

Dr. Hanson lives in Toronto.

Cover photograph by William Baumgartner/Denver.
Cover design by Salli Ratts.
Printed in the USA.

The Joy of Stress

By Peter G. Hanson, M.D

The Joy of Stress

By Peter G. Hanson, M.D.

Forward from the late Sir Edmund Hillary, KBE

www.stressipedia.com

 Address inquiries to the publisher: StressWorks, 7343 El Camino Real, Suite #164, Atascadero, CA 93422

Hanson, Peter G. (Peter George), 1947-
The Joy of Stress

Bibliography: p. 301
ISBN: 978-0-9884620-0-7

1.Stress (Psychology). 2. Stress (Physiology).
3. Health I. StressWorks (Atascadero, California)
II. Title

BF575.S75H36 2005 158'.1 C84-099758-2

Printed in U.S.A.

Illustrated by Barrie Maguire

This book is dedicated to the memory of Sir Edmund Hillary, Conqueror of Mount Everest

This book was inspired by all the good things that can come out of stress. One of my greatest examples of this spirit was Sir Edmund Hillary, with whom I was privileged to spend much private time over our three decades of friendship. He said he would have had no interest in climbing Everest if it was just a quiet walk in the park. Without the formidable stresses of this climb Ed would never have learned the great strengths that were inside him. Even in late age, he would continue to test himself against the elements.

But Sir Edmund's greatest pride was in the work he did with his beloved Sherpas in Nepal. When he arrived in Nepal in the early 1950's, the local Sherpas suffered from basic illnesses like goiter, caused by the lack of iodine in the diet. They also had a very high childhood mortality rate, and many deformities from untreated fractures. He started a program of medical aid, as well as establishing an infrastructure for clean water and reforestation. However, at no time did he work for the Sherpas; he always worked with them. Instead of airlifting pre-fab structures, he enlisted local labor to carry in supplies from the nearest airport, and to build the stone walls and doors needed. He always knew that the sense of shared efforts (and stress) would generate lasting results. The Sherpas have now established schools, nursing clinics, and hospitals, and have even started sending high-school graduates to foreign universities, returning with vital skills in agriculture, medicine, and engineering. This book is dedicated to his great legacy.

Contents

Foreword

by Sir Edmund Hillary, K.B.E., conqueror of Mount Everest (1919-2008)

All my life I have been attracted to adventure — Mount Everest, overland to the South Pole, driving jet boats up the Ganges River, and a multitude of other challenges. There has always been an element of danger. But if there hadn't been, I doubt if I would have gone to the trouble. Danger is stimulating, and challenge makes the effort worthwhile. So in a way, I have enjoyed stress, and life would have been rather boring without it. In reading *The Joy of Stress*, I was relieved to find that my involvement in stress has probably been to my medical benefit.

Peter Hanson's approach to stress is unique. It is refreshing, positive, and practical. If I had the courage to try myself against all his recommendations, I would probably fail miserably. But I have the feeling that his program for managing stress will enable most people to live a happier and longer life, and they'll be a little more successful, too.

Dr. Hanson and Sir Edmund Hillary share a humorous moment in the author's backyard.

In the years I have known Peter as a friend, I have noticed that he practices what he preaches. Peter is quite a "goer", who seems to thrive on stress. As a busy medical doctor, entertaining public speaker, author, publisher, and fund-raiser, he always tries to achieve excellence. Yet he still finds time for his family, and for energetic sporting and musical activities.

Peter believes it is far better to actively master the stresses in one's life than to be oppressed by them. His principles can help all of us to become successful and still enjoy life to its fullest.

— Sir Edmund Hillary

Preface

Modern medicine seems to have a miracle for every disease. Cumbersome and risky surgeries are now replaced by high-tech office procedures. Blurry vision? We can toss away our eyeglasses and have a laser restore perfect vision. Heart attack? We can open a clogged coronary artery without any surgery, just inflate a small balloon at the end of a catheter. We can remove gall stones and kidney stones by smashing them with sound waves, without ever having to cut through the skin.

Diagnostic innovations such as the MRI and PET scanners are saving millions of lives with early detection of cancers and other diseases. Stem cell research promises amazing options for diseases now untreatable. The Prescription Drug Industry is dazzling us with new cures for everything from the degeneration to inflammation, giving the elderly back their athletic prowess, as well as their youthful libidos. Our senior citizens are getting more senior than ever before, living much longer than the biblical "three-score-and-ten" or seventy years. With today's inflation, the age of sixty is the new forty, eighty is now the new sixty, and record numbers are celebrating their hundredth birthdays. It would seem that Medicine has finally found the fountain of youth.

However, if we look beyond the adult headlines, we see a disturbing picture. Our children are getting bigger than ever before. Obesity has become the new epidemic of modern life. Even in third world countries, obesity has become a bigger threat than hunger. For the first time in history, the rich are thin, while the poor are fat. Diabetes that used to be called "old age" is now so common in children that it had to be renamed "type-2". The childhood culture of exercise in playgrounds and sandlots has been replaced by a cult of sitting, in front of flat screens. The rosy "apple" cheeks of fitness have been replaced by the sad eyes of couch-potatoes. The two fastest growing categories of profit for the Prescription Drug Cartel are for obesity and depression, *in children.*

Today's bloated and out-of-shape children will not live long enough to benefit from our medical miracles. In fact, if a ten-year old child is a hundred pounds overweight, there is a very good chance that he or she will die before the age of fifty, while both parents are still alive. Estate-planning will not only need to provide funds for the kids' college and weddings; extra money could be needed for the kids' funerals.

So what are we doing wrong? Primarily, we have viewed our health as something we acquire *passively*, instead of something we earn *actively*. The media celebrates this paradigm with "reality make-over" shows, demonstrating that it is easier to reshape a flabby body with surgery than with sit-ups. When television broadcasts its regular programs, the actors are all beautiful, making the viewer want to be thin; but the ads are for products that will make the viewer fat and slothful. Schools have taken daily exercise out of the curriculum, and replaced it with soda-machines, fast-foods and Ritalin. Many doctors are enabling the passivity culture; instead of telling a sad, obese child to start exercising and stop over-eating, the doctor reaches for a prescription for Prozac and Lipitor.

To make matters worse, our bodies are programmed for the wrong kinds of stress. Our evolution gave us primitive reflexes for the stress of attacks in the jungle. Our grandparents left us primitive rules for the stress of assembly lines in the industrial age. But today our stresses are from a new source; the information age. We need to reprogram our antique defenses to protect us from modern stress, and to let us thrive.

As a family doctor, and, more recently, as a specialist in pain management and sports medicine, I see what kind of a *disease* each patient has. But, far more importantly, I also see what kind of a *patient* each disease has. When someone falls ill with a heart attack, dies of lung cancer, or simply seems to be catching one virus after another, it is wrong to blame passive "bad luck". Most likely, these examples of poor health come from active mismanagement, usually in response to stress.

The easily correctable nature of this mismanagement does not diminish the tragedy. Under stress, mismanaged people do not *feel* at their peak. On the job, they do not *perform* to the best of their abilities. Inside their bodies, their immune systems are not offering full protection. As a result, mismanagement of stress is the biggest cause of anxiety and depression, illness, and, ultimately, premature death.

In spite of countless books on stress, health, diets, success, and motivation, most people still don't get it. *Passivity may be popular, but it sure doesn't replace activity.*

Actively managed, stress can be defused as a danger, and can be harnessed as an ally. On a personal level that means stress can make us happier and healthier. On an economic level, good stress management techniques can vastly reduce the costs of health care, as well as the costs of accidents, absenteeism, and absent-mindedness.

Many books on stress are written by specialists with a narrow view—cardiologists, psychologists, nutritionists, and esoteric researchers. But most patients still turn to their own family doctors to find out how this specialized advice relates to their personal circumstances.

In my decades of active medical practice I have been privileged to have a unique window on the practical aspects of people's lives. I have delivered over one thousand babies, and seen thousands of patients in the Emergency Room. In my office, I have seen everything from pediatrics to geriatrics. I have also done thousands of house calls, which gives valuable information as to the context of the patient's lifestyle. In the past decade and a half, I have specialized in pain management in Denver, using acupuncture to give patients back their lives, and to get them off many of their prescription drugs. With patients as diverse as professional athletes (such as the NHL's LA Kings, Colorado Avalanche, and the NFL's Denver Broncos) and chronic sufferers of migraines, back pains or arthritis, I have seen people at their most stressful times. In my current office in Toronto, I continue to see the universal nature of stress in family practice. Resolving patient symptoms by focusing on root causes is indeed gratifying. And stress is certainly a ubiquitous root cause, that effects almost every disease we see.

I have traveled the world as a motivational speaker, helping corporations and business associations improve their performance when they are under stress. Corporations are only as strong as the people that work for them, so I often do pre-speech diagnostics with questionnaires as well as interviews.

The results have added to my base of patient input, giving me a very large and practical sampling of the effects of stress in the real world.

An experienced teacher can soon predict which students will excel and which will fail. In just the same way, a medical doctor can foretell which patients will live long and healthy lives, and which will suffer premature (and, these days, largely self-induced) disasters.

I've given my advice and seen it work consistently when heeded. I've also tilted at a few "windmills" when I knew my advice was falling on deaf ears. But through it all, I've been on the front lines, not in the research libraries. I've seen the grief in the eyes of a young mother when I told her that her husband's "mild heartburn" during snow-shoveling turned out to be a fatal heart attack. I've had to console two young children after a fatal car crash; their parents had buckled them safely into their car seats, but had died on impact with the front seat-belts left unattached. I've seen the shocked look on the face of a thirty-nine year old cancer victim who knew all about the risks of cigarettes in general, but didn't think these risks applied to her in particular. I've had to confront the family of a suicide victim, telling them that their son's "cry for help" overdose of a seemingly harmless bottle of iron supplements turned out to be fatal.

I don't mean to imply that all deaths can be prevented, or—as in the case of childhood cancers—even explained. But a casino can thrive by stacking the odds just a *little* in its favor. You owe it to yourself, and to those who love you, to stack all the odds you can in your own favor. The stakes couldn't be higher; your health, your wealth, and your happiness depend on it.

It is the objective of this book to help you turn

the tables, to do your part in shattering the current standards of longevity as well as quality of life. This book will give you practical advice that you can put to work immediately, and continue to use forever. If you are active about your health choices, you will get control over your life. If you stay passive, you will get the consequences.

Some of the points raised in this book are self-evident. Many others are known by your doctors, and have already been explained to you. However, there is much here that will be new, both in terms of facts as well as perspectives.

To begin at the beginning, we will review your basic anatomy. Under stress, certain physiological changes take place. Unless you understand these, they could be to your detriment. Second, you must identify and measure the stresses that are facing you. Many of these are well hidden, and, unless recognized, cannot be conquered.

Third, you will learn how to rate your own resistance to stress. Find out if you are "bullet-proof", or a "sitting duck". If you are the latter, you will learn how to make ten simple choices to maximize your resistance to your stresses.

Next comes a brief consideration of the subject of nutrition; a simple bodily requirement that has spawned a litany of silly to dangerous "fad" diets.

We will discuss the modern scourge of obesity, and learn a workable approach to learning to eat normally. After seeing all the failures experienced by serial dieters, I realized that a simple solution was needed. The approach that I recommend is one that can be followed for a lifetime, without hardship, and without having to say goodbye to tasty foods.

Moving on through the book, we review the subject of self-induced stress (Type A behavior).

New insights into harnessing it are presented.

Are you a success? If not, you will probably shorten your financial horizons, as well as your productive life span. With the help of this book, measure your success in the quadrants of finances, personal life, health, and job. Find out how you rate. Learn Hanson's Three Principles to cope with your stresses and to pamper yourself at the same time. See how others fail to solve problems by passively blaming the uncontrollable. See if you can do better, by actively focusing on the controllable truths behind the excuses.

It is my hope that this book will entertain, teach, and motivate you to take control of your life, both in terms of longevity, as well as quality.

Acknowledgments

It took almost a village to help me propel the self-published "Joy of Stress" into the million-seller category, and to have it translated into almost two dozen languages in the past twenty years. This new edition owes much to their help.

I appreciate the fine skills of Salli Ratts who did all the layout and design for this book. Rodger Mohme, my partner in www.stressipedia.com, has been instrumental in helping me edit this book, and transform materials into great information for on-line users. Barrie Maguire did a great job on the art work and layout.

I was fortunate to spend some time at an early age in the presence of a few great icons. The late Dr. Norman Vincent Peale advised me to have positive dreams, and to dare to follow them. (He also told me it was easier to "change the audience" rather than "change the speech", even though I resisted that format for my own subject matter!) The late Dr. Hans Selye visited our hospital in Toronto while I was a young Intern, and he motivated me with his then-radical views on stress and aging. The late Sir Edmund Hillary, K.B.E., conqueror of Everest, gave me the inspiration to climb my own mountains of endeavor, and was gracious enough to offer to do the foreword for his book. Dr. Ken Blanchard offered his guidance, and helpful "one-minute" tips. Dr. Deepak Choprah has also been a great inspiration with his mind-body approach to medicine. I also thank John Elway of the Denver Broncos for spreading the word about my acupuncture after I treated his throwing arm before he went on to win two Super Bowls. Phil Anschutz was also instrumental in exposing me to more professional athletes, when he asked me to treat his LA Kings of the NHL, and his professional soccer players in the MLS. There is much that we can all learn from the elite athletes, especially in terms of performance under stress.

Acknowledgment is also given to the McGraw-Hill Book Company for permission to use the General Adaptation Response from *The Stress of Life* by the late Dr. Hans Selye; to Pergamon Press, Ltd, for permission to use the Holmes-Rahe Social Readjustment Rating Scale; and to Larry Wilson, of the Wilson Learning Corporation, Minneapolis, for permission to use the Social Style Summary and Guideline for Recognition (Appendix A).

Introduction

What's so joyful about stress?

Stress is an individual reaction. A single event, for example speaking to a large audience, can give a positive stress to one person, and a negative stress to another.

Stress can be *fantastic*. Or it can be *fatal*. It's all up to you. As well as respecting the dangers of stress, you can learn to harness its benefits.

Olympic records are not set on the quiet training tracks, but only with the stress of stiff competition, in front of huge crowds. The most efficient work done by a student is often during the stress of facing a deadline for a term paper or exam. The most electric performances don't come out of actors during rehearsals; they occur when the curtain rises before a live audience. The best performance of a trapeze artist will probably be without the safety net.

Serious poker players will play only if significant amounts of money are bet on each hand. With only pennies or toothpicks at stake, the stress of losing is gone, but so too is the intense concentration, the enjoyment of bluffing, and the excitement of winning. Many people with low stress levels at work feel understimulated and seek stress in their spare time. This could take the form of extreme sports such as rock climbing, bungee jumping, sky-diving, or simply riding a roller coaster. Such stresses distract them from their boredom and bring more joy into their lives.

Too much stress, however, can become a negative force. We see evidence of this in our daily news. With the threat of suicide bombers in their midst, fit soldiers in hostile countries can easily have insomnia, anxiety, depression, and ultimately Post Traumatic Stress Disorder. Sadly, we have learned this tragic lesson from the wars in Iraq and Afghanistan, where more of our soldiers are killed by their own hand than by the enemy. Back home, the extra stress of a broken relationship can easily subvert the performance of a singer or athlete, and distract a student during their exams.

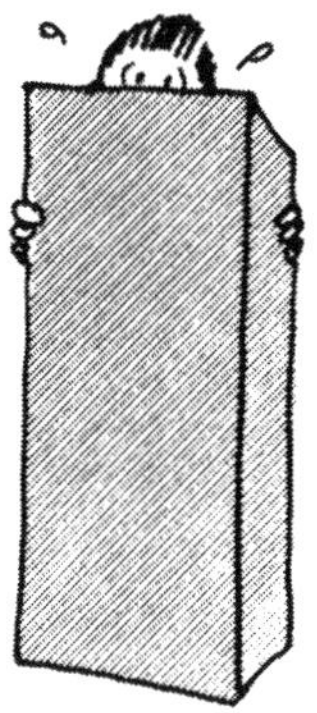

Too little stress can be just as disastrous. The sudden silence gained by retiring from a demanding job into a life of idleness usually promotes death or senility within a few years, unless new stresses and interests can be found. Some retirees find, to their chagrin, that little tasks they used to do well during a busy working day now take all week to complete. What's more, they often end up being done poorly.

As you can see from the graph, increasing stress serves to increase efficiency toward its maximum. Up to this point, it is correct to use the old adage, "If you want something done, ask a busy person."

However, past the critical line, your efficiency rapidly falls, even to below zero. This means that, with too much stress, you can actually become counterproductive-worse than useless! If you are close to this critical line, then even the addition of a minor task to your hectic schedule (for example, trying first thing Monday morning to find where your dog buried your car keys) could be enough to push you past your peak. When you are in that state, even things you normally do well will be beyond your grasp.

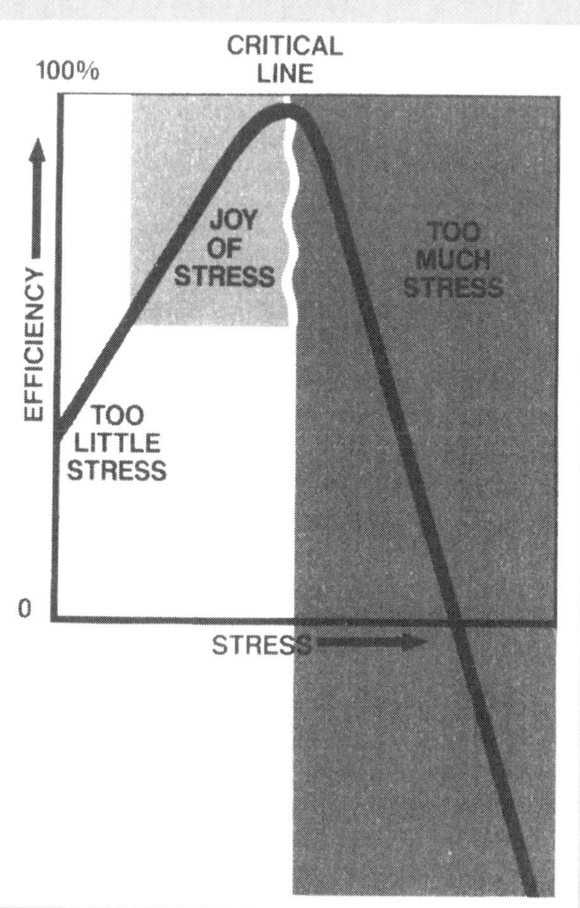

To find where you are on this graph, simply ask one question: "Will the added stress of a new responsibility at work or at home (no matter how small) increase my efficiency, or decrease it?" To make the best use of your energy, make sure your tasks are essential to your health, wealth, and happiness, and not a waste of time.

This graph applies to everyone, but the amounts and kinds of stress needed to reach maximum efficiency are different in each individual. The graph is also dynamic—it changes with every change in your life. Thus you should refer to it frequently.

If you are in the area of too little stress, you should say "yes" to extra duties at home, at work, or in your recreation. You could say "yes" to educational courses on line, or to immersion into hobbies or volunteer work. If you are spending too much time alone, you can interact with others in classes or sports teams, to meet new people while focusing on new stresses. If you love animals, consider adopting or fostering one of your favorite breed. Such extra responsibilities will add needed stress, and can improve your overall efficiency (and happiness) dramatically.

If you are in the area of too much stress, part of the solution will be learning how to simplify your life, and learning the power of saying "no." It is all too easy to have events fill your calendar, and to have data coming at you around the clock. Set aside some portion of your spare time where the cell phone is unplugged, and you have time for yourself and those around you. Even if you just enjoy the silence, you will find that some low-tech time is rejuvenating, and will empower you when you turn your internet back on.

In this book I will give you some practical tips on identifying your stresses, and selecting strategies to improve your defenses.

(See the Hanson Scale of Stress Management, Chapter 3.)

Strive to maximize success by investing your energy and time in all four quadrants of your life—financial sufficiency, personal happiness, sound health, and respect on the job. (See Chapter 9.)

Once you have mastered these life management skills, you will come to know the true Joy of Stress. As an added bonus, you will extend your good years longer than you thought possible and your personal and financial success to new heights. That's all there is to it. You don't need to buy expensive food supplements or throw your money into complicated health schemes. And you certainly won't need a bag full of prescription drugs to cope with your stresses.

However it doesn't always come easily. For many of you, making strong choices instead of weak ones will take tremendous courage, at least initially. But after you become used to the strong choices, the weak ones will become less and less attractive.

Well, if stress can be that simple to manage, why don't most people do it correctly? The answer as I have seen from my patients, is simply perspective. If people only think of the moment, then the consequences of this cigarette or that bag of junk food are invisible. If people think ahead, then they consider the cigarettes will rob their lungs, and they will be sucking for oxygen instead of enjoying fresh air and exercise. If they look at others who are on the obesity path, they will see that their short term "high" from sugar will quickly lead to a long term "high" in weight and risk of early death. Also, people who make poor choices seek solace in numbers, not unlike lemmings headed for the cliff. If those around you are all obese and depressed, then it seems natural to overeat and take prescription drugs. If those around you eat well and exercise often, then that will become the new "peer pressure". Unfortunately, statistics show that most people are bumbling into the wrong habits, simply because they are looking through the wrong end of the binoculars. They minimize the dangers of their bad habits, and magnify the difficulty

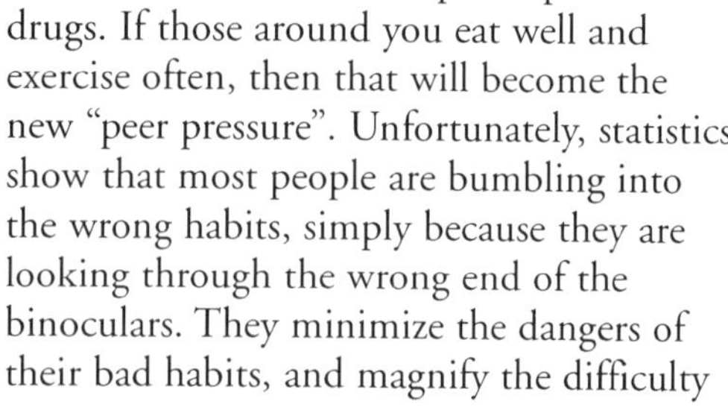

in making good choices. The reality is the good choices are extremely easy and fun, while it is the bad ones that are complicated and deadly.

What I am advocating to each of my patients and to you the reader is to be selfish: get everything you can out of life, for as long as you can. Be spontaneous. Be funny. Eat normal (organic) foods. Enjoy a drink of alcohol, beer, or wine if you wish. Walk tall, with a spring in your step. Run or ride with the wind in your face. Be proud of your fit body and enjoy each stride with your children and their children.

Continue to learn. Take time to use all your senses to soak up the beauties of color, texture, sound, and smell. Conduct your affairs with integrity. Earn the respect of your peers, the loyalty of your friends, and the love of your children and spouse. Push back the boundaries of senility, and extend your productive prime years as far as you can. This is *THE JOY OF STRESS.*

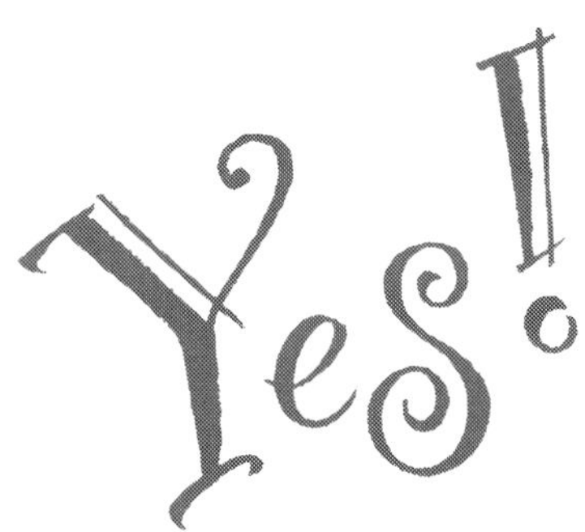

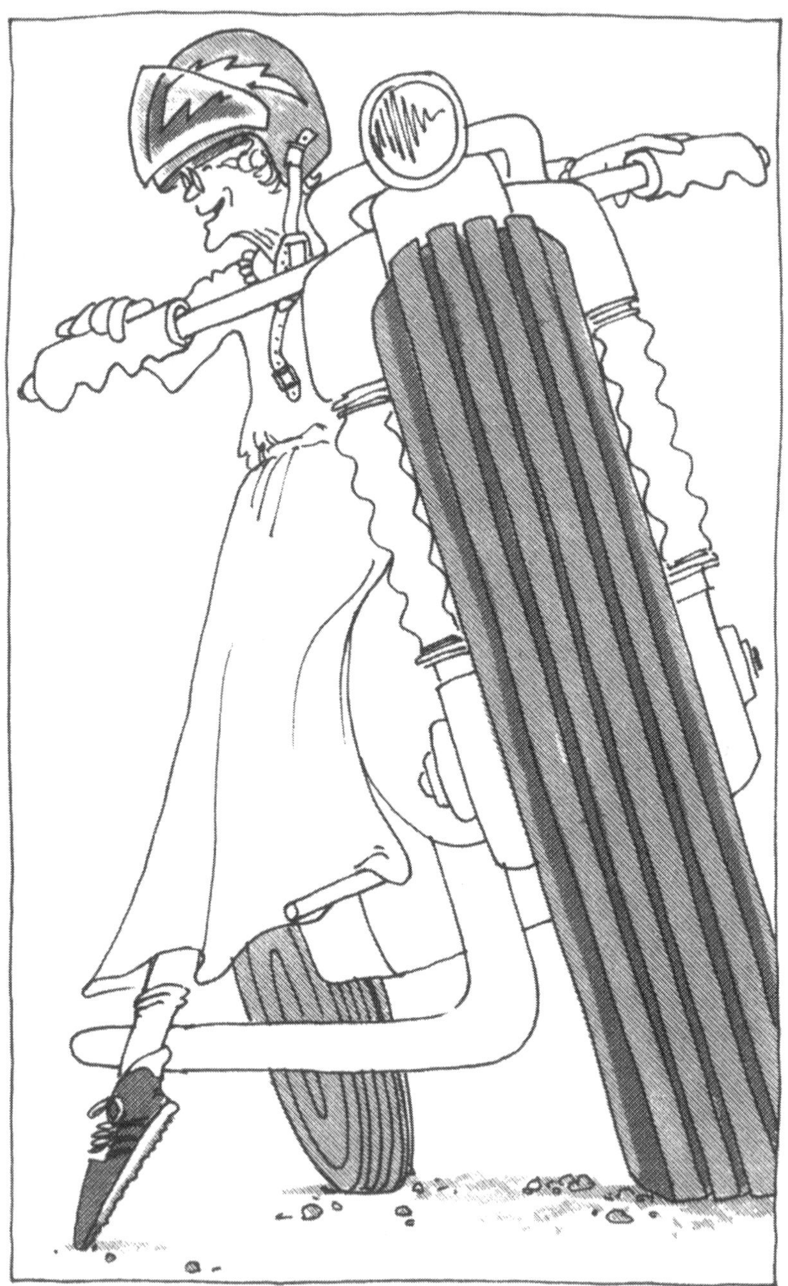

1. Stress: The Secret Fountain of Youth!

"Aging should be a reward, not a punishment!"

No one wants to die today, but most people say that they don't want to live to be one hundred either. Why is this? In Western society we have a terrible image of aging. We picture the hundred-year-old: weak and decrepit, dusted off and propped up in front of a blazing birthday cake, and then presumably returned to their green felt closet to be ignored until next year. For that matter, most adults are not that thrilled about their next decade. (For some reason birthdays that end in "0" seem daunting!)

With today's advances in medicine, nutrition and fitness we should be able to update our fears of aging, and re-boot our expectations for ourselves. We only have to look at the media to see great role models that shatter our stereotypes. Sexy icons like Madonna and George Clooney are in their fifties. Meryl Streep continues to dominate movies in her sixties. The top grossing Rock and Roll acts are in their seventies: Paul McCartney, and the Rolling Stones. Clint Eastwood is still active in his eighties. The late comedians George Burns and Bob Hope kept their sharp wits past the age of 100.

Most of what we used to accept as normal aging is now known to be simple disuse or misuse of the body. In my three decades of medical practice, I have seen that the biggest cause of illness and premature death, is not bad *luck*, but bad *management.* To put it bluntly, most tombstones could add the engraving "died of incompetence", based on what we now know about diseases and about stress.

As we all know, bad management can cause a company to go bankrupt, and it can cause your car to fall apart prematurely. Similarly, bad management of your body can cause your muscles to feel "old and stiff", your brain to become "senile," your arteries to harden, and your entire body to die prematurely.

Not everyone will live past one hundred, but everyone can certainly strive for his or her maximum "good mileage." No one should die before his time.

In the United States today, we lead the world with the most sophisticated advances in medical investigations, surgery, drug therapies and diets. But we do not lead the world in longevity; we have only about three one-hundred-year-olds per one hundred thousand people. In more primitive parts of the world (such as Abkhasia in Georgia, Russia, and Hunza in Kashmir), there are as many as forty to sixty per one hundred thousand, and the elders get around with vigour instead of with walkers.

Western scientists, always striving to find the mystical "fountain of youth" have naturally focused on these isolated areas, and tried to catalog any common ingredient that would explain the discrepancy. They examined the water supplies, the foods (even the yogurt), and the climate, but could not bring back any "magical" ingredient that would

confer their longevity onto us. However, there is one element that does explain it all: *stress*. The village elders face more stress each year they age, and play an active and respected part in the business and culture of their community, both physically and mentally, until the day they die.

In our own society, the same principle obtains. Those of our elders who continue to face stress live the longest, and stay physically and mentally sharp much longer than their peers. Symphony conductors and solo performers live longer than the regular orchestra musicians, primarily because they don't have an enforced retirement. Leaders who stay involved in the arts, business, politics or religion similarly stay youthful into late age.

The one group conspicuously absent from our list of admired elders is those who retire into total inactivity, free from all stress, which is all that many people have planned for their "golden years." The whole premise of our "assisted living" homes has been to "protect" our elderly from the stresses of daily life (shopping, traffic, household chores, gardening, or having to interact with neighbors of different generations). It is now clear that removing such stresses might well be to the detriment of the elderly (unless medical problems physically prevent these independent activities).

But stress alone is not a magic elixir, without good management of it. Life spans can be shortened in groups that generally do not have much control over their stress, for example, firefighters, air traffic controllers, police, and assembly line workers. And even a good match of the right kind of person and the right kind of stress will not overcome bad self-management; for example workaholics who love their careers but choose to smoke, and to overindulge in food and alcohol will not likely live as long as their peers. However, with good management choices, stress can indeed become the answer to Ponce de Leon's quest: the secret Fountain of Youth!

The "mythology" of aging

Let's take a closer look at our current "stereotype" of the elderly. They are often assumed (by others and even by themselves) to be:

1. ***Useless.***

   Discarded from the work force at the early age of sixty or sixty-five. No longer part of the decisions made in the workplace, in the community, or, often, even within their own family.

2. ***Inactive sexually.***

   Made to feel "old and ugly" by the mass media. Now that ads abound for drugs to cure male impotence, and hormones to restore the female libido in late age, there is a certain hint that the elderly might still have sex lives, but we still don't see octogenarians modeling in swimsuit catalogues.

3. ***Sequestered.***

   Placed in old-age communities such as nursing homes, "assisted living" apartments, golf neighborhoods or trailer camps. With no kids allowed to live with them (except for special visitations on holidays)these elderly people have little interaction with a normal cross-section of age groups. In fact, there are only two stages of life when we sanction age-matching of our citizens: in housing, for our seniors, and in little-league sports, for our kids.

4. ***Poor.***

   Many of our elderly are poor. This is especially devastating since the collapse of the economy in 2008, with most homes losing value, and most investment portfolios devastated. With low interest rates, savings in the bank don't generate much income. This can be compounded by the soaring costs of drugs and medical care. This means they may have to surrender their independence to their families or to society for financial reasons. Many are joining the ranks of entry-level workers who flip hamburgers in fast food restaurants, in order to earn some extra money to survive.

5. ***Senile.***

   Once sequestered from the stresses of everyday life, the elderly tend to lack short-term stimulation and memory. Thus they naturally fall back on topics of conversation relating to the "good old days." In fact, the memories that often give elderly people the most stimulation are those that involved a *lot* of stress, both happy and sad, such as weddings, births, wartime, epidemics, the Great Depression (and how it compared with the current one!), droughts, blizzards, and floods. In fact, the mental characteristics of "old-timers" disease are easily seen at any age when stress is absent, and people are isolated and bored. This has been seen on winter expeditions to the Antarctic, where healthy explorers who had months of time on their hands actually got very little work accomplished. (If you want something done, ask a busy person, not a bored one!)

6. ***Burned out and depressed.***

   Although it seems an unscientific approach, I can usually tell when an old person has given up. It's when he or she voluntarily stops buying new clothes, or making future plans, such as renovating the house, or updating the car, or the computer.

   Their attitude of depression and impending death seems to render such purchases pointless to them. Such negative thinking, mirrored in the shiny seat of their pants, (and in the stale décor of their homes) is a classic signal that life is over. With alarming regularity, people who have given up on themselves in this way follow their depressed attitudes right into the grave.

7. ***Shriveled physically.***

   Aging does cause destructive changes in the body. It is well known that connective tissues begin to degenerate and elastic tissues lose their resilience. For example the ear lobes and tip of the nose tend to droop. Thinning occurs between the discs of the vertebrae, reducing a person's overall height by as much as several inches, even while the bones of the arms and legs stay the same. The spine tends to turn "hunch-backed", often from a lifetime of hunching over a work surface, or from insufficient attention to exercise, massage, and alignment issues (chiropractic, pilates, yoga etc).

   The vocal cords tend to harden, raising the voice from perhaps a C to an E flat. Wrinkles appear as the skin thins and loses elasticity. (This is made much more severe by excessive sun, alcohol, and stress. See Chapter 10.)

Changes in the lenses of the eyes (causing cataracts), thinning of the hair and skin, and a host of related aging signs are well known to us all. By and large, they cannot be prevented. *However, a good deal that is accepted as normal in old age is actually just poor management.*

Muscular wasting is an example. Basically, your muscles don't know what the date on your birth certificate is. They know only whether or not they have been exercised recently. Our stereotypical elderly person has not done any regular physical exercise for decades, or possibly ever.

An exception is obviously seen with those who have resisted the call of modern sloth, and have continued to exercise their muscles doing physical work or athletics. There are many examples of masters-athletes that can compete favorably with youngsters half their age.

Arthritis is often equated with the elderly, but in fact this disease knows no age boundaries. Many old people have atrophy from disuse of muscles; for example, on hands and legs. This makes the joints look correspondingly larger, without their actually being arthritic. Knee joints, if not properly supported by good muscle tone in the thigh muscles, often "rock" with each step and can get puffy and painful. But again this is quite preventable through proper exercising.

Aging research shows that lessening of the immune resistance, mediated by the ever shrinking thymus gland through hormones called *thymosins*, does decrease the elderly person's ability to fight infections and even cancers. Someday we may see a thymosin substitute, to be taken along with vitamins and other supplements, if levels of thymosins in the blood are seen to fall.

Besides mediating the immune resistance, thymosins also release ACTH, which produces cortisone from the adrenal glands. As well, they release beta-endorphin, the "feel good hormone," which imitates morphine in the body. Both of these substances are produced in the hypothalamus of the brain. It is now well documented that their levels fall as we age.

Complaints of poor tolerance for aches and pains in the elderly do have a real basis in physiology. With the lack of regular movement, the joints dry up their secretions of joint fluids. These fluids carry not only a lubricant, but feed the joint cartilages vital supplies of food and oxygen. Also, when our muscles cool, as during sleep or inactivity, they stiffen. The result is an ugly "slow-motion" scene when we get out of a crowded airplane seat, stand up after a long session on the computer, or when we wake up first thing in the morning. This is not because the body is getting older, it is because it is getting colder. A few moments of flexing and extending our limbs after any period of inactivity will encourage self-lubrication of our joints, and resupply oxygen and food to our cartileges; at any age this will make us feel younger when we take those first few paces!

Interestingly, for thousands of years. the ancient art of acupuncture has been used for these symptoms, and is now known to cause the release of ACTH, as well as endorphins into the bloodstream. In my current medical practice in Toronto, I include medical acupuncture to treat pain, inflammation, and stress, and often can avoid having to prescribe strong medications. This can be dramatic in athletes of all ages, and because it has no side-effects, it can be remarkable in the elderly.

I have also seen the effects of acupuncture in rejuvenating old dogs, some of whom are so severely afflicted by arthritis that they are taken to the vet for consideration of euthanasia. Instead of putting the dog down, the vet treats with acupuncture, often with instantaneous and dramatic results; a rejuvenated old dog that can chase puppies all over the yard for the next couple of years. We see the same stunning rejuvenation of human patients, many of whom come into our offices for regular visits every month, just to keep up the "magic".

According to Hans Selye, every individual is born with a certain amount of *adaptation energy*. It is something like a bag of coins. Once spent, it cannot be replaced. Lord Moran, personal physician to Winston Churchill, in his studies of shell-shocked soldiers, referred to this quality as "courage." Every individual may inherit a different quantity of adaptation energy, or courage. However, once it is gone, burnout occurs. Senility in the elderly and shell-shock in young soldiers are alike in a sense. They both seem to result from having spent all one's adaptation energy.

Women and longevity

Today, most of our elderly tend to be women. The men in their lives, in many cases, have succumbed to wars, higher incidence of smoking and alcohol abuse, and to excess *stress*. This stress has been brought on largely by the "hurry sickness" that attends the twentieth-century production line. (This will be discussed in detail in Chapter 8. Those of you who just flipped ahead to see Chapter 8 have identified yourselves as type A's. You are the very ones who can least afford to skip whole sections of *this* book!)

Women in the past tended to be insulated from the battlefield, not allowed to drink in bars, and forbidden from smoking cigarettes. Before WWII men did most of the assembly line work, and did most of the driving through traffic. Pressures of child-raising and home-making, to be sure, are not to be minimized as a source of stress. However, they have generally not involved constant conflict with the time clock.

It would be wrong to assume that women will continue to outlive their men. Before the industrial age, men actually outlived women consistently. This was due to:

1. The high incidence of death among women at childbirth. (Note that before the age of birth control pills, women could not chose to delay or avoid pregnancies like they can today.)
2. Men did most of the vigorous work, in plowing fields, chopping wood, or hunting. This meant they had constant physical exercise, but not time-clock pressures. It also meant they had more control over their finished product (in this case, food) than the modern assembly line worker.

3. There were fewer temptations; cigarettes were not yet available, and alcohol consumption was much less than with today's binge-drinking crowd.
4. There was no such thing as "idle retirement", men continued to exercise during work until they died.

But the pendulum is swinging. Today, women are gaining improved status in the workforce. As a result, they are now fighting the time clock in increasing numbers, both on the job and commuting to get to the job. Although still restricted from the military battlefronts, women are being given active roles in police and military work. Cigarette smoking is now as socially "acceptable" for women as for men, and in fact the majority of teenage smokers are female. Binge drinking is now a huge problem for women, as well as men.

Our whole Western economy, including the price of houses, is built upon the expectation that most couples will be bringing in two incomes. Thus women are staying in their careers for longer than ever before. It is still expected that the major task of child raising with its extra pressures will be handled by women, who must thank goodness for the smaller sized families that birth control has permitted.

Working mothers in today's society were brought up at a time when it was less common for women to be working. The belief was instilled in them that they should assume the primary role in child-raising. Thus they are often made to feel guilty for doing otherwise. In reality, when both parents are working, it is obvious that the dynamics of the family must change radically from the former model. However, many women are still caught by guilt (the gift that keeps on giving), and end up with even higher stresses (and less control) than their men.

Thus women today are beginning to fall prey to the same stress-related illnesses as men—evidence that the possession of ovaries is not a guarantee of a longer life. We can no longer assume that tomorrow's young executive who dies of a heart attack will always be a man.

Why not live longer?

Physiologically, based on the number of cell divisions in each organ, the human body should be capable of living to between 100 and 150 years. Anything less should be considered an "early death." True "middle age" should not even start until age sixty!

The example of Winston Churchill is sometimes cited by people defending their own bad habits. Churchill lived to the age of ninety in spite of his smoking, drinking, obesity, and lack of exercise. However, he could well have enjoyed another few decades of useful life. That Winston Churchill lived as long as he did is a tribute to his constitution and to the effects of constant stimulation with stresses. He did not even start his career as prime minister of England until age sixty-six, and was re-elected at age seventy-seven.

His resistance to stress was also bolstered by some very good choices such as a loving relationship with his wife, and the ability to take efficient cat-naps. (See "How to Take a Power Nap," Chapter 4.)

Obviously, with many of our elderly living productively only into their mid-seventies, and with many of our obese middle aged dying of "old-age" diseases in their forties, we are doing something wrong. To correct this carnage, active prevention needs to replace passive mismanagement.

Health and stress

It has been estimated that illnesses and accidents related to stress account for three-quarters of all time lost from work. Stress is also implicated in the majority of cases seen in the doctor's office, hospital beds, and ultimately the graveyard. In spite of all the media attention to health, stress-related problems take the vast majority of people by *surprise*. They might have known that stress can harm others, but never fully realized what it could do to *them*. Purely uncontrollable (or bad luck) accidents or illnesses leading to death are fortunately rare.

It is at the very time when people are under great stress that their bodies are in the greatest jeopardy Dr. Hans Selye found that he could cause illness, premature aging, hardening of the arteries, and subsequent early death in his experimental rats by simply stressing them excessively. (For example, he would teach them a trick and then punish them for doing it.) The exact cause of death might not be a major catastrophe such as stomach ulcers, colitis, or heart attacks from stress-induced cholesterol deposits in the arteries. With the predictable and

The "Stupid-Light" is on: Things people do to put themselves into the hospital:

1. Don't fasten their three-point seatbelts. This is also known as volunteering to use your face as an air-bag!

2. Choose poor responses to stress, such as drug abuse, smoking, obesity, and excessive drinking. (See Chapter 3.) Many of these habits affect innocent victims as well.

3. Fall prey to careless accidents due to their increased error rate. (See Chapter 2.)

4. Undervalue time management, both at work and at home. (See section on Type A behavior, Chapter 8.)

5. Take their health for granted, ignoring the needs of their bodies (such as exercise) in their daily list of priorities.

dramatic shrinking of all the lymph glands as well as a decrease in their general immune response, the rats could just as easily die from a minor infection that would advance into a severe pneumonia, septicemia, or meningitis.

So be warned: Something similar can happen to you under your stresses. If you don't learn how to handle stress, you may be unnecessarily courting ill health, illnesses, or even early death.

This has been shown countless times. Following an earthquake in Athens, there was a sharp rise in the number of deaths from heart attacks and other illnesses. Increased deaths, particularly among the elderly, are often seen during spells of extreme heat or cold.

To cite an example from my own practice, I saw an eighty-two-year-old woman die of cancer within a few months of the death of her husband. She had had a slow growing cancer in remission for decades, but in the last months it spread like wildfire through her whole body. The true cause of her death was the stress of her husband's death—had he lived, her cancer would quite likely have remained in its containment.

Control

The key to surviving and thriving on stress is *control*, not avoidance.

An interesting piece of research done recently demanded tasks of concentration of two groups of workers. Both groups were exposed to very distracting background noises of machinery, horns honking, and people talking loudly in languages unknown to the workers. One group had a button placed on a desk, so that they could shut off the background noises any time they wanted to. The other group had no button.

The productivity of the group with the control button was as expected: consistently and remarkably higher than that of those without control. The interesting point is that *no one actually pushed the control button.* Just knowing it was there seemed to be enough.

The lesson here is an important one: It is essential to have some "control buttons" in your own life. They help you live satisfactorily with the stresses that are around you. If you have very little sense of control, the stresses will surely get to you.

The media headlines tend to bombard you with spectacular disasters, bad news, and frustrations, all beyond your control. This is likely a commercial recognition of the realities of human nature; most people just love to slow down to see roadside disasters in real life, and they love to identify with trivial stories such as a runaway bride (if she's pretty) or a depressed celebrity (if they are famous).

As a stress-reducing principle, try to avoid all stories of sensationalized violence in the media, and instead spend your time on the more productive stories. If you have a particular area of interest, such as business or foreign affairs, use the internet to read newspapers from around the world. Pick a specific time limit, say a half-hour, and catch up on all the relevant news you need or enjoy. But just do it once or twice a day. Most people are ***passive***, and let themselves be bombarded with the same stories all day long, on the car-radio, in the office papers, in magazines, and the televised news bulletins. Instead be ***active***, and use modern technology to program your own agenda for down-time: build your own archives of portable music, comedy, or audio books or courses. Given the number of hours most commuters spend in transit, one could learn a whole new language every year!

A good way to handle stress is by the Hanson method: Learn to ignore what you can't control, and learn to control what you can. You can't always control life's stresses, but you can control most of your choices.

Let's begin your active defense against stress by learning about your basic anatomy.

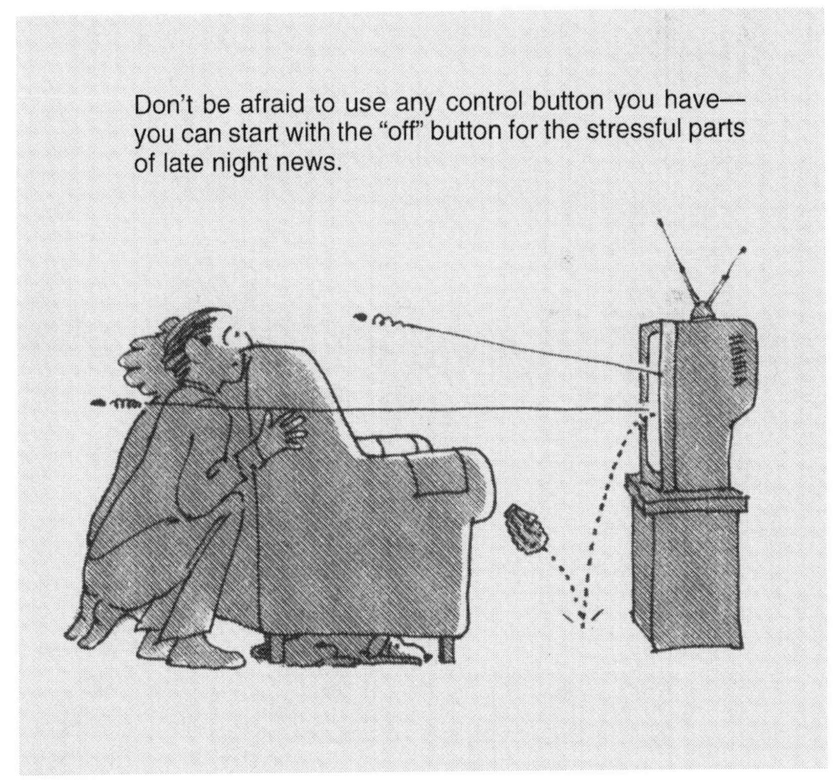

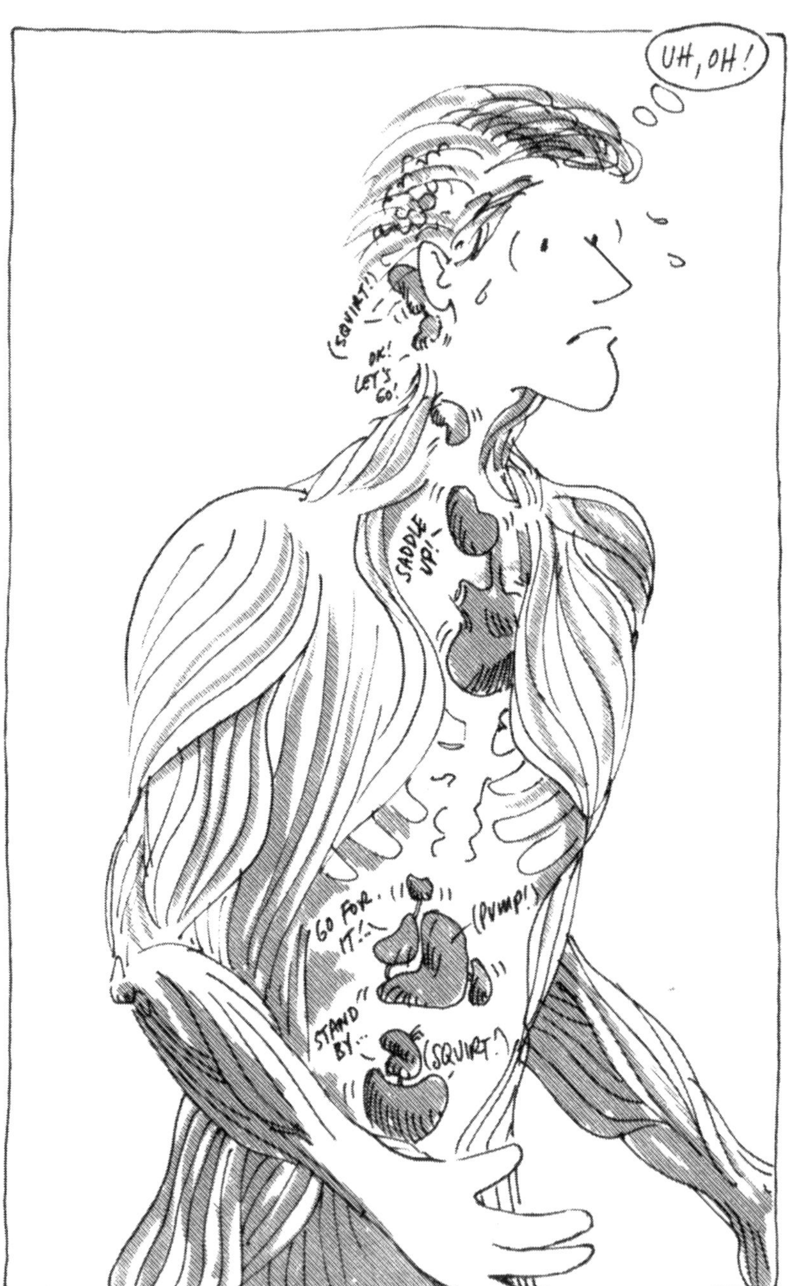
UH, OH!
(SQUIRT!)
OK! LET'S GO!
SADDLE UP!
GO FOR IT!
(PUMP!)
STAND BY...
(SQUIRT!)

2. The Anatomy of Stress

Your body as a battleship

Think of your body as a magnificent but outdated wooden battleship. It has many powerful and intricate weapons to use in response to the "enemy," stress. As you read on, you will become quite impressed by the superhuman "fight-or-flight" powers that can be unleashed. For example, soldiers in battle can summon amazing strength to lift a wounded comrade to safety, or to leap or jump farther than they ever could in routine practice. Stress magnifies our primal powers.

The problem is that stress brings out the same resonses as it did thousands of years ago, even though times have changed radically. We have witnessed three stages of civilization, each requiring new and specialized stress responses.

1. Originally, in the **Agricultural Age**, primitive man faced obvious stresses, like being attacked by wild animals. This required a set of a dozen automatic ***reflexes*** for "fight or flight", programmed to react with emergency speed.

2. Then, with the onset of the **Industrial Age**, stresses were all about coping with the time-pressures of the assembly line world, and our responses had to be ***rules***, memorized by all, just like soldiers obeying orders. Creativity and original thinking

were deliberately suppressed, and this culture persists in most of our school systems today.

3. Since about 1971, when we entered the **Information Age**, our stresses are once again morphed into traffic jams, computer viruses, and sensory overload from the media. These new stresses need more than old ***reflexes*** and ***rules***, they demand new ***strategies.***

To become active in our own stress defense, we need to understand the primitive reflexes our bodies have as "standard equipment". Then, when we understand the dangers of leaving these reflexes untended, we can better start our active involvement.

Stress responses are both physical and psychological

Quite apart from the obvious physical stress responses such as sweating and racing of the heart, there are some important psychological responses to stress, as have been seen throughout the history of warfare. For example, during the Second World War, Army doctors began to notice that a few soldiers would develop psychosomatic symptoms in order to get out of active duty. Air Force doctors noticed that pilots might present with psychosomatic eye pains or even hysterical blindness, which would obviously prevent them from flying a plane

over enemy territory. Parachutists were noted to suffer psychosomatic pains in their feet or ankles. Quite conveniently, these would prevent them from making jumps. We can only speculate as to the nature of the symptoms suffered by tail-gunners!

In much the same way, our physical responses to stress can be helpful in times of "old-fashioned" danger. In fact, they can even be life-saving, as could be attested by anyone who has found a sudden burst of speed in his or her legs while being chased by an angry animal. But the old "fight or flight" program is not much help against modern stresses, because there is no one to hit, and nowhere to run. Our automatic emergency responses do not help us when the ATM machine eats our card, or when we lose our keys, sunglasses or password codes.

It seems that our bodies are wired for the wrong war; for the first time in history, we need to understand its shortcomings before we can be safe from our modern stresses.

Let's take a closer look at some of the body's specific responses to stress, and how the *original benefit* can become *today's drawback* if left to your unthinking reflexes.

1. Cortisone
2. Thyroid
3. Endorphin
4. Sex hormones
5. Digestive tract
6. Sugar and insulin
7. Cholesterol
8. Racing heartbeat
9. Air supply
10. Blood
11. Skin
12. Senses

Natural responses to stress

Automatic Stress responses: the Obsolete Dozen

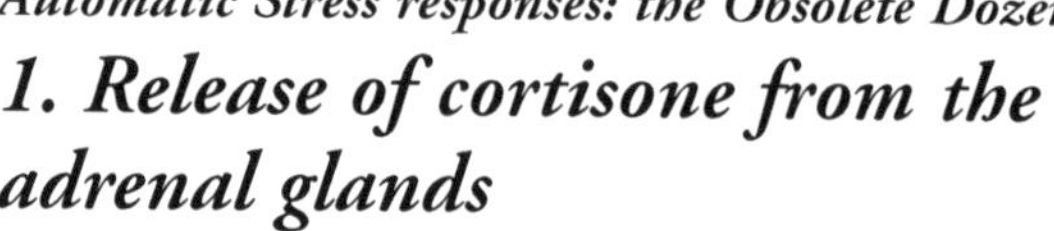

1. Release of cortisone from the adrenal glands

Original benefit

Protection from an instant allergy reaction (such as asthma or closing of the eyes), from a brief dust-up with an attacking foe.

Today's drawback

If chronically elevated, cortisone destroys the body's resistance to the stresses of cancer, infection, surgery, and illness. Every lymph gland in the body shrivels up; the immune response weakens. The ability to fight off even minor colds (as well as major illnesses) is greatly impaired.

As a common example, young children are usually brought to their doctors with one infection after another for the first five or six years after starting daycare or school. Partially, this is due to contagious diseases from the other children, but mainly it is due to decreased resistance, from the stress of leaving the womb-like comfort of the home for the general brouhaha of the society of their peers. Adults will also notice this phenomenon when in new environments. Teachers suffer frequent colds caught from their pupils during the first five years on the job. Pediatricians, however, have it even worse. They often go through five years of diarrhea while getting their training!

Chronic cortisone elevation also dramatically reduces the stomach's resistance to its own acid, leading to gastric and duodenal ulcers. Farther along the bowels, colitis can be aggravated.

Bones are made more brittle by cortisone, eventually leading to osteoporosis. Thus they could fracture much more easily.

Blood pressure can be elevated by the retention of sodium, which can also push a borderline heart failure case into trouble. (The common stress response of eating salty "comfort" foods is thus even more harmful than usual.) Adrenaline is also released by the adrenal glands, and mediates a host of bodily reactions, as we will see.

2. Thyroid hormone increases in the bloodstream

Original benefit

Thyroid hormones speed up the body's metabolism. The body thus burns its fuel faster, to provide extra energy, much as a supercharger helps your car. Great for that emergency get-away chase!

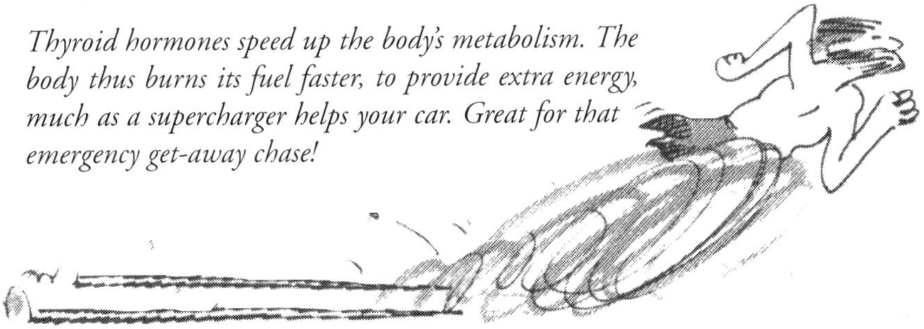

Today's drawbacks

Intolerance to heat, shaky nerves to the point of jumpiness, weight loss under stress (if food intake remains constant), insomnia, and ultimately exhaustion or burnout. While some obese people react to stress by gaining weight, this is only because they actively work at overwhelming their thyroids with extra calories.

3. Release of endorphin from the hypothalamus

Original benefit

Identical to morphine, this is the body's "feel good" hormone. It is a very potent pain killer as well as a natural mood elevator. Under acute stress the soldier doesn't feel his wounds. The boxer doesn't notice his (or her) cuts or broken bones. The mother in labor feels much less of the pain of childbirth than she otherwise would. The marathon runner gets a "second wind" in which the pains lessen. Depression can fade into the background while the body and mind focus on an acute stress response. In all of these conditions, the levels of endorphin are elevated as part of the wisdom of the body.

Today's drawbacks

Chronic relentless stresses can deplete the levels of endorphin. This has been shown to aggravate migraines, backaches, and even the pains of arthritis (although not the actual disease itself.)

Acupuncture, with needles placed strategically into anatomic target points, has been shown to dramatically increase endorphin levels, to reverse the effects of stress. Not only will aches and pains improve, but the mood elevation will effect anxieties, depression and insomnia. Dentists can use these techniques to provide enough of an anesthetic effect for dental work. Veterinarians use acupuncture on injured race horses (thus no trace of prescription drugs show up in the urine). Injured Olympic athletes are now being treated with medical acupuncture, because most drugs used can be detected on urine or blood testing, and might cause disqualification. In my own practice, I have treated many elite professional athletes, as well as the weekend warriors, and have seen an amazing response when we stimulate the patient's own endorphin production. Doctors in China and now in many other countries use this technique to anesthetize some patients for major surgery.

4. Reduction in sex hormones: testosterone in the male; progesterone in the female

(In the male there is the added response of retraction of the testicles for protection.)

Original benefit

Decreased fertility. In times of drought, overcrowding, or decreased food supply in the past, this was a critical response since it reduced the number of mouths to feed. This applied to the whole animal kingdom, as well as humans. With soldiers and hunters away from their mates for long intervals, a decreased libido made both partners' lives more bearable, and allowed energies to be focused on the job at hand, without distraction.

Today's drawbacks

Usually unrecognized by either partner, a predictable decrease in libido accompanies stress. This leads to obvious anxieties and failures when intercourse is attempted. The most common problems are premature ejaculation or erectile dysfunction ("E.D") in the male, and failure to reach orgasm in the female. Because couples are often not aware that their sexual downturns are a physical result of stress, I have found many transfer their anxieties inappropriately.

They may start nit-picking at each other, or develop obsessive-compulsive behaviors. They may develop phobias regarding such conditions as cancer or heart attacks. Ultimately they may even seek new partners.

For couples who are infertile, the paradox is that the stress of wanting to get pregnant can actually be misinterpreted by the body as a general stress, and will trigger the infertility response. (This is why acupuncture can be an effective adjunct to infertility treatments).

It was well known to doctors several generations ago that an infertile couple could benefit from a cruise, or trip abroad. The idea was to get away from routine stresses, and let the body restart its hormones and regenerate its libido. Not only would the opportunities for intercourse increase, but the actual sperm counts and ovulation rates would benefit from the resurgence of the testosterone and progesterone respectively.

This effect has certainly been well noted by the travel industry, in which the whole tenor of advertising for sun holidays is to make people feel "sexy," to leave their inhibitions and stresses behind them.

5. The shutdown of the entire digestive tract

Original benefit

Blood could be diverted to the muscles, and the "engine room" of the heart and lungs. Thus this reflex would act as a vital "self-transfusion," enabling one to perform extraordinary feats of muscular power (for example, as in Olympic competition or in the case of the woman who lifted the tractor off her son).

When the digestive tract shuts down, the mouth goes dry, to avoid adding more fluids to the stomach. (Even these fluids will be needed elsewhere.) The stomach and intestines virtually stop their secretions and movements. The rectum and bladder are programmed to empty their contents to lighten the body's load for fight or flight.

Today's drawbacks

The highly stressed public speaker can't get even enough moisture going in his or her mouth to unstick the tongue from the roof of the mouth, unless he or she uses the glass of water placed on the lectern for just this purpose. The dry mouth phenomenon is so consistent that it has been used effectively as a lie detector test in parts of China. A "line up" of suspects were forced to take a large spoonful of cooked rice, and then answer questions. The innocent ones would make enough saliva to swallow the rice. The guilty one, as a direct result of the stress response, would have a dry mouth, and no luck swallowing. At this point the perpetrator presumably makes a rather muffled confession.

People who eat on the run under stress do themselves a lot of harm by forcing food at high speed into their inactive stomachs. One look into any food court confirms that most people are swallowing at the speed of a pie-eating contest. The results are predictable: the stomache bloats, cramps, burns and burps. When gas does not come up, it creates spasms in the lower intestines, and can cause significant pains in the chest and abdomen. Swimmers are well aware of these reactions; that is why we were all told as children not to swim within an hour of a heavy meal.

The pre-programmed gastro-colic "dumping" response is another problem for modern stresses. Today's public speaker is not pleased by this embarrassing stress response, as he or she rises to address the audience.

6. Release of sugar into the blood, along with an increase in insulin levels to metabolize it

Original benefit

Quick "short distance" energy supply. Fuel for the sprint.

Today's drawbacks

Diabetes can be aggravated, or even started, by excessive demands on the pancreas for insulin. Today's common stress response of over-eating foods high in sugar is thus even more damaging, as the bloodstream already has high levels of sugar as part of its natural response to stress. "Comfort" foods are not so comfortable! Insulin responds to high blood sugar by forcing it into the body's storage cells (as fat or "cellulite"). This leaves the blood low in sugar (hypoglycemia) which then encourages the body to crave a quick fix (more sugar). That's why it's so hard to stop after only one Oreo. This makes life difficult for the pancreas to say the least, not to mention your teeth, and the girth of your stomach or hips. (See Chapter 5.)

Consult your doctor if you think you have any symptoms or signs of hypoglycemia or diabetes. If you do, consider:

1. Diet; eat natural foods, and restrict "junk" foods such as white sugars, and simple carbs.

2. Exercise; burn off the calories you take In, so that you have a muscle mass, and less fat to deplete your insulin stores.

3. Weight; strive for your ideal weight, as measured by how you look in the mirror.

Make sure you do not follow the crowd, skip items 1-3, and head straight for drugs. Even with anti-diabetes medications, you should still eat the right foods, burn them off with exercise, and get rid of any excess fat on your body.

7. Increase of cholesterol in the blood, mainly from the liver

Original benefit

Helps to transport "long distance" fuel, to power the emergency responses of fight or flight. This is particularly clever, because stress shuts down the stomache, and muscles need to draw fuel from elsewhere, namely stored fat.

Today's drawbacks

On a chronic basis some of this elevated cholesterol can tend to deposit in the blood vessels, including the coronary arteries. It can cause hardening of the arteries (arteriosclerotic heart disease), or even a fatal heart attack. The dietary cholesterol controversy is a big issue on its own, and will be discussed in Chapter 5. One word of caution—if the doctor drawing your blood is a sleepy, overworked, rookie intern who stabs the needle into the bell cord instead of your arm on the first of many attempts, the stress generated can elevate the patient's cholesterol by as much as 40 percent in just a few seconds. (I know, because I was once that rookie intern!). An artificially high reading could also be obtained in a doctor's office or lab if you cheated on the fourteen-hour fast requirement (for example, by sneaking a coffee with cream on the way in). Or it could be obtained by eating a very high fat diet for the week prior to the test.

In spite of occasional artificial readings, blood cholesterol studies are still useful. They should be done by your doctor as part of your regular physical examination. In high-risk cases, they should take place at least once a year. High-risks cases would include women on birth control pills, people who are obese, and anyone suffering high levels of stress (if you are not sure of your stress levels, see Chapters 3 and 4. In addition, extra scrutiny should be given to people, even children, who have a strong family history of heart disease or high cholesterol levels.

It is clear that the last thing you need to add to your blood supply in times of stress is excessive cholesterol. Yet with most fast-food diets this is exactly what happens. The average person in this country takes in about 45 percent of all calories in the form of fats. Most of this is from unnatural processed foods or meats and fish, with untold quantities of added steroids, hormones, antibiotics, and other pollutants, none of which show up on the label (and you thought the government was looking out for your health). The worst side-kick for cholesterol, like the hamburger, is starch such as white sugar or white flour, making the bun and the side of fries the devil's own combo-meal. (See Chapter 5.)

The occasional meal at your local hamburger chain is harmless, although this is becoming less true with the recent advent of supersized "belly-bomber" portions. These have turned out to be hugely popular with the public, and are contributing to the mass obesity epidemic. Obesity is now the basis for the health care crisis, and it is getting worse. A whole day's calories can now be taken in one giant burger, or a single Frappuccino coffee, and a month's rations of sugar (thirty or forty spoonful's) are served in barrel-sized soda cups. If one ate three meals of "fast food" a day, plus snacks, the results would be swift and damaging: obesity, inflammation of the liver, impotence, nausea, and other problems. Over time, the knees and hips need replacement, and the heart needs new arteries. Once again, "comfort" foods are proving to be not so comfortable.

8. The racing heartbeat

Original benefit

Pumps more blood to the lungs, to load up on oxygen, and to the liver (and other stores of energy such as glycogen deposits) to load up on fuel. The muscles are then "supercharged" for fight or flight emergency responses. This surge of circulation also serves as an efficient mechanism to flush out the products of this metabolism from the muscle cells.

Today's drawback

The reflex rise in blood pressure and circulation was only ever designed for quick emergencies, a few minutes at a time. Today, our stresses are chronic, often lasting for decades. If unchecked, the rise of heart rate and blood pressure could lead to serious consequences, such as strokes, the bursting of an aneurysm, or kidney damage.

High blood pressure from uncontrolled stress could also lead to the "big one"—a fatal heart attack—in anyone over the age of fifteen. If you already have cholesterol deposits in your coronary arteries (and autopsies of young American soldiers have shown that this is alarmingly common), your heart may be barely keeping up with routine demands. Any additional push from excess stress—such as a temper tantrum, pushing a car out of a

How to REALLY check your blood pressure:

Blood pressure can change abruptly during the day, depending on a number of factors such as stress, relaxation, anger, overeating, and, obviously, exercise. Often it is at its worst when you are at the doctor's office (this is known as "white coat" hypertension). That's why I tell all my patients to get their own blood-pressure cuff, and record multiple readings during random times of the day. Bring your cuff in to the office and let your doctor check its readings for accuracy.

Let's take a look at what the numbers mean. When you are told your pressure is 120/80, these two numbers represent the pressure (in millimeters of mercury) inside the heart during contraction, and during relaxation between the beats. The upper number goes up and down with your heart rate can often be as high as 100 plus your age. But the lower number should not rise above 100mm, and, ideally, should be under 90mm at rest.

It should be noted that this test relies on a "normal" resistance of the upper arm, as the mechanism involves using a balloon to compress the brachial artery next to the bone. The stethoscope or microphone is placed over the artery at the crease of the elbow. The balloon is inflated to completely shut off the artery, so the pulse is silent. As the balloon is slowly released, the turbulent sounds of the pulse can be heard at the elbow, which gives the upper number (systolic). When the balloon further decompresses until its pressure equals that between beats, the artery is no longer squeezed, and the sounds of turbulence disappear, This gives us the lower number, (diastolic). An artificially high reading can occur if the upper arm is huge from obesity, or from freshly "pumped" muscles after weight lifting. If your doctor suspects a bogus reading through the thickness of the arm, it is possible to get an exact pressure by inserting a catheter into an artery. If the arm is simply too big, you may need to get an extra large cuff for your machine.

It should be noted that many people are on unnecessary medications for high blood pressure, simply because of the above variables. The most important first step in correcting this problem in our obese population is to lose ten pounds. Then, recheck the pressures. Most often the restoration of fitness and correct weight will solve the problem. If medications are indeed the only way to reduce your pressure, make sure you see your doctor regularly to monitor any possible side effects.

ditch, or heat prostration—could be the last straw.

Remember, high blood pressure is a silent enemy. It can occur in fit athletes, it can start in childhood, and can go on for years without any symptoms that a person would notice. Checking it is easy, and is routinely done as part of a routine check-up at your doctor's office. If you are under excessive stress, or have poor lifestyle habits, or a bad family history, consult your doctor for more thorough checks. Even modern tools such as stress EKGs, echocardiograms, coronary angiograms, and scans are not completely foolproof. However, advance warnings are never a bad idea.

Cardiologists have become adept at miraculous rescues. If you end up with blockages in your coronary arteries, from high blood pressure, or high cholesterol from diet or genetic reasons, they can insert a catheter from your thigh up to the heart. The catheter tip enters the clogged artery, and a tiny balloon is inflated to squish open the blood vessel. A stent is then left in place to keep the artery open. If this fails, then cardiac surgeons can cut out part of a leg vein, then reinsert it in the heart muscle around the blockage. While these steps have become all too commonplace, they are largely safe, and certainly have saved many lives.

But before you give all your faith to medical technology, you should ask yourself the simple question: "Are you feeling lucky today??" Active management of your health risks will always be better than passively waiting for that miracle cure. The first warning of your next heart attack could well be your last breath.

Ultimately, seeing your doctor isn't going to be enough help unless you are willing to heed his or her advice. You must have the versatility to correct your weak choices, for example, smoking, obesity, wrong job. (See Chapter 3.)

9. Increasing air Supply

The nostrils flare, the throat dilates, all the air passages in the lungs dilate, and the breathing becomes deeper and more rapid.

Original benefit

Provides the extra oxygen for the body's combustion. Much like opening all the doors on a fireplace, to create more heat energy.

Today's drawbacks

Air pollution has greater access and can do even more damage to your lungs when you are under stress. This response can be very detrimental if you are a smoker or live with one. Even if you do not increase the number of cigarettes smoked under stress (most cigarettes smokers do), the penetration and damage that each stick of poison gas can wreak is greatly amplified during stress. It makes matters just that much worse when you choose to increase the actual number of cigarettes smoked in response to your stress.

10. The blood (and the plot) thickens

This is due to increased production of red and white blood cells from the marrow. It is also due to the squeezing of the fist-sized spleen to inject its thick paste of blood cells and clotting factors into the bloodstream.

Original benefit

More capacity to carry oxygen, to fight infections, and to stop bleeding from a wound. Could save your life by giving you extra strength and speed for an emergency attack, and, if you are wounded, it could save you from bleeding to death. (This natural reflex is the basis for "blood doping", where an athlete can cheat by transfusing packed red blood cells before a race.)

Today's drawback

Strokes, heart attacks, or an embolus can all be encouraged by having the blood turn to sludge under stress. (This is yet another reason why I recommend drinking at least eight glasses of water per day—unless you are an uncontrolled epileptic. It helps dilute your blood.) Blood thinning drugs have long been available, and studies suggest that even less than one baby aspirin per day helps. However, consult your doctor to have tests to see what might be appropriate for you. As a general principle, pills are not the first line of defense against stress. They do have a role, but one wants to make sure the side-effects do not exceed the benefits.

11. The skin "crawls," pales, and sweats

Original benefit

The skin, the largest organ in the body, has all its hairs stand up on end. This is a vestige left from some of our "fur-fathers." It was useful in increasing the overall appearance of size, like a cat frightened by a dog.. The bristling of hairs also heightens our sense of touch. It acts much like a cat's whiskers in the dark, providing a sort of "radar" to detect our closest environment. The skin blanches with stress to divert blood to the "war machines" (muscles, heart, and lungs). Bloodless skin also means less blood loss in case of lacerations. Under stress, the skin also sweats. This is to provide coolness for the underlying, overheated muscles.

Today's drawback

Social leprosy. The dreaded (at least in TV commercials) triad of clammy hands, pasty face, and stained armpits. Also, sweating decreases the skin's resistance to electricity (also known as the GSR or Galvanic Skin Resistance), which can be easily measured. This will give you away every time in the modern lie detector test (assuming you find telling lies to be stressful).

12. All five senses become acute

Original benefit

This brings the body to its peak of function. It explains why thrill seekers feel they are most alive when doing something very stressful. This is also why we all our most vivid memories are around times of stress (happy or sad); boring or routine days tend to be lost in the mental archives.

Overall mental acuity is also improved, with greatly increased concentration, as anyone who ever faced a deadline in school or work knows well.

Eyes—pupils dilate to allow better night vision, and give better peripheral vision when in battle. When our life depends on it, we can almost see sideways.

Ears—hearing becomes more acute.

Touch—enhanced by the hair response (see response number 11).

Taste, smell—enhanced

Today's drawback

The major drawback today is the high error rate that occurs after prolonged modern stresses. It seems that the senses are only switched on to high alert for the short duration of primitive stresses. With our modern chronic stresses these senses "burn out", and become less efficient. The person becomes less observant of details around him or her, pays little attention to tastes or smells, tunes out whole conversations, and ignores touch.

For years, comedians have found humor in this state of vulnerability. The very time one is trying to look one's pompous best at a society cocktail party is the time one will inadvertently thrust one's swizzle stick up one's nose.

Knowing when your stresses and this error rate are high could save your life. For example, if you have just had a heated argument at home, this is the worst time to jump into your car and squeal rubber all the way down the street. Another risky trip is the drive home from the hospital with a brand new baby, even though this stressor is a happy event. When under extreme stress, remember to be careful not to undertake any potentially dangerous activity such as working with power tools or machines, or climbing heights. Stress may also affect the eyes as its only target. I have seen cases in which stress overload first manifests itself with sudden blindness due to detached retinas, or imaginary blindness due to hysteria.

Another complication of eye dilation as part of the stress response is the exacerbation of glaucoma. An interesting sidelight of stressful pupil dilation is that your eyes can betray you when you tell a lie (assuming you find lying to be stressful). This is why the bad guys in movies wear sunglasses, and why people who don't look you in the eye during a conversation are perceived to be "shifty" and untrustworthy.

Your eyes can also give away your feelings when presented with pleasant stresses. See Figure 2.1.

Figure 2.1

Pupil size is easily measured, and a good indicator of the different stresses experienced by individuals. When presented with a stressor (in this case a pleasant one), consistent differences between men and women will usually be noted. The first picture will generally dilate the pupils of the women readers.

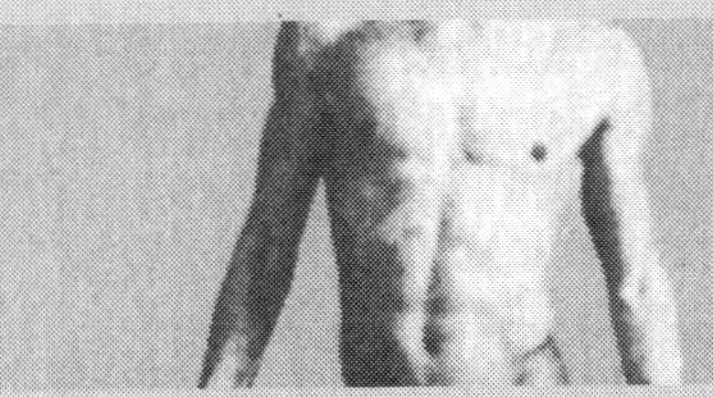

The second picture will generally dilate the pupils of the men.

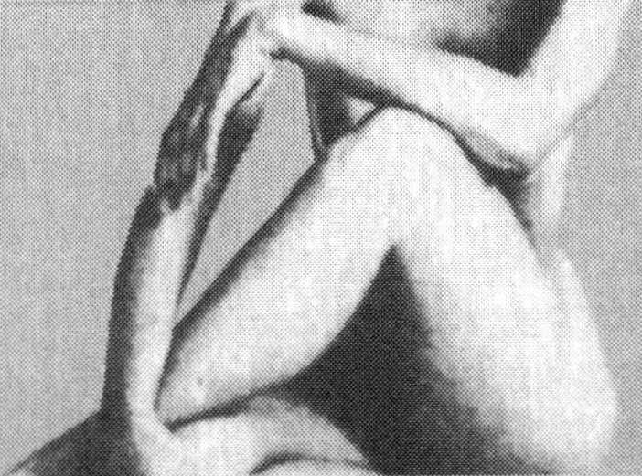

The third picture is a control. If this one dilates your pupils you may need glasses!

Stress: cultural and personal factors

Although we have spoken of responses to stress as being fairly general, there can be quite marked differences in response depending on cultural or personal background and differences in gender (see Figure 2.1). The stress of crowded families in North America tends to be equated with high crime and juvenile delinquency, but far greater crowding in Hong Kong and Tokyo does not seem to lead to similar crime levels there. (Could this be because everyone there knows karate and judo?)

On the day that the First World War broke out, there was mass hysteria in front of the Paris Bourse, with people angrily trying to withdraw their money from the stock market.

By contrast, on the same day in London, the scene outside the stock exchange was calm. People lined up in single file, quietly reading newspapers as they waited. The ingrained tradition of the British "stiff upper lip" obviously had an effect on how Britons responded. This, of course, is not to say that one response is better than another; we are merely illustrating differences in culture and upbringing.

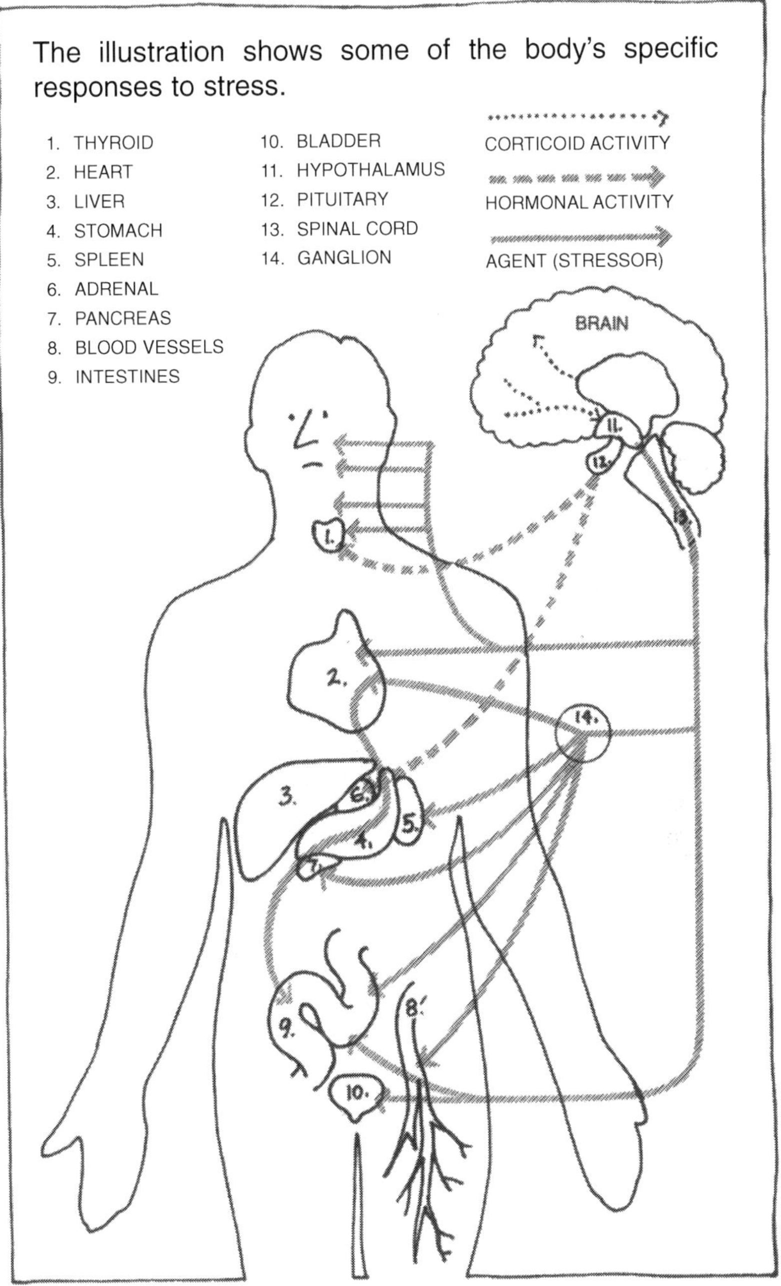
The illustration shows some of the body's specific responses to stress.
1. THYROID
2. HEART
3. LIVER
4. STOMACH
5. SPLEEN
6. ADRENAL
7. PANCREAS
8. BLOOD VESSELS
9. INTESTINES
10. BLADDER
11. HYPOTHALAMUS
12. PITUITARY
13. SPINAL CORD
14. GANGLION
CORTICOID ACTIVITY
HORMONAL ACTIVITY
AGENT (STRESSOR)
BRAIN
1.
2.
3.
4.
5.
6.
7.
8.
9.
10.
11.
12.
13.
14.

Paris Bourse, 1914, the day World War I broke out.

London Stock Exchange, 1914, the same day.

The Role of Stress in Child Raising

An individual's response to stress can be modified as early as in the cradle and all during one's upbringing. For example, many of the adults I see who do poorly under stress had parents who tried to "protect" them from all childhood stresses. Thus, the "protected" child who has never had to look a waiter in the eye and order his own food during family outings may never learn to look *anyone* in the eye during conversations. (One of my great pet peeves is trying to communicate with a fully grown teenager who shuffles and stares at the ground while mommy "helpfully" intercepts all my questions. This adolescent will still be getting wake-up calls from his mother when he is in his forties, just in case his alarm clock fails!)

This is also one of the reasons many self-made rich and famous personalities have problems with their children. The parent, having gone through considerable poverty on the way to success, wrongfully assumes that this stress was bad for him or her. The attitude of "I may have started out poor but no child (or spouse) of mine is ever going to have to worry about money" deprives the child of ever learning the value of hard work, and undermines the development of self-esteem and confidence. The child thus spoiled by a well-intentioned parental desire to save children from stress will eventually, when forced to meet stresses on his own, be certain to become a victim. Remember stress is not an enemy *if* properly managed.

On the other hand, children can be actively raised to *manage* stress, and develop winning responses that will last a lifetime. These are the children that we see to have "leadership" and "self-confident" and independent qualities that help them rise above the crowd in adult years.

How Parents can help kids cope with Stress

Stress is something every child needs to cope with, in order to be successful in dealing with stresses as an adult. But there are two perils of extremes for parents here, one offering the child too much stress,and the other offering too little stress:

Too much stress: This is seen when parents expose kids to adult stresses, such as obsessing on grades. In athletics, this has led to the total demise of "sand lot" games where the kids organize themselves and play for hours, or until the kid with the ball has to go home. Now the kids games are organized around their parents, and the kids have to listen to adults yelling at them from the sidelines. In some cases, little league sporting associations have had to ban parents who start fist fights in the stands, or who attack referees.

Too little stress: This is seen when kids are raised under the mantra of "everyone is a winner". This gives us a system where no student ever fails a grade in public school, no matter how little they study, and even the laziest athlete gets a huge trophy, just like the dedicated few that have a good work ethic.

The balance lies in exposing kids to stresses that are appropriate for their age and stage of development. When a child is old enough to speak, then he or she is old enough to speak *to* someone, and to look them in the eye when doing so. When a child is old enough to follow directions, then they should be responsible for finishing a task on their own, and not just blindly follow an older sibling. If a child is able to run and walk, then exercise should be encouraged, preferably without constant adult attention. Video-sloth, unless the child is quadriplegic, should not be the bulk of the after-school routine.

Response to stress

People have the ability to choose to respond to stresses in one of two basic ways. They can choose either the *syntoxic* response (the ignoring response), or the *catatoxic* response (fight or flight). A man could well choose the catatoxic response when his wife is being insulted from two rows back in the theater. When he confronts the heckler and learns that the man is six-feet-five-inches and a professional boxer, he may suddenly reverse his field and choose the safer syntoxic response: ignoring the heckler. Again, depending on your upbringing, one or the other of these responses could easily be ingrained to the extent that you do not need to consciously make a choice. It will be made for you by your own reflexes (unless you actively over-ride them). This is one reason why abused or battered children can sometimes grow up to abuse or batter their own children.

Human response to any stress, no matter how trivial, has been well documented by Dr. Hans Selye. His diagram of the G.A.S., or General Adaptation Response to Stress, may be seen in Figure 2.3

Figure 2.3

General Adaptation Response to Stress
(Developed by Dr. Hans Selye)
B.
A.
STAGE OF
RESISTANCE
C.
STAGE OF
EXHAUSTION
STAGE OF
ALARM

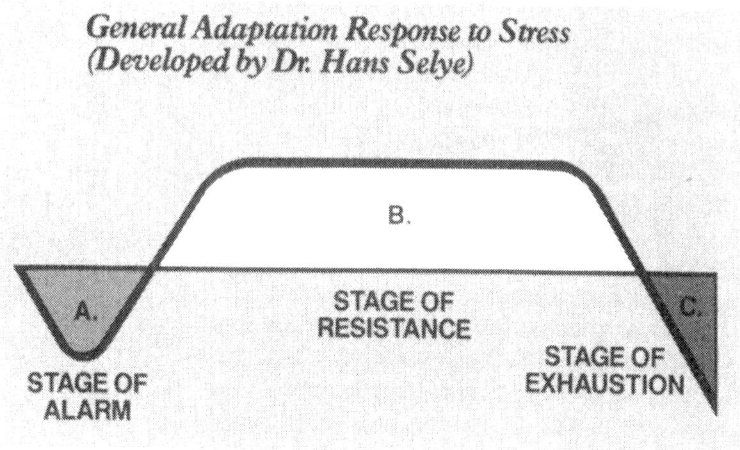

Stage A, the Alarm Reaction: all of the body's responses to stress come to bear. However, after the stress continues for long enough, the body becomes used to it and enters a Stage of Adaptation, or Resistance. If the stress is unremitting, there is a limit as to how long you can adapt before you enter the Stage of Exhaustion.

Morale studies on Allied bomber crews in the Second World War showed that the Alarm Stage lasted for the first five or six missions over enemy territory. Then the Adaptation Stage set in. But due to the extreme levels of stress, it lasted only about another five missions. After the eleventh flight, morale entered the final Exhaustion Stage. This was marked by a "shell-shocked," war-weary resignation, which was seen to make young men age almost overnight.

The same principles, although far less dramatic, are seen in response to the stresses you face during the day. That is why it is so important to take a break in the action and incur different stresses (notice I didn't say less stress necessarily). Alternate stresses (see Chapter 4) are better than just plowing on with the same ones, as workaholics are prone to do. The true workaholic's level of efficiency will decrease with his or her constant stress levels, to the point where the person will need sixteen hours to accomplish what he or she should be able to do in eight.

Selye's G.A.S. model also serves to illustrate the basic stages of your life. Childhood is the first Stage. The Stage of Adaptation or Resistance corresponds to your adult years of health, leading to eventual decline and the Exhaustion Stage at death. The trick is how to lengthen the Stage of Adaptation or Resistance!

3. The Hanson Scale Of Stress Resistance:

It's Your Choice

Now that we have seen what stress can do, both *to* and *for* your body, you need to know how much stress you are facing. It is therefore useful to have measurable "warning lights" for stress overload, to alert you to dangers before something breaks.

Because many stresses have an emotional component, it is difficult to assign an absolute value to them. (For example, the sight of a mouse may be so stressful to some people that they will faint; the same stressor might not even rate a yawn in others.) Other stresses are influenced by culture. For example, in some societies a failed marriage can be extremely stressful, as it leads to ostracism by family, friends, and coworkers. In some religions premarital sex can lead to a death sentence by stoning. In some societies, having a jail sentence could be a badge of honor, and not at all stressful: in others, such a dishonor could lead to suicide.

The now familiar Holmes-Rahe Scale (see Figure 3.1), published in 1967 attempted to provide some guidelines for stress measurement. It is still valuable today as a benchmark. Holmes and Rahe rated the death of a spouse as 100 units, and marriage as 50 units. Note that 10 of the top 15 stresses on the scale have nothing to do with work. This is a surprise to most people. They expect stress at work, and may be on their guard to defend against it. However, they usually assume that home life is harmless, thus undervaluing the stresses on the spouse who stays at home, or undervaluing their spare time if they both work. As we shall see later, it is only by being aware of your stresses that you can cope with them. You cannot fight an unseen enemy.

Figure 3.1

Holmes-Rahe scale of stress ratings

Use the blanks at the bottom to list any of your stresses that do not appear on the Holmes-Rahe Scale. You can assign numerical rating to your particular stresses by comparing them with those on the scale.

Please note that the ratings apply only to stresses that you have undergone within the past twenty-four months.

Once you have rated all stresses that apply to you, add the numbers to arrive at your total.

LIFE EVENT	VALUE	YOUR SCORE
Death of spouse	100	
Divorce	73	
Marital separation	65	
Jail term	63	
Death of a close family member	63	
Personal injury or illness	53	
Marriage	50	
Fired at work	47	
Marital reconciliation	45	
Retirement	45	
Change in health of family member	44	
Pregnancy	40	
Sex difficulties	39	

(continued on next page)

Gain of new family member	39	
Business adjustment	39	
Change in financial state	38	
Death of a close friend	37	
Change to different line of work	36	
Change in number of arguments with spouse	35	
Mortgage payment over one year's net salary	31	
Foreclosure of mortgage or loan	30	
Change in responsibilities at work	29	
Son or daughter leaving home	29	
Trouble with in-laws	29	
Outstanding personal achievement	28	
Spouse begins or stops work	26	
Begin or end school	26	
Change in living conditions (children/parents moving back in)	25	
Revision of personal habits	24	
Trouble with boss	23	
Change in work hours or conditions	20	
Change in residence	20	
Change in schools	20	

Change in recreation	19	
Change in church activities	19	
Mortgage or loan less than one year's net salary	17	
Change in sleeping habits	16	
Change in number of family get-togethers	15	
Change in eating habits	15	
Vacation	13	
Christmas	12	
Minor violations of the law	11	
Misc: Here is where you get to add and score any extra stresses that are not listed, or to increase the value of stresses that have a greater impact on you than the above scores predict…		
Enter your total here.		

If your total is over 300, then you have an *80 percent chance of a serious change in your health within the next year.*

You now have some objective idea of the amount of stress that faces you. If your total score is less than 150 units, you have a 30 percent chance of a serious change in your health within the next year. Up to 300 units gives you a 50 percent chance. More than 300 units gives you an 80 percent chance.

The exact nature of this change in health is highly individual, and will probably involve your weakest link, no matter how healthy you think you are. For example, some people are prone to ulcers, others to heart attacks or sudden alarming irregularities of heartbeat (such as palpitations). Yet others could have, mental breakdowns, colitis, asthma, retinal detachments or, by virtue of decreased immune responses, infections, and even cancers. By having regular checkups from your doctor, at least *annually* if you have a high stress score, you will gain insight into your own target areas and be better able to prevent crises. Depending on the reasons for your high stress levels, regular visits to other professionals could also be therapeutic or even life-saving. These could include your bank manager, financial planner, fitness trainer, nutritionist, or psychologist.

When I first read this classic Holmes-Rahe Stress scale, I had no doubt that the high scores caused high risks. But why was high stress only harming 80% of the people and not 100%? Why do 20 percent of the people in this high-stress group have no damage to their health at all? To discover the answer, I had to turn to my own patients. Some had very high stress levels, yet stayed healthy. Others were a predictable health disaster, even from early childhood, yet had very little stress in their lives. In both extremes of the spectrum, there was a pattern of choices that determined the outcome. (Remember, the trick in medicine is not just to figure out what kind of a *stress level* a person has, but what kind of a *person* the stress level has!). So in order to make proper sense of these stress scores, , it was necessary to devise an additional scale for personal choices—the Hanson Scale of Stress Resistance. This scale measures your choices in response to stress, and shows you where you can improve.

The Hanson Scale of Stress Resistance shows you 10 choices to weaken yourself, and 10 to strengthen yourself against stress. Once you realize that your life is on the line, and that these choices do not just deal with unimportant habits, it becomes easier to manage your life better and thus tolerate higher levels of stress.

Now let's look at the significance of each of the 10 weak choices on the Hanson Scale.

Figure 3.2

Hanson Scale of Stress Resistance

WEAK CHOICES	SCORE	STRONG CHOICES	SCORE
1. Bad genetics	-10	1. Good genetics	10
2. Insomnia	-20	2. Sense of humor	20
3. Bad Diet	-30	3. Right diet	30
4. Obesity	-40	4. Alternate stresses	40
5. Unrealistic goals	-50	5. Realistic goals	50
6. Poisons (including caffeine)	-60	6. Understanding of stress	60
7. Smoking	-70	7. Relaxation skills and efficient sleep	70
8. Wrong job	-80	8. Thorough job preparation	80
9. Financial distress	-90	9. Financial security	90
10. Unstable home	-100	10. Stable home	100
	-550	Resistance Score	+550

Using the Hanson Scale:

You can use the Hanson Scale to determine your stress resistance, which can then be added to your current stresses (Holmes-Rahe score). Note that while you may not have much control over the stresses in your life, it is here that you will count your reaction to all the things you can control.

Although there will be different *degrees* of each category, assume for the initial purposes of this exercise that any degree gets the full number of points.* (For example, whether you smoke forty cigarettes per day or ten, you still get –70 on your score sheet.) Once you have your basic picture, you can adjust the fine focus by changing these numbers a few points up or down.

*These numbers are somewhat arbitrarily assigned, and serve to provide you with a rough guideline only.

We have seen that we share many common animal responses to stress. Of course, as humans, we have one key advantage over the baboon: *intelligence*. We can use it to make ourselves much stronger than the so-called "dumb" animal. However, as we can see in medical clinics and hospitals across the country, most people's choices in response to stress leave them *weaker* than the animal. Whether such choices are active or unwitting matters not—the results are reduced enjoyment, impaired health, length of life, and, not coincidentally, reduced efficiency and profits in the workplace. However, by actively choosing strong responses, you can conquer stress, live *better*, and live longer. This empowerment not only effects the individual, but the company they work with, and the country they live in. The only hope for reducing the escalating costs of medical care is to have some active participation from each patient; the solution cannot rely on passive help from private or government sources.

The popular "herd instinct" of wrong choices isn't due to the lack of information. For example, world hunger is now replaced by world obesity as the major nutritional threat, yet we have never seen more books available on diet. Nor are wrong choices always due to the lack of opportunity. I recently toured a modern air traffic control headquarters, where the latest of stress reducers were at hand: a library, exercise equipment, and video games. The controllers are under intense stress, and are usually allowed to work only half of their eight-hour shift, the other half being set aside for relief of tension. At the time I visited, the thoughtfully provided outlets were being completely neglected. People on breaks congregated in the coffee room for fast food, sugar drinks, and chain-smoked cigarettes. If you are like most people, your exercise bike and fitness-club membership card are both gathering dust. Fitness depends on *active participation*, not the *passive possession* of tools and toys.

Weak Choice Number 1

Bad Genetics—Minus 10 Points

Although the quality of health and the lifespan of your ancestors is not within your control, it has been said that the key to a long life is to "choose" your parents carefully. This may not be as important as once thought. Thus a history of relatively early deaths in your family has been given the lowest rating on the Hanson Scale of Stress Resistance. Although this may seem odd, it is generally true that most people's ancestors died prematurely because of what could now be seen as mismanagement (not necessarily of their own doing) of their stresses. In many cases, lives were shortened because of the direct trauma of war, famine, or diseases, which, even if survived, took a very high toll of adaptation "coins." This—along with mismanagement in other areas such as lifestyle, financial, environmental, and retirement planning—may well have contributed to their early demise.

Until very recently, it was virtually unheard of for the majority of the population to do regular and proper exercise for any appreciable part of their lifetimes. Although people on farms tended to derive the benefits of exercise from their everyday labor, their lifespans were shortened by famine due to drought, floods, insects, and fires. Medical care for infections was primitive, and average lifespans were shortened by maternal and infant mortality. With the advances in modern living, most of the causes of your ancestors' deaths would now be treatable. Also, our knowledge of public health has improved. Thus if your family died young of lung cancer, but worked in an asbestos mine, this need not be reflected in your own health, assuming you are not being exposed to the same risks.

Of course, if all the males in your family died in their thirties from the same heart disease, and you do not bother seeing a doctor yourself until you are twenty-nine, it is quite likely that you could inherit their "bad luck." The low rating accorded to the genetic factor is nor not intended to demean the very real risks to those with inherited diseases, but rather to emphasize the numerical rarity of such cases.

BAD GENETICS.
If your parents or grand-parents died before 65, your score = -10.
Enter your score here.

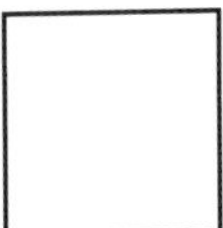

Weak Choice Number 2

Insomnia—Minus 20 Points

Although this may not seem like a choice, the fact that sleep can be gained without drugs makes it so. Occasional insomnia, such as on the eve of an exciting trip, is not harmful. Often people will have a couple of nights a week where they don't sleep well, but fully catch up by sleeping in on the weekend; this too is not a harmful pattern. But if you are chronically unable to sleep efficiently and awake refreshed, you will not be in very good shape to withstand the following day's stresses. One of the most common causes for regular insomnia is unresolved stress. We will discuss ways to correct this later.

Before you label yourself as a true insomniac (and take the minus 20 score here), we must take into consideration how much sleep you need in the first place. I receive many requests for sleeping pills from elderly patients because they are sleeping only four or five hours per night. Actually, it is quite normal for people to require less sleep as they grow older, and yet the ingrained habit of thinking one requires eight hours is still present. I tell these patients that the only way they could be given the additional three hours of sleep a night would be through a general anesthetic. Sadly, this was precisely demonstrated by the late pop icon Michael Jackson, who died following one of his regular such anesthetics. Many great achievers in history, such as Winston Churchill, never slept more than a few hours out of a 24 hour day, taking catnaps as needed. Their achievements would not have been enhanced, and nor would their quality and quantity of life be enriched if they were forced to sleep longer with prescription drugs.

Stimulants such as caffeine and alcohol will interfere with a good sleep, as will Type A behavior (see Chapter 8), a large meal before bedtime, a snoring spouse, or a crying baby. However, for those who wake up each morning feeling fatigued, and the only deep sleep comes after hitting the "snooze" button on the alarm, put yourself down for minus 20 here. Don't despair however, we will show you some drug-free options soon. (See Chapter 4.)

INSOMNIA.
Your score if you have chosen it = -20.
Enter your score here.

Weak Choice Number 3

Bad Diet—Minus 30 Points

If you eat too many or too few calories, the wrong foods, or if you eat too quickly, you are choosing to greatly weaken your resistance to stress. Eating too much will be discussed in the obesity section. Eating too little, while far less common, is still a bad diet choice. Anorexia (self-starvation) and bulimia ("bio-food-back") can be dangerous, and, if untreated, potentially fatal.

Far more commonly, bad diet choices are made unwittingly, by people suffering from a "time famine". As cooking skills and dinner hours at home are subverted, people are eating pre-made foods out of the microwave, or eating take-out foods, often with poor ingredients. The biggest inflammatory element in our environment is white sugar, or white flour (which turns to sugar after absorption into the blood stream). These form the basis for "comfort" foods, that offer the opposite of comfort. If you are looking for another reason to reduce or avoid these unhealthy elements in your diet, just consider that all disease is either caused or aggravated by inflammation at a cellular level. This is true of infections, cancers, pain, chronic fatigue, just to name a few. My patients find that a good visual aid here is to imagine standing beside a bar-b-que, spraying a bottle of gasoline near the flames. White sugar and flour will have the same explosive effect on the cells in your body.

Another bad choice can be chemically altered vegetables and other foods. The secret to good health is to eat foods as close to their natural state as possible. In today's terms, we should be wary of all foods that are not organic. (see figure 3.3)

Figure 3.3

Our ancestors did not need to have a treasure hunt to find organic foods. In the old days, *organic* food was known as something else: *food*. It is only recently that we have figured out how to give growth hormones, antibiotics, estrogens and other additives to the feed of our cattle, chickens, and farmed fish. (Note that the FDA does not require any of these additives to be listed on live produce). Also, it is not natural for animals to be raised with zero exercise, such as in the modern "factory" production lines. Remember a couple of new rules for organic eating:

New Food Rule: aerosol spray cheese, in neon colors, is not one of the basic food groups. Cheese does not come from a cow in any color other than basic white, and it does not come naturally between plastic sheets in burger-sized squares that last seven years without refrigeration.

New Food Rule: Food is SUPPOSED to have a stale date. Any food that stays "fresh" for years can't be good for you. The best way to keep real food fresh is simple: leave it in the store, until the day you need it. In case of "emergencies", try keeping a short list of storable foods, such as whole wheat pasta, frozen vegetables, and wild canned fish.

New Food Rule: Kitchens are meant to *make* meals, not just to *store or reheat* them. One great stress defense is a low-tech involvement with your own food preparation. With good ingredients, great meals can be made as quickly as reheating frozen "fast" meals. This results in great quality, prices cheaper than a restaurant, and conversation with significant others during the process.

New Food Rule: Presentation is (almost) everything. Use your good dishes and silverware every day; even the humble fried egg will look better! Eating out of the fast-food container with the lid pealed back, standing at the sink, spoils the whole effect. Elegance can also be economical. Canned or bottled drinks are actually quite pricey. Ordinary tap water can become much more marketable if served in a fine glass, with ice cubes. If it still looks unappetizing, add a slice of lemon and a paper umbrella.

New Food Rule: Egg yolks are supposed to be dark yellow, not pastel pale, as in the factory hen-house. Often the organic eggs are not much different in price as from the factory hen house, and are well worth their value.
New Food Rule: Fresh fish should have fins with jagged edges, not rounded smooth by collisions with neighbors in a densely packed fish-farm. Fish are supposed to swim thousands of miles and be caught with a line or net, not be trapped in a pond where they can be killed with a hammer.
New Food Rule: It is OK for natural fruits and vegetables to have imperfect colors on the outside. They are not supposed to look like the plastic ones on your grandmother's hat. The only way to enforce uniform orange color onto an orange peel, or perfect reds on every apple and tomato is to use dye or other artificial means. If you are going to insist on perfection in foods, go for the taste inside, not the color outside.
New Food Rule: It's ok to use a knife to cut through meats and chicken. Don't expect food additives to do the work for you. The point of hormones like estrogen in cattle feed is to make the meat so tender you can cut it with a plastic spoon.
Bad diet choices can also include too much salt (which in some people can cause hypertension) and, very commonly, too little water. Insufficient fluid intake (less than eight glasses of water per day) is detrimental to the viscosity of the blood and the function of the kidneys. When doing cardio exercises like running or biking, don't wait for thirst to tell you to rehydrate; drink often. If your urine is dark after you finish your exercise, then you are dehydrated.
If you are not sure if you have a bad diet, enter your score after you have read Chapter 5.

BAD DIET.
Your score if you choose to have one = -30.
Enter your score here.

Weak Choice Number 4

Obesity—Minus 40 Points

Obesity is a *choice*, not *"bad luck"*, no matter what advocacy groups pretend. My old professor of internal medicine served as a young military doctor in Europe in the post WWII years. He made an untactful but true observation: "nobody ever comes out of a concentration camp fat". The body's weight indeed is a simple product of arithmetic. Calories **in** must equal calories **out**, or your weight will change. The choice of obesity can thus be from taking in too many calories, or from burning off too few. So even if a person is not guilty of gluttony, they can still be obese because of sloth. Most commonly, however, we see the full combination effect. Once a person is carrying too much weight (like a hiker carrying a full back-pack), it is difficult to have any spring in their step, meaning few calories are expended in shuffling through daily activities. (If the hiker puts down the heavy back-pack, he can feel as energized as a tap-dancer!).

Obesity is now the biggest preventable health threat in the world, and it is especially prominent in children. It is on track to bankrupt our medical insurance plans, whether private or government operated. Paradoxically, stress tends to make us lose weight, if the diet is unchanged. So it actually requires great determination to stay fat when you are stressed. This determination, if harnessed in a positive direction, could be better used to combat the root cause, namely our poor choices in response to our stresses!

But let's take a closer look at obesity, and try to understand it better. Obesity is not a problem: it is only the result of a problem. Usually the root problem is one of these top ten causes:

1. Boredom
2. Anxiety and/or depression
3. Badly managed stress
4. Pain
5. Lifestyle habits
6. Poor Self Image
7. Addiction to refined sugar (and flour)
8. Massive Passivity
9. Can't cook
10. Had no idea this was fattening

Treatment for obesity obviously begins with its recognition, and with its underlying cause or causes. Start with your doctor, and be aware of any additional "spin-off" problems, such as diabetes, high blood pressure, etc. Sometimes it can be helpful to see a Bariatric specialist, a psychiatrist, or to join a peer group that is losing weight. Surgical cures, which include everything from wiring the teeth shut to bypassing part of the stomach and loops of intestines, are not usually the long term answers (short of constructing a single tube to connect the mouth to the rectum.) If the underlying causes are not dealt with, there is no amount of surgery that will work for the long term.

Even being 10 percent over your ideal weight (not from insurance charts or the BMI calculation, but the weight at which you look and feel the best in your bathing suit) is a detriment to your health and well-being. Jockeys know that as little as a ten-pound weight gain can decrease the performance of the horse under the rider; just imagine the effect of even ten extra pounds on your own legs. For illustration, try loading up a back pack with ten or twenty pounds, and see how it feels to climb stairs, rise from a sitting position, and walk distances. Sure feels better to lose those weights!

Animals in the wild would not survive if they were as much overweight as most humans are. One exception could be the hippopotamus; its body is designed to help it float in water. Besides humans, the only other *pathologically* obese creatures are domestic pets fed by humans.

The effects of obesity are more than aesthetics, or the trembling of the knees under the massive weight of the body. The heart will not last as many years; other areas of the body that are harmed by obesity include the lungs, the liver, and the pancreas (diabetes type 2 will likely result). Even the bones feel the effects of extra weight. The obese are far more likely to need operations or replacements for knees and hips. Back pains are also frequent, especially with those with protuberant abdomens that pull the spine into a sway-back. For the morbidly obese teenager (double their normal weight), the warning is clear: if you don't take control of your choices, your choices will control your destiny. Not only will you suffer ill health as a young adult, you will likely not live long enough to be an old adult. If you are a parent of a seriously obese child, don't think it is healthy; you will not only need to set aside college funds, but you will need to plan for your child's funeral before your own.

OBESITY.
Your score if you choose to be fat = -40.
Enter your score here.

This subject, including the calculation of your BMI, or Body Mass Index, is dealt with more fully in Chapter 6; also see the "eat *normally*" way to lose weight in Chapter 7.

Weak Choice Number 5

Unrealistic Goals—Minus 50 Points

Consider a group of teenagers in a career counselling class. Each has different capabilities and limitations, and each has a specific career goal. The short one who dreams of being a basketball center, and the tall one who wants to be a professional jockey are both are being unrealistic. The one who is tone deaf will likely never achieve a dream of being an opera singer. And the clumsy one will likely never make it into the high-wire act at the circus (at least, not for long). Unless their goals are realistic, and matched to their natural aptitudes and limitations, these teenagers will be doomed to failure, as measured by their own ambitions. They may idolize the "bling" possessions of popular celebrities, but without marketable skills (or an inheritance) they are never going to be in that league. The continual unhappiness resulting from

unrealistic goals can have a very negative effect on a person's self-esteem, and, ultimately, on their ability to resist stress.

Through the media's focus on celebrity-worship, most people now leave school with high expectations regarding their future lifestyles. In the culture of our public school system, we have evolved to the point where every child is told they are a "winner", and none can fail, no matter how little they study. In some school systems, teachers are reprimanded if they make 9-year old students memorize their multiplication tables, because it might interfere with their "self-esteem". In organized "little league" sports, children are passively "motivated" by their parents and coaches, and are all given the same huge trophy even if they came last and did no work. Once again, every child, even the laziest sluggard, is a "winner".

Once these kids become adults, they can no longer expect to have "winner" status follow them into the job market, unless they have a corresponding work ethic. With the flattening of the international marketplace, there is an entire world of ambitious competitors for every job imaginable. Not only does this apply to low paying factory jobs that are being done "off shore" from the markets of Europe and the US, but there is a great deal of outsourcing of high paying high-tech jobs to countries like India and China.

If you have unrealistic goals, your resistance to stress will suffer; enter your score here as minus 50 points.

UNREALISTIC GOALS. Your score if you choose unrealistic goals = -50. Enter your score here.

Realistic, as opposed to unrealistic, goals will be discussed in Chapter 4.

Weak Choice Number 6

Poisons—Minus 60 Points

I use the rather strong word *poison* to cover the broad category of toxins, drugs, and excessive caffeine taken in response to stress. Obviously some of these are much worse than others. Methamphetamines are now the most dangerous, followed by cocaine, and opiates such as codeine and heroin. Score the full sixty points here if this applies to you. But other substances are often deemed "harmless" and should also be considered in this category. If you only have a modest problem, just give yourself 10 of the 60 points; if you have a more serious problem, score up to the full 60.

Alcohol

Alcohol in moderation (one to two ounces per day, or one to two glasses of wine or beer) can be harmless enough except during pregnancy. In fact, some evidence now suggests that your cholesterol level can in fact be reduced by this sort of moderate intake. However, drinks in excess of this amount quickly cross over into the toxic side. This is especially true of today's binge drinker: no drinks at all during the weekdays, then countless shots on Saturday night. The body does not average out the math. You can go all month with no drinks, then take thirty all at once and still kill yourself. Excessive alcohol interferes with sleep patterns and the integrity of the stomach lining. It can cause cirrhosis of the liver, headaches, and a host of other problems. It can lead to atrophy of the testicles in males and of the ovaries in females, to the point where libido is nonexistent (in ironic counterpoint to "sexy" alcohol ads). Most importantly, excessive alcohol consumption can destroy irreplaceable brain cells.

Alcohol at bedtime-with its paradoxical delayed stimulative action-interferes with efficient sleep; it may help you nod off after a "nightcap" drink, but you will have a "wake-up" effect about two hours later. Alcohol in excess also causes unbelievable *premature aging*. If you could see the birth certificate of the typical street "wino," who looks about ninety years old, you would be truly shocked. He might be only in his thirties; at autopsy every internal organ would show advanced aging. Whenever I see someone who is much older in appearance than in stated years, alcoholism is the first condition that I suspect.

Tranquilizers

Another major type of poison is the mood altering family of drugs to treat anxiety and depression. These are not illicit drugs, but usually obtained from the medical establishment. While they are perfectly appropriate in the short term for grief or crises, and in the long term for a select few cases of psychiatric disease, they have become a widely overused panacea. The Prescription Drug Cartel has done a masterful job of marketing, with ads to patients and with clever marketing to doctors. Consumer ads are now being seen everywhere, with the punch line of "ask your doctor" if you want to get your smile back. Not only are these ads seen in adult media, but also in magazines for parents, targeting children as potential lifetime tranquilizer users. Bribes to doctors are finally getting more scrutiny; they were verging on the unethical, often running to over ten thousand dollars a year per doctor. The FDA (in the US) and other national agencies are now clamping down

on the more obvious "inducements", such as subsidized tuition to "educational" courses, free steak and wine dinners to doctors and their dates for medical "education" evenings (with live infomercial for their chosen drug), and free "toys" for the doctors offices, like coffee mugs, pens and clipboards).

To be sure, these drugs are being given because of stress. The public is bombarded with stressful news, none of which can be controlled by the individual. We wake up to television images of the carnage from suicide bombs around the globe. More of the bloody details are found in the morning papers or on the internet news sites. In case we missed *that*, it shows up on FaceBook and Twitter. As we commute we are further given audio updates of global atrocities, corruption, and disasters. In most cities, traffic itself is becoming more stressful, all the more so when we hear of bombs going off in subways, trains, and busses. While we are at work, we are stressed by the realities of global competition, which affects all of us, from manual laborers to executives. When we travel, we are reminded of terrorism at the airport, and even at our resort destinations. When we try to unwind by going to the movies, all hell breaks loose; special effects and violent explosions seem to have replaced plot and acting. Try to unwind at home by turning off the news, and you are bombarded with "reality" television, which is to say a combination of fear, lust, and low budgets. Try to relax with music on the radio dial? Its very hard to find, in between the screaming talk shows, the blaring ads, the car-shaking bass, and the unintelligible lyrics.

So the stressed-out patient wants a passive way to treat anxiety and depression, and turns to the doctor for a soothing, fast-acting prescription. As a result of this huge demand, doctors are ladling out record numbers of prescriptions to the general public. As a long term strategy for the masses these drugs become detrimental, addictive and expensive. Especially when we consider that the fastest growing users of these drugs are our children, we need to consider the implications. Help for stress does not come passively, in pill form. Your treatments should aim at the *cause* of the stress, not the end *result* . If taken daily, prescriptions for mood elevating drugs are never cleared from the body, and often become a lifetime habit. Instead of helping your stress defense, it dulls the wit, making it even harder to organize your stress defenses. While some patients with specific pathology will truly benefit from such medications, they are not meant for broad distribution to all.

Caffeine

Reaching for that nice hot cup of coffee or tea when under stress has become one of life's more popular pleasures. Certainly two cups of drip coffee, a couple of shots of espresso, or two cups of tea per day will not cause any real harm to a healthy person. However, as with alcohol, excessive caffeine can become detrimental.

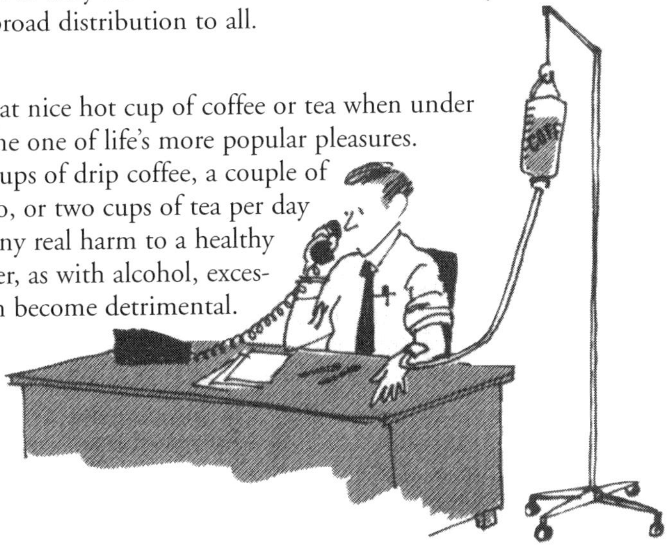

Some of the main sources of caffeine are:

	mg of Caffeine per serving
Coffee	
Instant	*65-100*
Percolated	*135*
Strong Drip	*175*
Espresso—2 ounces	*100*
Tea-US or imported	*40-60*
Green tea	*15*
Hot Cocoa,	*15*
Red Bull (8.2 oz)	*80*
Jolt	*71*
Pepsi One, Mountain Dew	*55*
Pepsi Cola	*37*
Diet Pepsi	*36*

Coca Cola Classic *34*
Diet Coke *45*

(See a more complete listing from the US Food and Drug Administration, appendix C.)

Note that, contrary to public perception, real espresso is actually lower in caffeine than drip coffee. Of course it can be diluted with water (called an Americano) or by milk (latte, or cappuccino), and, at the rate of a few per day, can be enjoyed without adding to your stress risk. In fact, just as with alcohol, a small dose of caffeine can be helpful. Caffeine can offer help to an asthmatic, as it can help release some of the bronchial spasm. If your breathing is tight, a shot of espresso would likely help, either straight or diluted with water (don't add milk, as it might thicken your mucous). Small amounts of caffeine are routinely added to pain medications, because caffeine helps "transport" the drug to the end organ.

But it is in the high levels of intake that caffeine can cross over into a risk instead of a reward. Over 400 mg per day (three cups of drip coffee) can double your adrenaline levels in the blood stream. I

have treated patients who admit to drinking over a dozen cups of coffee a day. This excessive consumption can produce risks if you have certain heart conditions, or hormonal imbalances such as an overactive thyroid gland. Epilepsy could also be triggered by such high doses. Many women have benign breast cysts that can flourish with high doses of caffeine; while this does not cause cancer, it could certainly make it difficult to feel a new lump. High doses of caffeine can also aggravate inflammatory conditions such as colitis, dermatitis, and acne. Naturally, excesses can also cause insomnia. Even hemorrhoids are adversely affected by caffeine.

So if you love caffeine, first identify how much you take. If you are over 400 mg per day, or if your doctor suggests reducing your intake, switch the rest of your consumption to caffeine-free options. I love my morning espresso, but I switch to water the rest of the day.

If you have trouble "selling" yourself the idea of drinking water, try it hot (with lemon wedge), or cold (flat or fizzy). Since coffee or tea and cigarettes are a two-handed habit in most smokers, switching to water may have the added benefit of reducing the automatic urge to light up during "coffee" breaks.

Surprisingly, excess caffeine consumption rates as the easiest of all habits to give up, according to my patients.

POISONS.
Your score if you choose to abuse = -60.
Enter your score here.

Weak Choice Number 7

Smoking—Minus 70 Points

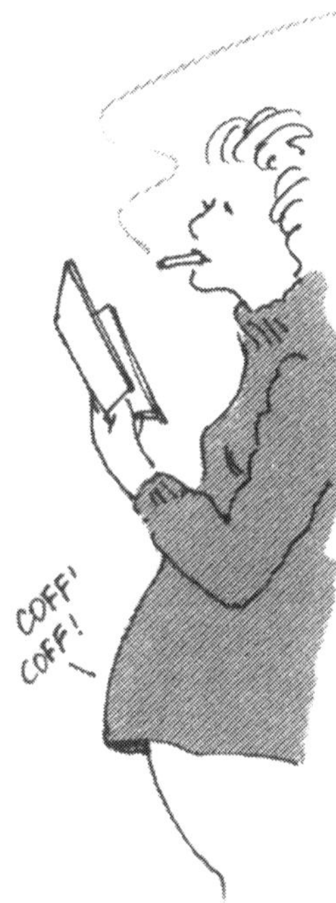

This is a common and disastrous response to stress, and is the number one preventable health hazard in the world. Although it seemed to be in decline several years ago, the rate of smoking among young people, especially teenage girls, is quickly rising. The very idea of rolling up a leaf, sticking it in your face, and setting fire to it does seem to defy intelligent explanation. But the tobacco companies are very clever about marketing. They may not be able to advertise on television, but they can have the same impact by paying movie companies to have the leading actors smoke cigarettes. The other pressure to smoke, especially with young women, comes from the disparity between the obesity of the public, who are bombarded by media with images of thin "role models". The implication here is that smoking stops snacking; so if you want to lose weight, start puffing. While smoking is very easy to start, it can be extraordinarily difficult to quit. Nicotine is actually much more addictive than cocaine or even heroine, and would never have been granted government approval if it was proposed today.

I have often seen pregnant mothers with conscientious concerns about what foods will be best for the unborn baby and whether the water should be boiled before drinking. Often such mothers stoically refuse to take even the safest medication to relieve a migraine. These concerns are welcome, and in most cases fully justified.

Yet it is a source of amazement to me that some of these same mothers-to-be will blithely inhale a pack of cigarettes per day, ignoring the incredible, constant, and devastating damage to the developing fetus. Smoking during pregnancy is nothing other than a prenatal form of child abuse. Many obstetricians today are even refusing to accept responsibility for prenatal patients who continue to smoke during pregnancy.

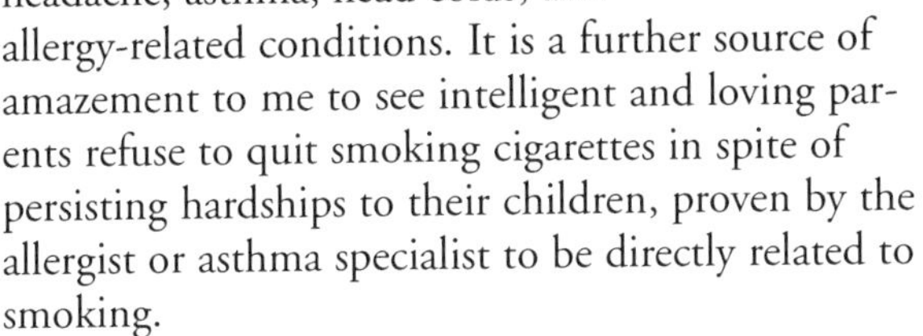

The effects of this child abuse-in-utero, of course, persist into childhood if either parent smokes in the house. Evidence now shows that second-hand smoke can stunt a child's physical and mental development, and cause a much higher incidence of children's visits to the doctor for bronchitis, headache, asthma, head colds, and allergy-related conditions. It is a further source of amazement to me to see intelligent and loving parents refuse to quit smoking cigarettes in spite of persisting hardships to their children, proven by the allergist or asthma specialist to be directly related to smoking.

Even more significant than their role as an agent of child abuse, cigarettes are an unparalleled form of self-abuse. I have seen conditions of peripheral gangrene that are dramatically linked to smoking, where the tip of a toe has to be amputated. If the patient quits smoking, the problem never comes back. If the patient starts back, more gangrene appears at the stump, and serial amputations have to be performed, all the way up the leg (even to the hip).

During stress, when lungs are already being dilated and sucking in air to the maximum capacity, the inhaled cigarette smoke is able to do its maximum amount of damage. The fact that all the blood vessels in the body, including the coronary arteries, are known to clamp down severely when even one cigarette is inhaled makes it easy to see why smoking can push you closer toward heart attack pains.

We have all seen vivid pictures or films about the effects of cigarettes on the circulation of blood to the heart, stomach, skin, limbs and other organs. Literature abounds on the subject of the ill effects of cigarette smoking, to the extent that public financing of even more studies on smoking are wasteful of medical research dollars. We all know by this time that cigarette smoke is a proven killer. However, cigarette sales have remained relatively stable. They tend to decline only when taxes become too high for the market to pay.

It is interesting to note that when teenage girls are left out of the calculations, statistics show the majority of North American adults do not smoke. This is certainly a sign of discretion, and an improvement over the past. It is also a clear indication that smokers are killing themselves off faster than new recruits can be found.

Smoking badly damages virtually every organ in the body. It is responsible for thousands of deaths from heart attacks and stomach ulcers. Approximately 30 percent of all cancers are related to smoking. This includes lung cancer, throat cancer, and cancer of the bladder, to name but a few. Even second-hand smoke can be very dangerous, particularly to patients with angina. Such patients often get chest pains simply by walking into a smoky room. "Careless" smoking is also a major cause of fire, causing burns, deaths, and damage to forests and homes.

Remember, if you are a smoker, you may think your lungs are in great shape. You may be falsely lulled by the memory of an aged family member who smoked. But until you try to do extensive exercise (like running a few miles or skiing at high altitudes) or have your pulmonary functions measured by your doctor, you will probably have no idea how bad your lungs are. You may not notice your lung deterioration until you can no longer climb stairs without having to pause for a breath, and no longer finish a sentence without sucking for air. These are predictable and irreversible manifestations of late stage emphysema, and have nothing to I do with the state of your muscles.

The only way to salvage the remaining lung tissue at this stage is to quit your cigarettes. There is no dietary supplement, series of exercises, vitamin, or magic potion that will negate the poisonous effects of inhaled tobacco smoke.

SMOKING. Your choice if you choose to do it = -70. Enter your score here.

Weak Choice Number 8

Wrong Job—Minus 80 Points

Picture a window-washer on the outside of an office tower, swinging high above ground level on a scaffold, suspended by rope. He loves his job, and is good at it. He enjoys the freedom of fresh air, the sunshine, and the constant exercise. In addition, he has a sense of personal accomplishment, and no boss looking over his shoulder. He looks inside at the office workers, each in their own "Dilbert" cubicle, and wonders how anybody could choose to work under such claustrophobic and stressful conditions.

Inside the glass sits a skilled IT specialist, who loves her job. She gets great satisfaction out of problem solving, and helping her customers stay in business in a competitive market. She uses all of her learned skills from school, but, more importantly, has a great sense of creativity. She looks through the glass at the scaffold and gasps at the thought of stepping outside.

Neither worker in this analogy would do well if they traded places, as both would be in the wrong jobs. He would probably have a stress ulcer in the first month in the cubicle. She might have a panic attack or even a cardiac arrest in the first minute on the scaffold.

If you are in the wrong job, you are committing one of the worst "offenses" against your stress defense. Try to plan some other options, even if you feel "trapped" by a good salary, and don't want to downscale your lifestyle. Such plans help even if they can't be implemented without prolonged periods of extra work or study. Prisoners of war always felt better able to deal with their stresses if there was an escape tunnel being dug underneath their compound, even if ultimate freedom was years away. (See the classic historical movie "The Great Escape" for a good insight into the improved prisoner morale during their tunnel work.)

Lack of satisfaction on the job breeds discontent, lowered self-image, brooding, moody behavior, and often increased arguments at home with the family. This can be just as true if you are "over-educated for the job," as if you are undereducated and poorly prepared.

It may seem unlikely that anybody would willingly choose the wrong job for himself or herself. But in fact it does often occur, for various reasons. For example, Dr. Laurence Peter, author of *The Peter Principle*, has demonstrated that it is all too common for people in a job hierarchy to continue to be promoted until they reach their level of incompetence.

The corollary of this is that, in any hierarchy, each person tends to rise until he or she becomes incompetent at a job. It is at that level that he or she stays, being considered unsuitable for further promotion. (If this is commonly true, the majority of jobs are held by incompetents.) This situation would impair the stress resistance of the corporation as a whole, and would certainly impair the individual's ability to resist stress.

Keep in mind, you need not be a passive bystander; you can say "no" to a promotion above your area of competence. You can ask for your old job back if you recognize unhappiness resulting from your last promotion. Or you could even quit and find more suitable work elsewhere.

Inadequate education often prevents people from doing work they enjoy. Sometimes too much education does the same thing. I have seen kids sent to expensive schools by wealthy parents, but who would much rather have spent their early years becoming a skilled artisan or craftsman. But it is possible to go into retraining programs, at any age. You can still be the architect (or draftsman) of your own destiny to a large extent.

WRONG JOB. Your score if you have one = -80. Enter your score here.

Never underestimate the importance of knowing yourself in order to assess the types of work that are best suited to your strengths and weaknesses. See the appendix to find out which social style quadrant you are in, and to help you find job categories that would be appropriate.

Weak Choice Number 9

Financial Distress—Minus 90 Points

As evidenced in the stock market crash of 1929, a financial crisis can evoke a lot of ledge-jumping. Since 2008, the global slump in real estate and a tightening of credit has sharply curtailed family spending, and left many retirement plans in ruins. This spills back onto the job market, with many senior citizens forced to stay in the workplace, competing for jobs with recent high-school or college graduates. The detrimental effects of having the financial "alligators" snapping at your heels are seen both in the acute fall from wealth and the chronic oppression of poverty. Financial distress may also apply to those between the two extremes--people who are working hard and making a good wage, but lack perspective, discipline, and organization in managing their money. The seductive lure of credit cards and "no money down" purchases of cars, holidays and furniture also lays a trap for the unwary. The ease of refinancing one's home also provides cash that can be temptingly squandered. In some cases, financial distress comes from a poor relationship, where excess spending is thought to "buy" improved self esteem, whether for oneself or one's spouse or kids. The difference between spending 5 percent more than you earn and spending less than you earn separates financial distress from comfort.

Money that is wasted on frivolous purchases could often be enough to finance stress reduction measures such as vacations, treats, or part-time help around the home. Without making time and priority for financial stress reduction, burnout is the likely result. In health, this burnout can be disastrous or even fatal; at work it can lead to even worse financial stress, and, ultimately, ruin.

When I see a patient with chest or stomach pains, headache, depression, or other signs of stress related conditions, I always ask how things are going financially. Very often the rest of the medical history will be negative, but the health crisis will be caused because there is too much month left at the end of the money.

FINANCIAL DISTRESS. Your score if you have it = -10. Enter your score here.

In a case like this, a good financial planner can often help more than a doctor. If you have significant financial distress, enter your score here as minus 90.

Weak Choice Number 10

Unstable Home and Social Support—Minus 100 Points

This rates the highest score on our list of conditions that reduce your resistance to stress. Yet the typical workaholic, when under stress, tends to undervalue his or her personal time with family and friends. Nothing could be further from the truth. Such an attitude is likely to end in marital strife or even breakup, which will further add to the Holmes-Rahe stress score. As anyone who has suffered the legal fees and emotional costs of a divorce will tell you, an unstable home life can be ruinous to your other stress defenses as well. No resources left for vacations, health club memberships, or golf games. Then there is the predictable

trouble with relatives and friends who take sides. Usually the household splits, with one or both parties moving to smaller quarters. Finances quickly become depleted, especially if one cannot find extra work or overtime to make ends meet. Insomnia at night, and lack of focus during the day serve to impair relationships with kids and new dating prospects.

Beware of the workaholic trap; spending all of your waking hours thinking about work, and then ignoring your family and friends. By demeaning your important support team, you will inevitably make your work more difficult, and burnout more likely. In case that is not enough motivation, it should also be noted that this support will also keep you healthy, happy, and alive for many more years.

Make if a priority to connect with those who matter to you, including pets. There are a few people in this world who deliberately choose to be "loners," but they do not tend to be among the long livers. (Although loners that are alcoholics may *have* long livers!)

UNSTABLE HOME AND SOCIAL SUPPORT.
Your score if you choose this= -100.
Enter your score here.

If you have children, try to spend some quality time with them, even if you don't have much quantity time. If your home life is truly beyond redemption, don't stay miserable forever; consider divorce.

If your home life is unstable, enter your score here as minus 100.

How did you do?

WEAK CHOICES	POSSIBLE SCORE	ENTER YOUR SCORE
1. Bad genetics	10	
2. Insomnia	-20	
3. Bad diet	-30	
4. Obesity	-40	
5. Unrealistic goals	-50	
6. Poisons (including caffeine)	-60	
7. Smoking	-70	
8. Wrong job	-80	
9. Financial distress	-90	
10. UNSTABLE HOME	-100	
Total score if you made all the wrong choices = -550		
	YOUR TOTAL	

All right, now you have a minus score total. To put this in perspective, keep in mind that the best score is zero. Anything over -10 should be improved. Now you're ready to start calculating your positive responses to stress-to work out your plus score on the "strong" side of the Hanson Scale. Read on…

The benefits of touching

In a recent experiment, a young schoolgirl was asked to give a poetry reading to a group of peers in her home. Blood pressure and pulse monitors were connected to a graph. Predictable, with the "stage fright" of performing, both of these parameters quickly rose and stayed high throughout her reading. However, when the girl's cat jumped up on her lap for a cuddle, she absent-mindedly began petting it as she continued reading. Both her blood pressure and her pulse rate plummeted back to normal. Similar experiments with adults and the elderly confirm the universality of this effect. Pets do help counteract the effects of stress.

4. The Hanson Scale:

Ten choices to be strong

Now we have considered your total stress score (fig 3-1). We have also learned of 10 weak choices you could make in response to these stresses, which will only add to your health risk. So let's now take a look at 10 positive choices, that will help to make you impervious to your base stress levels.

These choices won't change your stresses, but they will change the outcome of these stresses in your body. I have been impressed by some of my patients who are under incredible levels of stress, but fail to buckle or have their health break down, while others around them wilt under the same strain. These ten choices illustrate the reasons for their resilience.

The stresses around you may be beyond your personal control, but each of these choices is entirely within your grasp. Initially, if you are in the habit of making a lot of weak choices (chapter 3), it may seem a bit difficult to adapt to new options. You might have even convinced yourself that all of the fun in life comes from the bad choices, and all of the good ones are horrible. However, it all comes down to "selling" the good choices, and "un-selling" the bad ones. Mercifully, this is not difficult, because good choices really are more enjoyable, and none require odious self-denial. The end result will be to add more years to your life, and more life to your years. If you master these, you will be able to thrive under pressure, and learn the true Joy of Stress.

Strong Choice Number 1

Good Genetics—Plus 10 Points

Although this is the only item on the scale that you can't choose, I include it for its undeniable (if minor) relevance. Just as we have seen that bad genetics need not spell out an automatic shortening of lifespan, a good genetic history by itself should not give false confidence. For example, if all your ancestors lived into their nineties, that cannot be a bad influence on your lifespan. Their stresses were probably simpler than our modern pace. But if they were making good choices, and now you are making bad ones, your family history alone can't help you now.

In any event, rather than dwelling on ancestors, it is better to plan for a lasting close relationship with your peers and descendants. If you make the rest of the good choices in this chapter, you will be on your way to winning the longevity lottery!

GOOD GENETICS. If your ancestors lived to a ripe old age, your score = +10. Enter your score here.

Strong Choice Number 2

Sense of Humor—Plus 20 Points

Research shows us that laughter is indeed good medicine, for reasons both physical and chemical. Physically, a good explosive laugh provides both exercise and relaxation for our muscles. Exercise from laughter is given to the muscles of the chest, diaphragm, and abdomen. By increasing the abdominal pressure, laughter can encourage the propulsion of the intestines, thus helping digestion. Laughter also provides exercise for the facial and neck muscles, and, even the rest of the body as well. Laughter provides relaxation to muscles that create the tense body language of stress, such as those involved in a chronic frown, the hunched posture, or the raised shoulder-tips. A good laugh helps release the tension in these muscle groups, and allows the return of a good blood supply.

At the chemical level, laughter puts the pituitary gland back to work, enhancing our natural production of the body's defenses against pain and inflammation: endorphin and cortisol. Endorphin (endogenously produced morphine) is a famous pain killer, but also a mood elevator (which is why people get addicted to the "high" of morphine derivatives like codeine and oxycontin in the first place). As the other part of the pituitary's "two-pack", we also release ACTH (Adrenal Cortico-Tropic Hormone), which stimulates the adrenal glands (above each kidney) to make cortisol, the best anti-inflammatory drug in the world. Thus laughter (along with exercise, acupuncture, music, meditation and massage) helps our stress defense in terms of mood elevation, physical aches, inflammations and even our immune responses. This is why a doctor with good bedside manner usually gets better results. Not only does a little humour put the patient at ease, but it will also help the body in defending itself. Patch Adams, the MD immortalized by Robin Williams in the movie of the same name, has an impressive record of helping patients with a little dose of humour as part of his interaction.

But note that laughter is hard to teach. If you didn't have it as a child, it is hard to learn humor as an adult. One of the most boring lectures I had in medical school was on the subject: "Laughter : the Best Medicine?". It was delivered in a monotone voice by a sad-faced professor who was totally bereft of any of his subject matter. He dimmed the auditorium lights to show us fifty minutes of slides and graphs illustrating all the physiological improvements in the body's organs during laughter. Then he swept on to his grand finale, complete with his favorite (and only) amusing anecdote, one that encouraged us to tell each patient we would encounter. Unfortunately his punch line didn't get any reaction. When he turned the lights back on, he found the entire student audience had fallen asleep.

Norman Cousins became famous for his ability to laugh in the face of a crippling medical prognosis (a painful back from anklyosing spondylitis). He taught the medical profession a great deal about the value of laughter as medicine. He collected all the humorous material he could in the form of books, movies, and so on, and then literally laughed himself back into health. Humor certainly ignites the will to live, which if missing, makes the recovery process much more difficult. Humor also helps balance our perspective, giving us vital relief in troubled times. Soldiers in battle (and doctors in MASH units) have historically used humor under fire to break the tension. During the blitz in World War ll, Londoners famously kept their senses of humor amidst devastation. During stock market crises, we see the value of "black" humor in keeping people from jumping out the window. During the great depression of the 1930's, one of the few industries to thrive was the movies, which carried the audience away from their poor reality into a few hours of uplifting laughter or storytelling.

So it seems we should not begrudge the high salaries of entertainers. Part of the value of laughter is that it enables you to gain new perspectives on your problems. It often makes you realize that others have the same problems, and that you are not alone. A popular style of humor is to use the technique of making the listener feel superior... to others, such as minorities, spouses, mothers-in-law, bosses, etc. However, the benefit of humor cannot be maximized until you can laugh *with* others, and *at* yourself, not the other way around. (If you cannot laugh at yourself, you will find plenty of volunteers to do it for you!) Remember, you don't need to develop the skills of a professional comedian, but it would be helpful if you could learn to enjoy being in the audience! You could even do this during time you would be listening to news on the radio. Once you have heard the day's events, switch to a comedy channel, or downloaded recordings of your favorite comedians.

SENSE OF HUMOR. Your score if you've got one = +20. Enter your score here.

Strong Choice Number 3

The Right Diet—Plus 30 Points

The best diet for stress is one that is:

1. Natural (with as few additives as possible).
2. Energy appropriate, matching your fuel needs with enough calories to maintain your ideal weight (your doctor can help you here).
3. Eaten at a reasonable pace.
4. Balanced in its content of protein, fats, carbohydrates, and fiber. (see Chapter 5).
5. Supplemented if needed (ask your doctor for personalized advice; blood tests are a better guide than just your symptoms). Some people with anemia need extra iron, some with bad skin need extra vitamins, some with weak bones need extra minerals. Most people need at least a modicum of vitamins C, E, and the B complex to simply replace those food elements that have gone stale between the farm and your table. Vitamin D can be helpful in winter, if your blood tests show a deficiency.
6. Hydrated. Most people, especially when they are exercising,drink only when they are thirsty. This usually means chronic under-hydration. Thus the rule is better stated as "drink before you become thirsty". At least eight glasses (or two liters) of water is healthy for most circumstances. More is obviously needed if you are sweating gallons in extreme heat or prolonged exercise. One good way to tell is through the color of your urine. If you are dehydrated the urine tends to be dark and concentrated; well hydrated patients have light colored urine, and lots of it.

Remember that there is no one diet that will work for all body types. In just the same way, there are multiple blends of fuels that suit different cars, from diesel to high octane gasoline and ethanol formulas used at the race-track. The same is true for humans. There are carb-loaded diets that are designed for long-distance runners, for storing glycogen prior to a Marathon race. More protein and larger servings will be needed for the sprinter, to put on the huge muscle bulk needed for explosive starts and quick times. Some (most) patients need to lose weight. If they can't (or won't) control portion sizes, a high protein and carb-free diet might be ideal. Diabetics and the obese all need to avoid the so-called "white death" (refined sugar, flour, rice), and need to be careful to eat or snack at regular times. Some patients are vegetarians, and some have religious or allergic reasons for avoidance of certain foods from milk to gluten. An elderly patient with heart failure may need to have a salt restriction. Discuss your specific dietary needs with your doctor, and make sure that you are putting the right fuels into your "engine".

RIGHT DIET. Your score if you have it = +30. Enter your score here.

EAT SLOWLY: Remember a meal is not a race.

On a stressful day, as we have seen, your stomach is likely to be shut down. Thus poorly chewed food, and drinks consumed in a hurry, will tend to sit like a take-out container under your rib cage for several hours.

We all know that good manners dictate a slow rate of eating, but most of us find the admonishments to chew your food at least twenty times to be a little pedantic. One look into the food court of any mall or office building will reveal the obvious: most people eat while distracted, and at the speed of a pie-eating contest. What is clearly needed is a new list of *adult* tips for slower eating. Based on thousands of patient interviews, I have distilled the following hints:

- Sit down.
- Turn off your cell phone. Your texts and emails can wait a few minutes!
- Try chewing your food before swallowing it. Not only will it make the pieces smaller, you will produce the salivary enzyme amylase, which begins to digest foods before entering the stomach.
- Wait until the server has finished placing your meal in front of you before you start eating.
- If you are in a self-serve line, wait until you pay before you start nibbling!
- Relax your death grip on your fork—no one is going to take it away.
- Cut your food into more than two pieces. The knife can help your digestion if you use it often!
- Remember to take the foil off your burrito before eating it.
- Leave time for breathing between mouthfuls, not during them.
- Try to engage in a conversation, to pace your rate of eating. It is hard (and rude!) to eat and speak at the same time.
- Never try eating to fast background music. Have a playlist of relaxing dining music ready if you can plug in during mealtimes.

Strong Choice Number 4

Alternate Stresses—Plus 40 Points

If you're under a lot of high-intensity stress, it may seem tempting to "veg out", doing absolutely nothing at all. No problems for a few minutes or hours, but trying to erase your stresses by emptying your agenda does not work for long — an empty brain will quickly fill up its screen with tape-loop replays of all your stresses.

As far back as 1960, researchers showed that sensory deprivation is a tough sell. Volunteers were paid to stay in bed, each in a dark room, and do nothing for as long as they could stand it. Sounds like a great break from life's stresses? Not so much. After a couple of days the volunteers cried "uncle", and surrendered. The absence of stress does not protect you from stress. While intervals of zero activity are fine for sleeping or napping, or even for "recess" in between activities, it is clear that having an alternate stress will offer a valuable defense in the long term.

This alternate stress should be something that compels your full concentration, and involves different circuits of the brain and body. Thus, such obviously stressful activities as amusement park rides, mountain climbing, white water rafting, parachuting, skiing and surfing can all have a great ability to get your mind off your routine stresses. Of course, the operative word here is *alternate* stress. Nobody talks about their office stresses when they are hurtling down the roller coaster; it is worth the price of the ticket to "escape" from those stresses, even if only for a brief adrenaline rush. However, if your job was to work all day test-riding roller coaster cars, then a ride on your day off would not have any such benefits.

Alternative stresses don't have to be scary (although this has always been the value of horror movies), they just have to keep your mind from constantly replaying your daily stresses. In other words we need to fill the vacuum, and prevent sensory deprivation. Throwing yourself into a gripping novel, or challenging yourself to finish some artwork or crafts could also be useful. Learning to play a musical instrument or enjoying the dance floor can also boost your stress defense. With the additional stress of a competition or recital at the end of the lessons, even greater benefits are obtained. Mercifully there are endless possibilities, from classes to hobbies and sports, but the main thing is to play to your passions, aptitudes, and interests. And, of course, to make sure that whatever you choose is completely different from your regular routine stresses.

Not only will alternative stresses refresh your immediate stress defenses, they will also keep you alive longer. When people retire, their work stresses all disappear. However, without a hobby or passion to fill up the time, prolonged sensory deprivation will soon lead to senility or to a premature death. The elders that we admire all have something stressful to stimulate their bodies and minds, to prolong their youthfulness.

In fact, when people of any age are chronically under-stimulated, they can simulate senility quite well.

Time management is obviously important here. If your job gives you no exercise, then spending your spare time reading or playing video games won't tone your muscles. If your job involves plenty of exercise, then some sedentary activity that challenges your different brain circuits could be a great relief.

The problem of fitness does not relate merely to adults. North Americans tend to start degenerating as early as age six, when they begin "organized" school. For reasons of legal liability, most schoolyards are now bereft of any exercise equipment. For reasons of budget cuts, exercise classes have been slashed. With the availability of in-school soda machines and dreadful nutrition choices for lunch, kids have never needed exercise more, yet they are getting almost none. With the distractions of cell phones and video games, it is hard to get them to burn off any calories at all. It behooves us to remember that fitness is an acquired lifestyle habit, and should start in childhood. If you have been out of shape since childhood, please consult your doctor before beginning any exercise program. Pay attention to any recommendations he or she might give concerning diet, smoking, degree of exercise, and general lifestyle.

Graduated exercise programs of the kind popularized by reputable health clubs across the nation have definite merit. They first do a fitness assessment, then monitor your progress at intervals through the year. They will create a program that suits your needs, and show you how to properly use the equipment. Personal trainers can also be a great help, as long as they are giving you exercises for you, and not just exercises that suit themselves.

Disorganized exercise is never smart. Even if your routine is haphazard, it doesn't mean you can't check your pulse, or take other measures to pace yourself. In the emergency department, I attended many patients who had heart attacks simply because they didn't check their "tachometer", or pulse rate. Not only could your heart rate elevate past the "red line" during vigorous sports, but it can do so while shoveling snow, pushing a car out of a ditch, or even walking on a hot, humid day. A gross guide is your breathing rate. Try talking conversationally if you are with someone, or sing along with a song you might have on your earpieces. If you can't finish a phrase without sucking air into your lungs, then your heart is likely racing. For more precision, check your heart rate. If you don't have a portable machine that does this for you, then manually check your pulse at the wrist, never at the neck (see figure 4.1). Your doctor will tell you what your ideal pulse rate would be during exercise. Do not exceed your maximum unless you ask yourself this question: "Am I feeling lucky today?" Special caution must be taken if you play demanding sports like squash or racquetball. I have seen many who are so focused on the ball that they completely forget to check their pulse after a long rally, or at least between games. Such an approach has all too often resulted in acute heart attacks while on the playing court, especially among Type A personalities. (See Chapter 8.)

Read the Speed:

Checking the pulse at the neck is fine if you are healthy, but dangerous if you have plaques of cholesterol lining the arteries like the scales on the bottom of a kettle. Pressure on the artery can cause a flake of this material to break loose, and lodge in the brain with a resulting stroke. There are only four arteries that supply the brain; two carotids in the neck, and two vertebrals beside the spine. At the level of the neck, each is about the size of your little finger. If three of these are plugged with cholesterol (which, in this country, starts as early as age 6) then sealing off the last remaining artery for a routine pulse-check will starve the brain of its blood supply. An excellent way to induce fainting. Not smart, especially if you are not wearing a helmet!

ALTERNATE STRESSES.
Your score if you have one = +40.
Enter your score here.

So here's how to check your pulse safely, at the wrist. While you could use either wrist, let's follow along with your left wrist, as in the illustration. Place the tip of your right middle finger over the radial artery as shown. This lies in the bony groove on the thumb side of the wrist crease. Continue to press here for about fifteen seconds, to shut off the flow of blood. This is like squeezing the far end of a garden hose, which causes the rest of the hose to become swollen with back-pressure. Now that your radial artery has been expanded in diameter, touch your index finger-tip gently to the skin, and feel the beat. Note that you can feel no pulse with your middle finger, because it is pressing hard enough to close off the artery. Check the rate with your watch, for just six seconds, then add a "0". So 10 beats in six seconds becomes 100 beats per minute. Checking your pulse for a full minute is technically a little more accurate. However one tends to lose count with three-digit numbers when your heart is racing during exercise. If your target rate is up to 150 beats per minute, it is a lot easier to count to 15 during six seconds. If you are at your limit, ask your opponent for a couple of minutes to walk it off, then recheck before resuming. Same point if you are on your own. Please see my video on this important skill, at www.stressipedia.com.

Strong Choice Number 5

Realistic Goals—Plus 50 Points

We have seen that unrealistic goals can make you feel like a failure in your own eyes. Realistic goals, on the other hand, will help your self-esteem and bolster your stress defenses. To have realistic goals, it is important to know yourself. Assess your strengths and limitations, both physically and mentally. If you are young and athletic, and have a body type and skills for a particular sport, then it could be realistic to try for a scholarship or a professional career. If you are physically uncoordinated, but have skills in music, math, or the arts, then seek goals in these areas, whether for hobby or career. If you are at a stage when you don't need to work and can retire, don't stop having goals, lest the brain and body start to atrophy. Take up a new sport, or get better at an old golf game. Learn or teach a new skill or language, or volunteer to help others in your community. If you are charismatic and intelligent, then a career in leadership could be a realistic goal. If you are in such a high pressure job, but are not suited to it, then a realistic goal could be to plan your escape, including downsizing your lifestyle if needed.

I treated a stressed patient in his forties right after his third coronary (having learned little from his first two such events). I asked him about his goals, assuming that an impending (albeit lavish) funeral wasn't one of them. He realized that the long hours and sales/performance pressures might have been realistic for him in his twenties, but might indeed be killing him now. He was working almost eighty hours a week, plus interruptions during his sleep. His time for family and friends was minimal, and he had no time for himself. He felt trapped, living "large", in a career that he now hated. I asked him what he did enjoy, and to think about how to make new goals that were realistic. He had always enjoyed the simpler life, and wanted to get his hands on something tangible. After his third coronary was repaired, he moved his family from the city to the lake, and bought a modest marina. Less income, and far less expenses. But because he was happy in his new goals, he had much better resistance to stress. Thirty years later he is still in touch with me, and still busy repairing boats. He is happy, enjoys his (now grown) family, and has never had another heart attack. Had he kept his former lifestyle, no amount of exercise, drugs, or cardiac surgery would have prevented him from dying young. Changing his goals saved his life.

Goal setting can be helped with professional career counselors, who incorporate tests of your intelligence, aptitudes, and interests. A personality assessment can also be very important in setting realistic goals. See Appendix A to find out what social-style quadrant you fit into best. If you like applause and contact with people, you'll obviously not find happiness working with a machine in a back room for the rest of your life. Similarly, if you have a more analytical personality and do not find it rewarding to work directly with the public, it would benefit you to pursue career opportunities that lead in other directions.

Realistic financial goals are also important to your happiness. Try to leave some room in your budget for simple rewards. But don't forget to allow for unforeseen expenses. For home owners, that means to allow for repairs, even if your home does not go up in value as much as you hoped. It is also realistic to aim for modest growth with your investments. This is especially true as you reach the end of your peak earning years, as it is hard to replace sudden losses once you retire from work. It would also be realistic to gradually pay off debts, in case you are earning less than you need ten years from now. If you want to pay down your debt, set a realistic pace that you can live with, not a pace that forces you to take risks with your career or your investments.

Realistic health goals are also important. If you wish to lose a hundred pounds, give yourself a hundred weeks (not days) to do it. If you wish to get into great physical shape, don't expect to do it overnight. Get professional help to plan gradual improvements in strength, flexibility, and conditioning.

Goals should also be realistic for your time, as well as for your priorities. If you are promising to be at your child's school play, be realistic in assessing your ability to leave work early, and in allowing time for traffic. If you are volunteering for too many activities in your spare time, you could undermine your defenses at work. The same could be said with the "little league syndrome" that plagues parents, where kids are signed up for too many sports and other activities, so that week-ends become frantic, and their school work suffers. Realistically, it would be smarter (for both kids and parents) to include some down-time, where you say "no" to interruptions. If you hate wasting time and energy in commuting, be realistic in your goals for housing. Granted, you get a lot more land and house space for the money if you are prepared to suffer through a long drive to get to work. However, considering the price of fuel, the cost of your wasted travel time, and the wear and tear on your vehicle (not to mention the high prices of parking and insurance), it could be an affordable option to find smaller living quarters much closer to work. A city public park can be just as good for stress defense as a back yard, and, as an added bonus, someone else gets to trim the grass! If your goal is to live in the country-side, it would help your stress levels if you could work some of the time from your computer at home.

REALISTIC GOALS. Your score if you have them = +50. Enter your score here.

Strong Choice Number 6

Understanding of Stress and Its Effects—Plus 60 Points

Once you have finished this book, you will have gained an important advantage in learning to harness stress. This includes knowing your own body, identifying the stresses around you, and learning to seek more or less stress as needed.

***More* stress:** You might need more stress, if you are languishing in a depressing job, for which you are overqualified and under-stimulated. This is often the case active career parents who give up their jobs to stay home with the baby. At the other end of the age spectrum, the same could be said for a person leaving a stressful career to sit through an idle retirement. Some people thrive on this new kind of lifestyle, but not all. I have seen many that were getting depressed, lonely for adult stimulation, and in desperate need of the stress of daily challenges. For these patients, the best answer was to return to their careers, or to some other form of work or study.

***Less* stress:** Some of my patients have told me their life's journey was turning into a death march, with too much stress coming at them from work, home, traffic, and relationships. Without a course correction, a medical disaster could easily await. In these patients, I ask them to look at the sources of their stress, assess their priorities, and consider escape options. This could include downsizing lifestyles to permit a less stressful career, or for example, if commuting was the problem, it could involve moving closer to work.

Better tools: Once you have adjusted your stress levels, you need to assess your responses. Habits can be changed if your eyes are open to problems, and your mind is not closed to solutions. If relationships are giving you trouble, then get professional counseling, or, if you are lonely, get a reputable online dating service. If you are bored, then turn off the television or internet and get a real life; join something, study or teach something, or do something you enjoy. If you are burning out, then stop feeling guilty when you pamper yourself (see chapter 10). If you are making a series of bad choices (chapter 3), then begin action steps to change your behaviors.

In other words, understanding stress empowers you. That's why it is important for a pilot to understand his plane, and the laws of gravity, weather and physics. Once you know what is happening, and how to fix it, you can correct even the worst tail-spin. Of course there is no value in understanding your stresses if you are not going to actively change any habits. Many intelligent people with a lot of understanding can still suffer and die prematurely from addictions, whether to drugs, foods, or sloth.

Understanding of Stress.
Your score if you
have it = +60.
Enter your score here.

Strong Choice Number 7

Relaxation Skills and Efficient Sleep—Plus 70 Points

We have seen that prolonged sensory deprivation is counterproductive, but in the short term it can be as restorative as oxygen. Many people who have very high stress levels can fight back with the skills of instant relaxation or sleep.

The modern work day is no longer physical labor, and it is no longer confined to daylight hours in the fields. Today our stresses are around the clock, around the globe, and live on the internet. We have gone from "hunting and gathering" in the wild to "hunting and pecking" at the keyboard. About half the country is suffering from fatigue or insomnia. Rest is a weapon, without which you will be ill-protected from your next day's stresses. The answer does not usually lie in pill form, even though there is a huge trade in prescriptions for anxiety, depression, and insomnia.

Insomnia, a subjective term, is based on results (fatigue the next day) rather than efforts (number of hours lying in bed). There is a great myth about the "8 hour" standard for sleep each night. Winston Churchill, in the most stressful times of World War II, never had more than a few hours of naps each day. He was not fatigued, and could not have performed any better had he slept an extra four or five hours. For most people it is useful to have the ability to take a restorative nap to supplement those days when your sleep is poor.

Most people can relax on a two week vacation, many can totally relax on the weekend, and some can relax every evening after work. But how many, during even the most stressful days, can count to ten, suddenly be at complete rest for a few moments, and then wake up refreshed? This is the power nap, and I will show you how to do it.

This does not mean you will necessarily put yourself sound asleep in the middle of the day, but simply that you can learn to slow your pulse and breathing rate, and reverse many of the natural stress responses in your body. Depending on the images or triggers that are designed for you, you could, for example, count to ten and place yourself on a nice beach with your hand in the warm sand for a few seconds. Then you could count back down to zero and be fully refreshed. Other people find success by closing their eyes for a few seconds and imagining a dial, set on high, when they are very tense. In their minds, they simply imagine the dial being turned down. In this way, they can gain control of themselves, and "command" their pulse and blood pressure rates to decrease.

Some of you already have skills to help you relax on command, gained from such diverse (and excellent) activities as prayer, yoga, martial arts, meditation, exercise, listening to music on your i-pod or 'droid, and doing favorite odd jobs around the house. But if you find that your current levels of stress are too high for even these methods, then you should have an ace up your sleeve: the power nap.

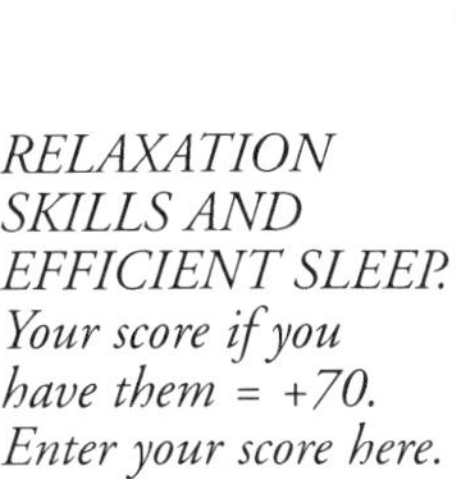

The power nap can be taken at the drop of a hat. It can break up your most stressful days with a few moments of total relaxation for your body (to the extent that you will be unable to prevent your jaw from slackening).

It also relaxes your mind (so that you are aware of none of your surrounding stresses). With practice and coaching, you may be able to gain an excellent recharging of your batteries in a few minutes per day, and spare yourself the burnout of the constant use of the same brain and body circuits. The same skills are also helpful in getting to sleep at night.

RELAXATION SKILLS AND EFFICIENT SLEEP. Your score if you have them = +70. Enter your score here.

Efficient sleep

As discussed earlier, efficient sleep is crucial, but it doesn't need to take all night. If you are one of those lucky people who need only four or five hours per night, consider this a gift of extra time added to your life, and make use of it. Don't waste it just lying in bed, glaring at the alarm clock, and wishing you could get back to sleep.

How to take a power nap

Many people have unfounded fears of hypnosis, and worry that they will lose control of their minds—rather like being on drugs.

In fact, hypnosis is not only harmless, but will help you to gain control of your mind. It can be used to great advantage when under stress.

The following is a typical example of what you might expect to hear when a professional is guiding you into hypnosis:

Just sit back and make yourself comfortable and allow your eyelids to close…

As you listen to my voice, you can pay attention to the growing feelings of relaxation and comfort in your body…

I am going to count for you from one to ten…

and as I do…

you can imagine yourself traveling down in an elevator to a private place of peace and tranquility…

one…

just beginning…

letting relaxation spread through your scalp…

and your face…

and your neck…

two…

going down deeper…

more relaxed…

down to tranquility…

three…

arms and hands relaxing…

breathing easy…

four…

every breath guiding you to deeper relaxation…

closer to your special place…

free from stress and tension…

five…

down the elevator…

stomach knots dissolving…

deeper relaxation…

calm…

comfortable…

six…

deeper still…

letting go of all cares and worries…

buttocks and thighs relaxing now…

relaxing deeply…

seven…

legs and feet joining in the growing relaxation…

all the way down…

to the tips of your toes…

eight…

journeying deeper…

to your special private place…

totally calm…

more profoundly relaxed…

nine…

almost there…

drifting comfortably deeper…

ten…

letting the elevator doors open…

step out into your place of calmness and freedom from stress…

enjoy the feelings…

let them soak keep into every part of you…

just let yourself drift with these feelings for a short while…

and when you're ready…

just come back up this elevator in your own way…

and bring these calm feelings with you…

all the way back to your everyday state of alertness…

refreshed and relaxed…"

In order to experience this more fully, you can put on soothing background music, and try to follow these steps. Someone could read the above passage to you, slowly. Or seek a professional hypnotist to try out a session. You will enjoy the experience!

Courtesy of Dr. Steven Crainford, Hypnotherapy Associates, Toronto, Canada.

Ways to fall asleep

1. Try and go to bed at the same time each night, preferably about half an hour before you plan to fall asleep. Obviously, try to use the same bed; if you are unable to, as when on the road, consider taking along a small neck-pillow, pillowcase, or other reminder of your own bed. As a last resort, small stuffed toys are not out of the question (just kidding!). If you drive to a holiday destination, take advantage of being able to carry more luggage; many of my patients have conquered "hotel insomnia" by packing their own feather-bed and duvet.

2. Compartmentalize: Your work environment, including the clothes you wear, should be designed for alertness and focus. Your sleep environment should be engineered for rest. Try not to mix these respective associations, or both will suffer. Never use your bed as a desk. If you have laptop or tablet work to be done, sit up at a proper table, or at least in a comfortable chair. Trying to do your work while lying on your bed reinforces bad sleeping habits, not to mention poor work habits. Its just as bad as trying to sleep on the top of your desk at work. Dress for the occasion. Don't wear work clothes while trying to sleep, and, if your office is at home, don't work all day in your pajamas. When you are trying to sleep, your whole environment, including clothing should be specifically suited to the purpose.

3. Don't eat a full meal late at night. A high protein meal at bed-time is especially bad; it switches on the adrenaline pathway, tending to increase restlessness all night. That's why a late night snack of pepperoni pizza tends to promote nightmares and poor sleep.

4. Eat your bigger meals earlier in the day, at breakfast and lunch. Snacks are fine, but not a big one at bed-time. For dinner, eat a light meal, and include a few carbs (whole grain, not refined sugars and starches). Complex carbohydrates, such as whole wheat pasta, tend to trigger the body's indolamine response cycle to encourage sleep.

5. If you must put something in your stomach just before bedtime, have a small warm drink such as milk, or a few spoonful's of cold (organic) applesauce or yogurt. Don't have alcohol or caffeine before you go to sleep, as both can wake you up a couple of hours later. Also, out of consideration for the bladder, don't drink too many fluids just before bed-time.

6. A relaxing warm bath an hour before bedtime can also help, by raising the body temperature, then letting it start to cool prior to turning out the lights. This will start your body's "temperature momentum" in a downward direction, where it tends to stay during sleep .

5. Invest in a good quality comfortable mattress. (Try all kinds, including pillow-tops and foam based beds, before deciding.) A mattress covering of real sheepskins, space-age foam, or featherbeds can also upgrade the comfort of most beds. Pillows should support the neck as well as the head, and could be made of down, or memory-foam. Presentation is everything in sleep, as in meals, so dress the bed up with a duvet and fresh linens, and good lighting (for last minute reading).

6. Your bedroom should be tranquil in noise levels, lighting, and decoration.

7. Use your "power nap" relaxation techniques to slow your breathing and pulse rates, and help get you off to sleep. (See page 114.). If you like technology, try a sound-effect machine that offers ocean noises or forest breezes, or can play soothing music or talk.

8. Spend a couple of minutes reviewing your day-timer, so you can be sure you have finished all your tasks for that day, and have a good idea of what you need to accomplish the next day. It is difficult to keep a disorganized brain from jolting you awake. Often my insomniac patients tell me they wake up in panic, remembering some important detail they forgot to enter into their calendar.

Strong Choice Number 8

Thorough Job Preparation—Plus 80 Points

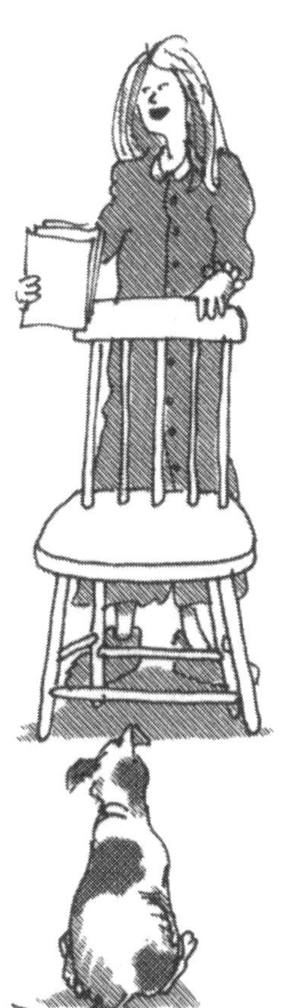

Thorough job preparation is vital to your defense against stress. That's why stage actors rehearse assiduously before opening night, making sure they know their lines, their cues, and their movements. Even before the rehearsals the actors have gone through a Darwinian process of selection, to make sure that those who don't have the aptitude are weeded out. A professional actor's pulse and blood pressure actually defy gravity, going down when the curtain goes up, because of this process of job preparation.

The same can be said for any line of work. Instead of a "dress rehearsal", you may need to think of a "stress rehearsal", both in terms of preparing for a presentation next week, as well as in selecting the right career options in the first place. To maximize your defense, you should work in a job you are well suited to, at your level of competence, with all the appropriate skills. You should know where you are on your stress curve (see page xxii in the introduction). If you are under-stimulated and a little bored, you may need to say "yes" to more extracurricular or work related responsibilities in order to increase your efficiency. If you are over the top of the stress curve, you might need to say "no" to such options.

By way of further illustration, just think of the different stress levels of students when writing final exams. Those who are ill-prepared sweat bullets; those who have studied well actually enjoy the stress.

Thorough preparation can also be augmented by developing skills of positive imaging. This has been shown to great advantage in the field of sports. For example, baseball coaches can reverse a team's slump by showing highlight videos of its best hits. Hockey coaches will often inspire a team the same way, by replaying films of scoring streaks.

A recent study of high school basketball players divided the students into three groups. One group practiced their free throws. The next group did exactly the same thing at the other end of the court, but in pantomime, without the ball. The third group spent its time sitting on the sidelines. Predictably, the last group did not show any improvement. The amazing thing was that the first two groups showed equal improvement, thus indicating that even in your imagination, and without a ball, you can still gain thorough job preparation.

In my career as a public speaker, I have had the privilege to meet many inspirational personalities. Some of the most amazing were former Prisoners of War from the Vietnam conflict. The ones who spent years in solitary confinement had to create virtual strategies to keep from having a mental breakdown. One, a handyman in civilian life, would build an imaginary house, one plank at a time, over several months, then tear it down and rebuild it again. Another, who was musically inclined, "played" the imaginary piano, covering every note of every piece he could recall. One who was a moderately good golfer, teed up his ball every morning, and "walked" thirty-six holes a day, playing each stroke and lining up each putt in his mind. They all noted that this mental exercise had a good effect after their release as well, once they had recovered their physical health. The handyman noted that he could keep up with his coworkers as if he had never been away. The pianist was not as rusty when he got back to his piano. And the golfer actually broke 80 in his first full round, which he had never done before. In other words, instead of getting the predictable decay in job performance, even a POW could help his otherwise uncontrollable stress by using the incredible power of preparation.

THOROUGH JOB PREPARATION
Your score if you have it = +80.
Enter your score here.

Strong Choice Number 9

Financial Security—Plus 90 Points

It is not necessary to have vast riches to qualify here. What we are talking about is having enough financial security (in the form of positive cash flow, assets, skills, or insurance policies) to avoid being thrown out on the street if you lose your job through changes in your health, or in the economy. This will give you a crucial "control button" to fight stress.

On a daily basis, if all your loans can be consolidated into a manageable repayment program and if your spending habits are within your net means, then you will be in an excellent position to withstand stresses.

No matter what your salary level, you should have a written budget, and allow some money for *stress defense.* This need not cost a lot: it could be as simple as downloading movies regularly, or hiring a young student to help with some chores around the house, including yardwork or babysitting. The important thing is to spend this money regularly, and in advance *before* you finally see your health suffer from excess stress. *Pamper yourself.* (See Chapter 10.)

A preplanned mini-holiday each month is much more valuable than one taken after a whole year of uninterrupted stress. With today's financial distress, many people are learning to be creative with "staycations", and avoid the costs and time of travel. Write out your priorities, list the stresses that bother you most, and coordinate solutions within the limits of your budget.

If you suffer from the modern curse of a "time famine", then you might save both time and money by doing some of your shopping on line. If you learn the rudiments and pleasures of cooking, you can save a lot of money from your restaurant budget for dinners, and by being creative with left-overs for breakfast or lunch the next day. If you buy a coffee every day at the local bistro, you could easily spend $1500 a year; a home coffee maker would pay for itself in just a month or two. If you quit cigarettes, you will likely save $15,000 in a decade. If you have an option of public transport (or bike), you will save thousands a year by not owning a car. If you could use the local pub less, you will also save more by serving drinks from your own fridge.

FINANCIAL SECURITY. Your score if you have it = +90. Enter your score here.

Prioritize your choices for stress defense, and try to avoid paying for things with high priced credit cards. There are plenty of stress relievers that money can buy, but high interest rates and late fees aren't among them.

Strong Choice Number 10

Stable Home—Plus 100 Points

This does not mean you have to live in a stable, keep pets, or be married (although the latter two help greatly). But if you invest enough of your energy and time in maintaining an adequate network of friends and support from within your family, the stresses of your day will be greatly reduced. This means you have a safe harbour where you can get away from work pressure each day, which is better than escaping just once a year for vacation.

It is important to bear in mind that the time and effort involved in maintaining good relationships with family and friends are well worthwhile. If this aspect of your life is working well, you have mastered the most valuable defense you can possibly have against stress. People tend to treat you as you treat them. A high code of ethical behavior will also sow the seeds of reciprocation (and good karma) from those around you. For many people, a strong spiritual belief system is also integral to stress defense.

Pets can help too. Animals have been shown to ease their owners' stresses by decreasing their blood pressure and pulse when they cuddle up for some touching. As a result, their owners tend to live longer. Married people also tend to live longer than single people (although sometimes it just seems longer). One common link is that we all need to be touched frequently. Those with partners live better than loners.

Of course, physical touching is only one aspect of close personal relationships. There are also many psychological, social, and spiritual benefits. It is important to communicate with your spouse or significant other, to share burdens as well as good times. If sacrifices have to be made, then your inner circle will understand and be supportive. Do not be afraid to broach difficult topics. By building up the negative consequences of problems to the point of silent paralysis, you can destroy a good relationship. Emphasize the strong positive benefits of sharing your stresses, and difficult topics become much easier to broach and solve.

STABLE HOME. Your score if you have it = +100. Enter your score here.

How did you do?

STRONG CHOICES	POSSIBLE SCORE	ENTER YOUR SCORE
1. Good Genetics	+10	
2. Sense of Humor	+20	
3. Right Diet	+30	
4. Alternate Stresses	+40	
5. Realistic Goals	+50	
6. Understanding of Stress	+60	
7. Relaxation Skills and Efficient Sleep	+70	
8. Thorough Job Preparation	+80	
9. Financial Security	+90	
10. Stable Home	+100	
Total score if you made all the right choices = +550		
	YOUR TOTAL	______

Enter your score from the preceding page.		*Strong Choices*
Next, enter your total score from the weak choices at the end of the last chapter (see page 74).		*Weak Choices*
Now add these two numbers to give you your net resistance to stress.		*Hanson Stress Resistance*
Finally, subtract your Holmes-Rahe stress score (see page 49.)		*Holms-Rahe Stress Level*
This will give you your grand total, your net stress score.		*Net Stress Score*

A score of more than -300 = an *80 percent chance of serious change in your health. Consult your doctor soon!*

Now we can get a realistic picture of your true risks from stress. The higher your net score (in a positive direction), the better you are doing at harnessing your stresses, and the less likely you will be to have any serious heart attacks, ulcers, or other health crises or to cause inefficiencies at work.

With a negative score (in excess of -300), your risks are deadly serious. Note that even with few recent stresses on the Holmes-Rahe scale, you could still be in the high risk group just based on your weak choices on the Hanson Scale.

Your stress level may not be within your control. However your choices are. So what will you choose? Bad management, which will leave you a "sitting duck", or good decisions, which will make you virtually "bulletproof" to all those stresses.

The punishment for bad choices can be severe, in terms of preventable health crises, poor relationships, and lack of success in your career. The rewards of good choices are amazing; greater health today, longer life tomorrow, and greater happiness at work and in your personal life. Remember that the one thing you cannot change is the stress level around you, so don't waste any energy wishing it would all go away. Focus instead on your positive responses, and realize the resulting JOY of stress!

5. Nutrition and Stress

Seldom has so much been written by so many, about so little. Nutrition, while important, is just not that complicated. Take a look at the diet section in your local book store. There, thousands of "experts" will complicate the simple beyond all possible belief. They will tell you how to analyze your breakfast choices according to whether you have Blood Type A, B or O. For lunch, consider whether you should be eating like the cave man, with all raw foods (warning, cavemen died very young by today's standards). Or, if you prefer more civilization, eat like the French (chocolate, wine, cheese etc.) For dinner, select portions of each food element based on your astrological sign (bound to work one-twelfth of the time). Count calories (carry a calculator, a measuring spoon and scale to the grocery store, and to every restaurant meal). Eat high proteins and fats. Eat low proteins and fats. Eat purely vegetarian foods; or purely meats, fish, and chicken (pick your current guru). Speaking of gurus, check out the author on the cover. Some diet experts are thin reedy aesthetics, and, while admittedly thin, don't look like they are very happy. Others, like Dr. Phil, are extremely happy, but don't look very fit. Confused about fiber? So are the bowel specialists, who have some of their patients on low residue and some on high residue diets. How about antioxidants and vitamins? Only the PhD chemist can calculate all the permutations and doses here. The list of dietary cults and fads extends infinitely, from yeast free "Candida" diets to fasting and colon cleansing. ARGGGGGH!

To paraphrase the basic principle of medicine, the trick with nutrition is not to ask the question; "What kind of a diet does this patient have?" We should instead be asking "What kind of a patient does this diet have?" We all have stress in our lives, (if you didn't, you would not have picked up this book). These stresses, and the choices we make in response to them have influenced our nutrition. For example some of my patients tell me that stress on the job leads them to eat absent-mindedly, while working through the meal hour. For some, stress makes them forget to eat altogether, and their weight plummets. Others admit to a two-handed eating and drinking habit while driving in traffic (before you know it, cars will soon have "platter-holders" as well as cup-holders). Some patients find their stresses lead them to excesses with alcohol, sweets, or junk foods. Others find the absence of stress can lead to boredom or depression, and this will lead to poor dietary choices. Some are driven to specific diets because of a disease or disorder, such as obesity, asthma, or arthritis. Many patients, including children, are otherwise healthy, but are driven to poor nutrition because of a lack of self-esteem, or because of cultural or peer pressure.

To read the headlines, it all seems rosy: we are setting new records for longevity every decade. We have almost doubled the life expectancy of an "average" adult in the past century. However, most of these statistics are misleading. For example, a lot of deaths used to occur in childhood, before immunizations and antibiotics could intervene. Also, there used to be a lot of maternal deaths during child-birth, most of which are preventable with modern techniques. Modern science has also increased life expectancy through advances in purification of milk, water and food. Medicines and surgeries can now cure most infections, heart diseases, and cancers. So each generation should be able to outlive its parents. Right?

Not so fast. Our youth are about to turn the longevity charts upside down. Poor choices in nutrition and exercise have seen obesity become the number one public health hazard. Most of our children are now overweight, fat, or frankly obese. Most are also slothful, getting no compulsory exercise at school, and none during their average 5 hours of video games/internet/cell phones per day. In addition to their gluttony and sloth, they are often drugged with antidepressants and anti-cholesterol medications, as well as "cures" for Attention Deficit Disorders and Hyperactivity. As a result, these unhealthy kids will grow into unhealthy adults, and suffer epidemic rates of diabetes, high blood pressure, heart disease, and many forms of cancer. They will also likely need new knees and hips, and suffer back pains from being so out-of-shape. This means they will likely die younger than their parents, and some will die before their parents. So not only do parents have to set aside money for their children's education, but they also have to budget for their funeral expenses. (This begs the question; will parents have to fly these kids around the country to visit prospective cemeteries the way we do campuses?)

To put the importance of nutrition in perspective, let's consider the following popular myths about foods, comparing today's realities with yesterday's facts:

Myth 1: We're getting smarter about fitness.

Then: Look at old movies including the black-and white ones. The actors from children to elders were thin. The extras that filled out the background scenes were thin. Even the stars we considered "fat" (like Fatty Arbuckle, Jackie Gleason, "Curley" of the Three Stooges, Oliver Hardy and Sophie Tucker) were relatively moderate by today's inflated weights.

Today: Turn on the television news, or pull up a seat at any sidewalk café, and watch the public waddle by with glazed eyes, sad faces, and double-wide pants. Fit people are the new visible minority. Exceptions are certainly seen, mainly in large cities with clogged traffic, where people walk miles every day. These people are visibly fit, compared to those in more rural centers where driving is the only means of locomotion. For example, New York City has many more fit people that upstate New York. Toronto, and Chicago have lots of fit people in the downtown core, but less fitness is seen in their rural neighbours in the surrounding countryside. Lists of fitness for each state of the US shows that some have an endemic fitness/obesity problem, while a few like Colorado and California fare better. But in ALL areas, obesity is growing. In the UK and Europe, the same phenomenon is also happening, and is starting to cripple the government health programs that pay for the resulting carnage. In third world countries that have imported our fast food habits, obesity is now becoming more threatening than starvation. This is the first time in history that the rich people are thin, while the poor are fat. Precisely the opposite happened in the old days, when royalty had the gout and "liverishness" from overeating rich foods, and the poor people were thin from working the land and eating unprocessed foods.

"Follow the money" ...as applied to schools. Some schools have revolutionized the lifestyle choices they offer, and have shown that healthy choices can be presented for each student's day. However, these are in the minority. In general, schools are underfunded, but stand to earn thousands of dollars profit from the school soda drink machines (each can of pop has eight spoonful's of sugar, and each student drinks an average of three per day). For reasons of economy, cafeteria foods tend to be "empty calories" rather than healthy choices. Thus the resulting trays full of donuts, white breads, greasy fries and pizza slices. To make matters worse, schools are so nervous of expensive law suits from scraped knees that they have removed daily (compulsory) exercise and play-ground equipment from the curriculum. In addition to all this, the growing sizes of classrooms, and the increasing number of "hyperactive" kids (usually under-exercised and on a sugar jag) has led to the epidemic of mood altering tranquilizers, such as Ritalin. The profits are so high for the drug companies that they can spend billions to brainwash doctors, parents, students, and teachers alike that all students need more drugs. Prescription drugs are now the first line of defense for obesity, depression, anxiety, hyperactivity, and even anger management. Passive management has replaced active participation. "Sensitivity" has replaced "truth". At no time are these fat, sad kids told to get up, turn off the computer games, and run after a ball. They expect doctors to passively feed them drugs to "cure" their "illness". They are also bedeviled by their unrealistic goals (see chapter 3) that will doom their dreams; you can't keep up with the celebrities unless you have their cash flow. The problem is that there will never be a passive way to cure for gluttony and sloth; the only road back to health requires some active participation.

Myth 2: Diabetes is under control, thanks to drugs.

Then: Primary diabetes, in the days before Insulin was discovered, did kill children, usually before they were old enough to have their own babies. Thus a family history of primary diabetes was indeed rare. The "secondary" diabetes that is now sweeping the world was unheard of until people arrived at senior age status. These people were born with good insulin levels, but over a lifetime ate enough sugars to eventually deplete their stores. That's why they called it "old-age" diabetes.

Today: Now, thanks to the soda machine and the junk food epidemic, kids are being fed a lifetime's supply of sugar before they are even finished elementary school. Because they are exhausting their finite supply of insulin within the first few years of life, we have had to rename the resulting disease, changing it from "old age" diabetes to "type 2" diabetes.

Myth 3: Our food is better than ever.

Then: People did not have to have an Easter-egg hunt to find "organic food". That's because they had a different name for it; they used to call it "food". They hadn't figured out how to mess it up. Everything they grew was organic, without chemicals or hormone additives, and without pesticides. Everything they caught, trapped, or hunted was also organic, as nature intended.

Today: Big corporations have figured out that animals (like humans) grow fatter if they don't exercise. Obviously, the quickest profit comes from the fastest weight gain. So chickens are being raised in factory cages, with artificial lighting, with their feet never touching the ground. Cattle are raised in feedlots that are so crowded that the stench of sewage can be smelled for miles around. Farm raised fish are crammed into pens so tightly that they can hardly move (you could go fishing with a hammer). To counter the resulting infections, the corporations spike the feed with antibiotics (that's one reason bacteria that cause human infections have become more resistant to common antibiotics). To make the animals grow faster, they also feed them more hormones than an Olympic weight-lifter. To make the meat more tender, they add birth control hormones (that's why young girls AND boys are growing breasts). If the color of the meat or fish is a little pale, well, that's what artificial colors are for. NONE of the above ingredients shows up on a label. The same is also true of our public drinking water; contamination with bacteria is largely solved, but there are new tests that show traces of prescription drugs in our tap water (another reason to use reverse osmosis water filters at home).

Myth 4: We are what we read (i.e. Education ensures health).

Then: Nobody read any books on diet, and most people were thin.

Today: The book stores are filled with books on diet, and most people are fat.

Myth 5: It takes money to be obese.

Then: Poor people were thin.

Today: Poor people are fat.

Myth 6: Doctors can save you from anything, including from yourself.

Then: Doctors were not much help against the main cause of death, which was bad luck. Infections such as TB or scarlet fever had no cure, as antibiotics were not yet available. Trauma and tumors were made more deadly due to the lack of surgical and anesthetic options.

Today: Doctors are much better at treating "bad luck", but are almost impotent at treating today's main cause of death, which is "bad choice." Medicine has become very sophisticated in detection of diseases and in treating infections and cancers. However, doctors can't save you from bad stress choices, such as drug abuse, gluttony, sloth, and smoking.

To review our progress in the past century, it seems clear that we now have greater knowledge about nutrition. Yet our number one health problem for our population is malnutrition, while they are simultaneously being over-fed. This even applies to third world countries, thanks to the introduction of fast food and sugar products; the World Health Organization now states that starvation has been replaced by obesity as the new modern health threat.

The jargon of nutrition is complex-guaranteed to include words beyond the understanding of all but the Ph.D. biochemist. Impressive sounding though such words may be, the truth is that the subject of nutrition is not a terribly difficult one at all. In fact, before the Industrial Revolution, when the science of nutrition was almost totally undeveloped, people probably ate a better diet than we do now with all our sophisticated knowledge of the subject.

If you have symptoms of ill health, you need a diagnosis before you need a diet or nutritional counseling. Once the diagnosis has been made, your doctor will then send you to the appropriate nutrition professional for specific advice if needed. This is the way the diet for a diabetic is chosen. The same is true for advice to post-heart attack patients, the obese, fatigued, anorectic, and so on.

An old professor of mine used to say that most people would improve their diet if they ate shredded cellophane sprinkled with essential amino acids. Of course, this rather unappetizing prospect is not meant to be taken literally.

The elements of a good, balanced diet can be divided into the following six categories:

1. Protein.
2. Fats.
3. Carbohydrates (complex, NOT refined).
4. Fiber. (see appendix).
5. Vitamins and Minerals. (see appendix) *
6. Water.

Precise measurements of your foods are not necessary. All six elements should be included every day, but don't need to show up in regimented order during each meal. The first three elements are where we get our calories to fuel our daily activities. The quantities of protein, fat, and carbs is controlled by your goals. Some people are trying to gain weight, others (more commonly) are trying to lose weight (see chapter 6). Some are training for a marathon run, and need to eat lots of carbs leading up to the race, to enhance stores of glycogen in the muscle tissues. Others are trying to make the football team, and need lots of protein and fat to increase their muscle mass. Some have insomnia, and cannot tolerate proteins for their evening meal or snack, yet need it in the daytime. Others react to stress with stomach symptoms, such as heartburn or indigestion; these people will do better with frequent small meals. Under stress, some "gut reactors" have very sensitive bowels, and need to pay particular attention to what they eat; some cannot tolerate much in the way of fiber without having loose stools. Others get constipated unless they have a lot of fiber.

---

* A separate section is devoted to the important subject of vitamins and minerals. (See appendix.)

Remember, just because a food looks and tastes good, that doesn't mean it is good for you. Your neighbors diet may serve him well, yet may have the opposite effect on you. Keep track of your progress with a pencil and paper, to record your food intake along with your exercise output, and general observations of how you feel. If you feel better with fish for your protein than you do with chicken or beef, then guide yourself accordingly. If some vegetables make you bloated, or some carbs give you headaches, you can make your own modifications. If you have allergies or preferences such as vegan, there are still plenty of good alternative foods that will serve your needs.

Consult your doctor for specific advice if you have any health issues or particular sports goals.

Let's take a closer look at the six categories to be included in a balanced diet**.

1. Protein

Protein is necessary for our bodies to function. It is also essential for growth. Protein forms the genes that are present right from conception.

Protein also gives us antibodies to fight disease.

It forms the microscopic enzymes that regulate all body functions. And it makes up much of our bones, muscles, organs, bloodstream, and hormones.

Everyone recognizes the importance of protein, but unfortunately many tend to overdo it. The typical North American diet has far more protein than required. Protein is found in most foods, not just meats.

Excess protein in the diet will be converted to fat, as will excesses of any foods. All mammals do this; that's how a bear stores energy for a winter of hibernation. Excess protein is also excreted—as nitrogen waste. The added "work" of having to eliminate it may cause harm to people suffering liver or kidney disease.

A chronic excess of dietary protein may result in decreased calcium, resulting in demineralization of bones. Thus it is important that protein be taken in sensible amounts; about the size of a deck of playing cards, or 8 ounces, represents a pretty good portion for an average adult. Servings of Brontosaurus-sized steak are not only unhealthful; they don't leave room for the rest of your food. If your meal can't fit on a single plate (and I didn't say "platter"), you are off to a bad start.

2. Fats

Fats are essential in building up important elements of our body, including a good immune system, as well as healthy hormones. Fats are very good at dissolving certain elements, including the fat-soluble vitamins. But fats also will store bad elements, such as toxins commonly added to the feed of factory raised grocery-store animals. Thus the food chain can easily carry insecticides, antibiotics, added steroids and estrogens in food that carries no labels. So the safest fats are the natural ones, from organic sources (meats, fish, dairy, eggs). A balanced diet can include both animal and vegetable fats, such as butter and olive oil (assuming your cholesterol levels are normal). Overreacting, trying to keep the fat intake near zero is not the answer. Some authorities, such as the late Dr. Nathan Pritikin, have noted that heart disease is extremely rare in Third World communities with a meatless and fat-free diet. However, this shows the dangers of drawing conclusions by looking at only one organ in the body. While it is true that these people developed little heart disease, most of them didn't live long

Butter versus margarine

Because of the public awareness of cholesterol deposits in the arteries in connection with heart disease, many people have erroneously come to think of margarine as a "health food," and butter as being "bad for you."

Many other factors are involved in heart disease. The extent to which ingested cholesterol causes deposited cholesterol is not clearly defined, and is still under investigation.

Many of the cheaper brands of margarine are actually high in saturated fats. If you wish to reduce your dietary intake of these fats, you must look for a top-quality margarine labeled as having more than 35 percent polyunsaturated fats.

Margarine, however, is not a "health" food, nor is it a wonder drug. It is just a fatty food, as is butter. Margarine may be included in the dietary recommendations if your doctor discovers that you have a problem (see page 115), and tries you on a diet restricted in saturated fat.

Following a repeat test, your doctor will assess whether it makes any difference in your blood levels. If successful, then he or she might suggest continuing to reduce dietary polyunsaturates. If the blood levels do not decline significantly, the doctor might well suggest that it would be pointless to change your usual (balanced) diet.

Margarine is also recommended for those who don't have access to refrigeration (for example, people on camping trips), and those suffering from allergies to dairy products.

Caution: Some margarines may contain skim milk powder. Check the label carefully.

Margarine does have a large number of food additives in it and, frankly, tastes inferior to butter. Margarine has exactly the same number of calories as butter. You will put on just as much fat if you overeat either one. As mentioned earlier, the average diet contains too much fat, and the principle of reducing fat intake to the recommended levels of 30-35 percent (divided between polyunsaturated and saturated) should be endorsed.

The areas of reduction of fats are entirely a matter of personal choice, but there is no need to make sacrifices in taste. Because many people either prefer the taste of butter as a spread, or in cooking, I suggest that you use it if you like it. It should be used on high-fiber bread, or in a high-fiber diet, in keeping with our suggested balance of dietary elements (see page 110). But remember that a good quality olive oil can be a great substitute in cooking, or at the table.

Reductions in fat intake, in general, can more easily be made by restricting hidden fats; for example, by broiling or baking instead of frying, trimming visible fats from meats, and avoiding gravy. Other ways of restricting hidden fats are by having more frequent servings of vegetables, poultry (without the skin) and white fish main courses; and by using corn and safflower oils in salads and dressings. In fact, using a drizzle of olive oil instead of either butter or margarine is the healthiest choice to enhance your breads, vegetables, and meals at the table; cooking with olive oil is also healthier than either butter or margarine.

enough to enjoy this fact. Their total life span was (and is) remarkably shorter than ours. Their rate of maternal and infant mortality was very high, and the death rate from what should have been easily defendable infections was appalling and tragic. Sometimes people in the Third World die young because of the lack of medicines, such as antibiotics. Other times they die from the lack of prevention, such as is seen in the HIV scourge (lack of condoms and education), and in the resurgence of malaria (lack of mosquito nets for beds). And some die young because of corruption, starvation, pollution, and poor sanitation. So, great news that they don't have much heart disease, but it's an unfair manipulation of statistics to assume all of this is because of their low fat diets!

Recently there has been a lot of public alarm about the high incidence of cholesterol in the coronary arteries of heart attack victims. Studies have concluded that this must be due to our relatively high cholesterol diet. Autopsies on young (eighteen-

The cholesterol (blood) test

A complete serum lipid profile should be done every two or three years if you are under stress. You should make your doctor aware of the stresses that you are facing. Also mention your family history. Make sure you fast for at least twelve hours (water is ok).

It is not good enough to just test the cholesterol to predict risk of heart disease. A complete lipid profile, including the levels of "good" (HDL) and "bad" (LDL) forms of cholesterol, and an indexing or "typing" should also be done. Certain familial types of high cholesterol, once identified, can be important to check in all your blood relatives, including children over the age of ten.

year-old) soldiers in the Korean War showed that the American boys had cholesterol plaques already clogging up their arteries, while the Chinese and Korean boys did not. Two glaring differences between the cultures were the high fat diet versus the rice diet, and the levels of serum cholesterols. In the U.S. these were 50 percent higher than the Korean levels.

The initial reaction was to blame only ingested cholesterol for the deposited cholesterol. However, other key factors have since been identified:

Fiber

This is found only in plant materials; it acts as a passive sponge, just visiting your intestines and not entering the rest of your body. If taken in adequate amounts (50 grams per day), it will carry out four times the average amount of stool each day. Stools get their brown color from bile salts, which are made by your own liver, and are rich in cholesterol (even if you are a total vegetarian). These bile salts are resorbed into the bloodstream if not carried out in stool. Thus, if a person eats more fiber, and quadruples the amount of stool, the blood levels of cholesterol are bound to decline. (The Korean diet was high in fiber; the American diet was low in fiber.)

Excess stress

If you choose to make yourself weaker in response to stress (see Chapter 3) and build up 300 points against yourself on the stress scale, then you will probably suffer the same deposits of cholesterol in the arteries that befell all of Hans Selye's stressed rats. In Western society, fighting the time clock, both on the assembly line and with office deadlines, is a big stress factor that appears to remove any possibility of control from the hands of the individual. (As we will see in Chapter 10, this is not necessarily irrevocable.)

What to do if your doctor tells you your cholesterol is high.

There are six steps to its reduction:

1. Stop consuming refined white sugar, as well as white breads, pastas and pastries. These are highly inflammatory elements, and, as they are all processed by man, have never been suited to the human metabolism. Aerosol spray cheese comes to mind as a good example. If Man makes it, don't eat it. And if you can't pronounce the ingredients listed, then you shouldn't eat it. Also, beware of the "Cholesterol-Free" treats like muffins, cookies, or ice-creams: these products may have no cholesterol, but they usually are filled with white sugar and other additives.
2. Consider your visible cholesterol, namely your body fat. If you have too much of it, start to lose it.
3. Reduce total dietary intake of fats including animal fats. After a trial period, your doctor will want to review your progress and reassess dietary advice.
4. Increase dietary fiber to 30 grams per day. It's not hard to do; just eat fresh vegetables, grains and fruit (see appendix). Fiber acts like a sponge to increase the volume of stool from a quarter pound to one pound per day. This quadruples the amount of endogenously produced cholesterol that you excrete per day.
5. Do regular exercise (after medical and fitness consultations). Cholesterol enters our blood stream, and carries energy to our cells. It is just a fuel, as we can all see when fat burns on the barbeque. Sloth burns off nothing but your resting metabolic rate; if you want to accelerate the reduction of cholesterol in your blood stream, burn more of it off with exercise.
6. Take steps to correct poor choices in response to your stresses. Perhaps you could learn to say "no" sometimes, if you have too many activities crammed into your schedule. If your life is getting too complicated, pause to reflect upon ways to simplify it. Are you spinning your wheels just because everyone else is, or are you truly happy in your work and relationships with others? Reduce unnecessary controllable stresses, such as type A behavior. Use the Hanson Scale of Stress Resistance to improve your resistance to those stresses you cannot control.
7. If none of the above steps is reducing your cholesterol, in spite of a good trial for at least three months, then your doctor may suggest medications. Drugs ike Lipitor and Crestor can help, but have a considerable list of side effects hat need to be monitored by your doctor.

Korean society at the time of the Korean War was slower, based on rural agriculture. The passage of time was measured by the season rather than by the millisecond. Levels of Net Stress score were much lower, primarily because the Hanson Resistance score was higher. This would tend to help keep the arteries of the Koreans freer of deposits of cholesterol than those of their U.S. counterparts.

The major role of fat is that of energy storage. Fat has nine calories per gram, whereas proteins and carbohydrates store only four calories per gram. Therefore, when a diet is high in fat, it is extremely easy to consume too many calories, without taking up much space in your stomach. Fats can be easily hidden in foods and in the cooking process. Many people are aware of animal fats, such as are visible in meats, gravy, chicken skin, and so on. But they forget that vegetable fats have just as many calories. The typical two-piece fried chicken dinner with French fries can have over one thousand calories because of the fats used in frying. A serving of French fries with gravy can have as much as eight hundred calories. Even worse with "poutine" or cheese sauce added to those fries.

Besides energy storage, fat does also play other roles in the body. It cushions organs such as the kidneys, and acts as a storehouse for fat-soluble vitamins (A, D, E, and K). Another lesser function of fat is insulation in the wintertime. Fats are also an essential building block for our cells, and for our hormones and other enzymes.

Studies have shown that Seventh-Day Adventist men between the ages of 35 and 64 have half the risk of a fatal heart attack that the overall population has. This can be explained by the Seventh-Day Adventists' emphasis on strong choices on the Hanson Scale of Stress Resistance, for example, balanced diet (which includes adequate fiber);

abstinence from alcohol, cigarettes, and caffeine; and the high value placed on a stable family life.

In conclusion, organic fats, both animal and vegetable, can safely make up 30-35 percent of your balanced diet, as long as you eat enough fiber, choose a good lifestyle with correct responses to stress, have regular checkups with your doctor, and have normal blood tests.

3. Carbohydrates

These are often viewed as being very fattening, yet that is a misconception.

However, carbohydrates have only four calories per gram, which is exactly the same calorie content as protein. There are two kinds of carbohydrates: complex and simple. Complex carbohydrates are found in whole foods; for example, wheat, beans, grains, fruits, vegetables. These starches are a very efficient source of energy, and are particularly valuable when you are under stress.

Simple carbohydrates are found in refined sugar, white flour, and alcohol. These are truly empty calories. In the refining process, most traces of fiber are removed. It is excesses of foods such as these, which typically form over 30 percent of the daily American calorie intake, that give carbohydrates a bad name.

This explains why carbohydrates have gained a reputation for being fattening without being filling. Under stress, the level of simple blood sugar is already elevated. Thus, the additional ingestion of excesses of simple carbohydrates is redundant.

Figure 5.1

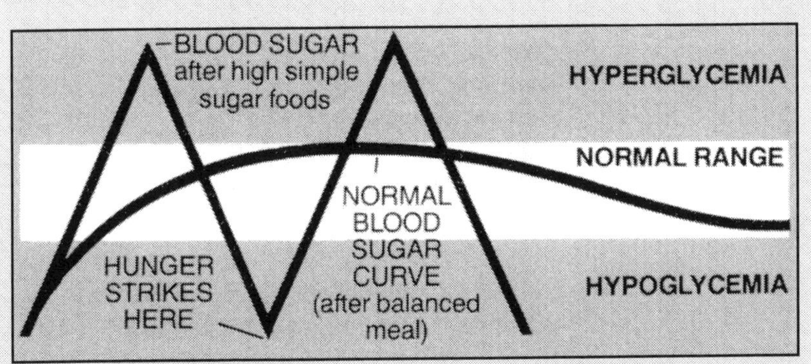

Complex carbohydrates or sugars with fiber, tend to be absorbed much more slowly than refined sugars.

A high level of refined sugar in your diet means that you will be a slave to your sugar graph. You will start out in a hunger crisis from low blood sugar, eat sugar, and then get hyperglycemic with a quickly passing feeling of "fullness." Very shortly thereafter, you will become hypoglycemic, and then have the panic rush for a "quick energy fix." You can't wait for regular foods to gently raise your blood sugar; therefore, you head for more sugar. This can be extremely habit forming, and explains why most people do not stop at just one cookie from a bag.

Complex carbohydrates (such as pastas, whole wheat bread, whole rice) and not pure protein (such as the traditional pre-game steak), are the most efficient sources of energy for any impending acute stress, both on or off the field of athletic endeavor.

Complex carbohydrates are the cleanest burning and easiest source of energy for your body to assimilate. Natural sugar cane (a complex carbohydrate) is actually high in fiber, and tends not to be fattening in spite of its sweetness. Because of the high content of fiber, natural sugar cane tends to be extremely filling; thus the stomach cannot physically handle an excess amount. "Refined" sugar, on the other hand, has almost all the fiber removed. Thus it is extremely easy to overdo the intake of refined sugar. The average person in North America consumes dangerous quantities of refined sugar a day, and thus inducing their own consequences.

Sugar is particularly harmful in drinks. A typical can of soda has up to eight spoonful's of sugar; impossible to imagine dissolving this much in a cup of coffee! A frappuccino at your favourite coffee shop can have a whole day's worth of calories. A drink with a high sugar content tends to be no more filling than a drink of water. A couple of hours later, the stomache will still want a meal. As a general principle, if one takes only those drinks that contain no calories, such as clear soups, herbal teas, and black coffees, then it is much easier to achieve a normal balance in sugar chemistry.

The ideal drink is, of course, water. If the tap water in your area is not ideal, use reverse osmosis filters as a cheap means of purification. Otherwise a bottle of spring or mineral water will be a good choice.

4. Fiber

Perhaps the most underrated element of our diet is fiber (roughage). This is simply the cell wall material of plant foods, and is not digested by mammals. Thus it cannot be found in any meat, or in animal products such as milk and eggs. Some fad diets for weight loss will have people omit all vegetables from their diet. This may work as an immediate weight loss method, but it soon leads to troubles with nitrogen overload of the kidneys, and other side-effects. The reason is that fiber only comes from plants, and cannot be produced from (or through) an animal. Fiber is also one of our six essential food elements for a healthy stress diet. This is one reason why I don't favour juicing machines, as all fruit is made of solids (fiber) and liquids (juice). If you are having trouble getting your fiber by eating five servings of green vegetables a day, then eat the whole fruit, not just the juice.

Fiber is the one ingredient you can eat plenty of, because it does not stay in the body. Eating fiber is something like swallowing a sponge. It passes unchanged through the bowels, and never enters your blood stream. Thirty grams of fiber can carry out almost a hundred undigested calories in every bowel movement.

Thus, if you eat fiber, you can "get away with" eating a bit more food without gaining weight.

Over the past century, modern methods of refining foods have taken more of the fiber out of the average person's diet. At the same time, total sugar consumption has gone from five to one hundred pounds per person per year!

Third World studies have shown that people who eat a lot of fiber have lower rates of heart disease, diabetes, and cancer. They also have fewer disorders of the bowel such as colitis. The late Dr. Denis Burkitt noted a strong correlation between these diseases and the size of one's feces. He traveled the side roads of Africa, and measured the weight of human stool specimens along the way. He noted that Westerners, eating a low residue "sophisticated" diet, produced only one-quarter pound of stool per day. The local African diet, high on raw vegetation, produced a full pound of residue, irrespective of race. He noted that certain diseases were common among westerners, such as hemorrhoids, appendicitis, gall stones, ulcers, and cancers. These conditions were much less likely to happen to people on the high roughage diets. His conclusion was intriguing: "The societies with the smallest stools have the biggest hospitals". I have referred to Dr. Burkitt's famous work as a "Turd World" Study.

British prisoners of war in Asia during the Second World War ate a diet high in fiber (husks, plant leaves, and so on), while their Japanese guards enjoyed a more refined diet including white rice. Even though the prisoners were under greater stress, they had fewer ulcers of the stomach and duodenum than their captors. Some were later transferred to Hong Kong, where they received a more "normal" Western diet. In these prisoners, the rate of ulcers climbed dramatically. When they were returned to more primitive camps, the rate of ulcers went down again.

Many patients initially feel that a high-fiber diet will be unpalatable, sort of like eating the wrapper along with their bran muffin. However, the foods richest in fiber may already be among your favorites. They include sweet potatoes, whole wheat breads, pasta, sweet corn, peas, and baked beans. You may even be denying yourself these foods in a misguided attempt to lose weight. Remember, fiber is extremely filling, (especially when taken with plenty of water), and it is (almost) impossible to become severely obese by eating foods that are high in it.

Where can you find fiber? All plants have it, but no animal does. So there is never any fiber in meats, fish, eggs, or milk products. But fiber is plentiful in almost all plants. Pure wheat bran is about half fiber. Bran is what is left behind during the refining of white flour. It is one of the best forms of fiber, but unfortunately most people find that it tastes a lot like kitty litter. Since it is difficult to take more than an ounce of bran per day, it is practical to seek out other sources of fiber. (But please don't eat this book!)

It is important to obtain fiber from a variety of plants, not just from one supplement. In general, vegetables (such as beans, peas, corn), whole grain breads, whole fruit (not the juice) and high-fiber biscuits are good sources. The following is a list of some specific foods that are high in fiber:

FOOD	GRAMS OF FIBER	CALORIES
Baked beans in tomato sauce-1 cup	16.0	180
Baked potato-medium	5.0	91
Raspberries-1/2 cup	4.6	20
Brown rice-1/2 cup	5.5	83
High bran health bread-2 slices	7.0	150
Large apple	4.5	80
100% bran cereal-1/2 cup (1 oz.)	8.2	72
Shredded wheat-2 large biscuits	4.4	190
Bran muffin, with whole wheat flour-no raisins or dates	2.3	78

In the intestine, the "sponge" action of fiber can slow down the rate of absorption of sugar into the bloodstream. This effect can significantly reduce insulin requirements for diabetics. As we have seen, a high-fiber diet can also help to reduce one's blood levels of cholesterol. For dieters, one of the most pleasing side effects of high-fiber consumption is that as much as 10 percent of the total calorie intake, or about 150 calories, will be passed undigested through the body in the form of bowel movements.

Benefits of fiber

In the mouth.

Fiber slows your rate of eating, simply by giving you more volume to chew through for the same number of calories. The obese tend to eat quickly.

Similarly, they often seek diets that will cause them to lose weight quickly. "Fast" seems to be their watchword in both senses of the word: speed of eating, and, as punishment, the absence of eating! The reason for eating quickly could be a sense of panic at not having enough hours in the day to take in the extra few thousand calories they are planning on eating. Alternatively, it could be a misplaced sense of guilt, a fear that someone will catch them eating. The old "hand is quicker than the eye" theory is operating here.

By increasing your fiber and thus having more volume to chew through, you will tend to eat more slowly. Certainly you will feel satisfied longer. Also, more saliva will be stimulated.

This aids in the preliminary breakdown of proteins, and improves digestion.

In the stomach.

A high-fiber load slows the stomach's rate of emptying. This means that, instead of being hungry an hour after a meal, your stomach will stay full for several hours. It also means that your stomach acid has more work to do, and tends to burn itself out. This is a natural protective device that is all the more important when you are under stress. When your body responds to stress by increasing your natural cortisol, as well as shutting down the motility of the stomach, fiber becomes a good buffer to prevent ulcers or heartburn.

In the blood.

Rebound hunger (hypoglycemia) following ingestion of carbohydrate loads lacking fiber has already been discussed. (See figure 5.1.) This is why the tendency to feel hungry an hour after a meal of Chinese food (with white rice) has some basis. In point of fact, people in China who live in rural areas do not have white "refined" rice. Their high-fiber rice keeps them full for many hours after a meal.

Initially, after a meal, insulin is stimulated in great amounts. Blood sugar stays normal for about two hours, following which there is a rebound phenomenon of hunger. This can be prevented by eating lots of fiber, which slows down digestion of the carbohydrates.

In the intestines.

Eating plenty of fiber means that more calories will be lost in the stool from undigested foods.

More protein and cholesterol will also be carried out of the body, in the form of digestive juices that are poured into the intestine to process the food.

It has been shown that the incidence of bowel inflammations (colitis and so on) and, most importantly, bowel cancer is directly related to the amount of fiber present in the diet. Although fiber increases the transit time in the stomach, it decreases the transit time dramatically in the large intestine.

One thing to remember, however, is that calcium absorption can be impaired by a high fiber diet. This is easily overcome by taking a couple of glasses of milk a day. Alternatively, other foods containing calcium can be taken, like green vegetables.

Zinc, magnesium, and other trace elements can

also be bound to the fiber. For this reason, supplementation with a daily multiple vitamin pill could be helpful if your doctor detects any deficiencies in your blood work.

Constipation: the sure cure

"Constipation" means protracted effort to produce hard, dry stool. The interval between stools is less important than their consistency, and the freedom from discomfort. Constipation is one of the most common problems that I see, particularly in the elderly. It is also, surprisingly, a problem in many younger people, often resulting from simple inactivity. While constipation may seem to be a lifelong problem, and a disease that knows no cure, nothing could be further from the truth. Constipation is not a disease; it is simply a preventable malfunction or a "disorganization."

There are three simple steps to follow in correcting constipation:

1. Eat enough fiber in your diet,

Aim for 30 grams per day, from foods. Consult Appendix C for more information. Fiber supplements are certainly safe, but should be redundant if you eat properly.

"An apple a day keeps the doctor away," is an old saying that makes sense. An apple is an excellent source of fiber, which helps prevent doctor visits for constipation.

2. Correct stomach muscle tone.

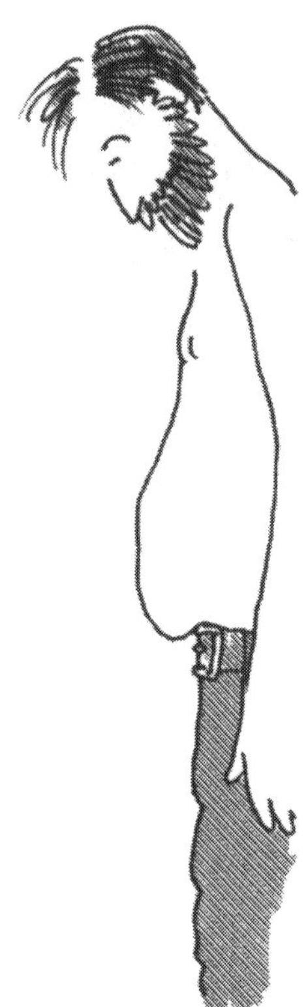

Having adequate stomach muscle tone is crucial to avoiding constipation, it increases pressure on the intestine walls. This is why even perfectly healthy young athletes may require something for their bowels when confined for extended periods to a hospital bed. Muscles are little used during bed rest, and consequently lose their tone. This is also true during pregnancy and the postpartum state.

As far as the elderly are concerned, stomach muscle tone presents a major problem m many cases, as the stomach muscles may not have had a good workout ever. Or, at least not in the last few years. Because more of today's elderly are women (for historical reasons discussed elsewhere in this book), and because they lived through a time when girdles and corsets were used as substitutes for aerobic exercises, the problem of constipation seems to be worse with women. In particular, it seems to be worse with women who are obese, and who have poor tone in their abdominal muscles.

However, the problem can affect any age or either sex if the abdominal wall muscles are slack. I have seen a surprising degree of constipation from lazy stomach muscles, even in children.

3. Timing.

Although it sounds rather distasteful, there is an aptly named medical function in your body known as the gastro-colic "dumping" reflex. This reflex occurs about twenty minutes after filling the stomach with a large meal, and is your cue to have a bowel movement. In many cases the reflex takes place while you are on a bus, in a meeting, or otherwise in a bad spot to act upon it. If you wait till a couple of hours after a meal to go to the bathroom, you lose the natural advantage of this reflex, and generally have less success.

Incorporating the above information, the simplest plan is to select a time during the day that is practical for you, such as breakfast. Start off your morning twenty minutes earlier than usual, which should allow you time to do some stomach exercises and general stretching exercises. Then have your breakfast, which should be high in fiber and fluid volume; for example, whole wheat toast, bran cereal, fresh fruit, and a glass or two of iced or hot tea, coffee or water. Make sure your schedule allows you to spend five minutes on the toilet when you get the "call of the sphincter" after breakfast.

I have never seen this plan fail for anybody, if adhered to on a regular basis. There is virtually no need to take any of the commercially available drugs. Constipation, as we have seen, is just a dysfunction. It is not a disease, and is certainly not caused by a lack of drugs or suppositories.

One other cure for constipation has emerged from the ancient Chinese art of acupuncture. There is one needle six inches long, which may work if all else fails. The doctor does not need to insert this needle into the skin. All that's necessary is to show it to the patient!

5. Vitamins and Minerals

Much nonsense has been written and claimed about vitamins and minerals. The R.D.A. (Recommended Daily Allowance) of these elements is found in most balanced diets.

However, there are cases in which the dietary source alone may be inadequate, due to the transit time between tree and table, or farm to plate. When food is eaten within a day of harvest, it has all of its vitamins, antioxidants, and other elements intact. After shuffling around the country on container trucks, then sitting on shelves for days, some of the natural elements have lost a little of their potency. This is yet another reason to buy fresh produce. (Remember, the best way to keep food fresh is to leave it in the store, then go buy it the same day you will use it. Failing that, try for frozen organic products). In general, most healthy people can get adequate vitamins and minerals with just their diet. But there are cases where supplementation can indeed be helpful, such as these:

- A strict vegetarian diet.
- Dieting for obesity, eating fewer than 1,200 calories per day.
- Pregnancy and lactation.
- Growth during childhood.
- Poor absorption in the elderly.
- Alcohol and drug addiction.
- Recovery from surgery, burns, or illness.
- Being under excessive stress.
- Being exposed to flu viruses, sore throats, and other contagious infections.

Get professional advice; if you have a symptom, start with a diagnosis, including a physical exam and blood test, then consider specific supplements as indicated. But remember that vitamins and minerals are not just benign. It is not difficult to take lethal doses of vitamin A, and even a simple bottle of pre-natal iron pills can prove fatal in the wrong hands.

I once treated a two-year old child in the Emergency Room who had eaten about thirty of his mother's pre-natal vitamins with iron (she was pregnant with her second child). The vitamins were left in an open jar on the kitchen table, within the toddler's reach. Tragically, in spite of intravenous fluids and stomach pumping for several hours by our pediatricians, the baby could not be saved. The iron was of a lethal dose. The chart in Appendix B, at the end of this book, gives some basic facts about vitamins and minerals. This chart is provided only for the sake of reference and completeness. Though it may sometimes seem so, the subject of vitamins and minerals is not really a complicated one.

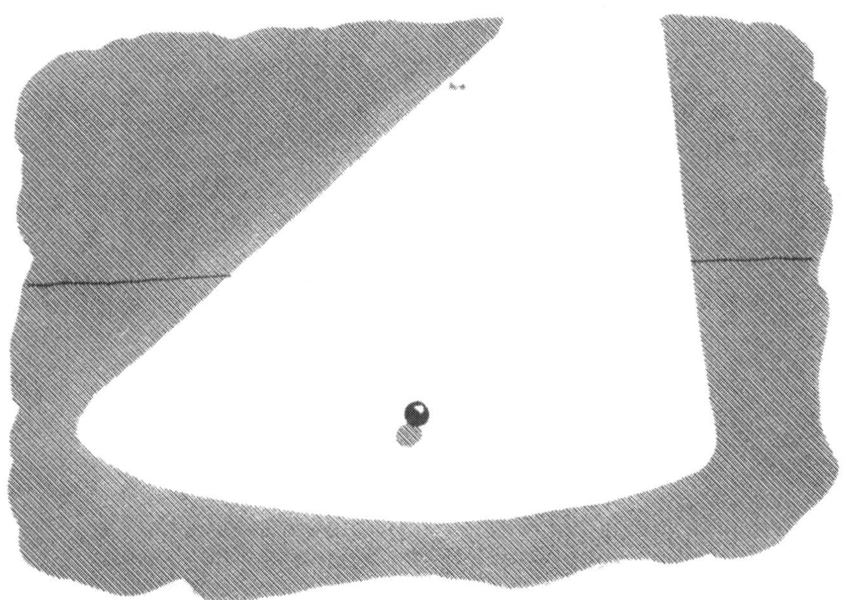

6. Water

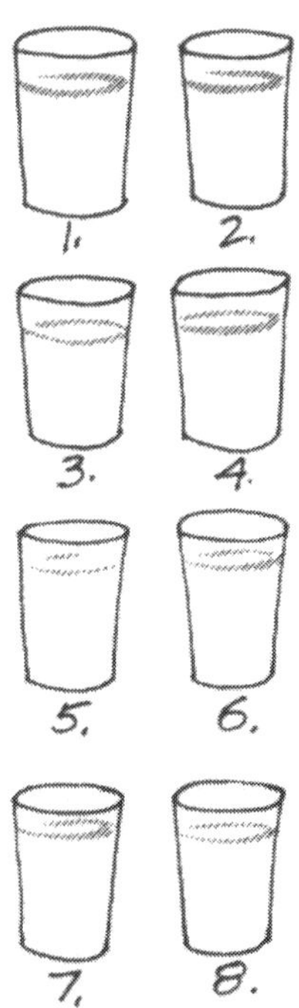

I recommend (and drink) eight glasses of water per day. This is particularly important for anyone experiencing a lot of stress. But remember that our general drinking water may contain more impurities than you think. Modern testing has become very sensitive, and can pick up traces of almost all the prescription drugs that the public is taking. These vary from hormones to antibiotics, antidepressants, pain meds and others. In many areas of the country, the tap water is fine, but if you are suspicious of either the water's taste or contents, consider filtration. Reverse osmosis filters can easily be fitted to purify your ice cubes, and your water for drinking or cooking. Bottled water is convenient, but expensive; a portable metal water canister is an easy way to keep sipping during the day. Adequate water consumption will benefit many areas of the body. Most people are, to use the car engine metaphor, "down a quart" in water. Eight glasses or two liters of water per day is just an average. Some people with certain medical conditions may need less, but most active people need lots. More should be taken if you are suffering a cold or flu, living in a dry climate, or if you are exercising vigorously. A crude but useful guideline is to drink until the color of your urine is very pale (unless you are on vitamins that color the urine). Let's take a look at the different areas of the body that benefit from full hydration.

1. The bloodstream

Water dilutes thickened blood. As we have seen in Chapter 2, one of the body's reflex responses to stress is to thicken the blood with extra clotting factors and red blood cells, both from the marrow and from the reservoir of the spleen. Having this "sludge" effect in your arteries can compromise the circulation and, in coronary vessels already partly occluded with early heart disease, predispose you to a heart attack. For the same reasons, emboli (blood clots traveling through the vessels, which get lodged in other organs) and strokes can also be encouraged by not drinking enough water.

There are drugs to help thin the blood, including the simple "baby" dose of 81 mg of aspirin.

Current findings suggest it is better not to routinely medicate young adults, as the long-term side effects of several decades of drug use in humans are not sufficiently known. Ask your doctor for your personal recommendations here. However, it is known that dehydration thickens the blood, and hydration thins it. Thus the simple addition of eight glasses of water to your daily diet can offer real benefits in your defense against stress.

"Water" pills are popular because of the prompt loss of up to five or six pounds of fluid in the first few days. As a result, they are increasingly being sought by dieters. However, as I explain to my patients, "water pills" are misnamed, and would more correctly be labeled "salt-losing pills." Wherever the salt goes, water will follow passively; thus it makes little sense to take a pill to lose salt through your urine if you continue to take in extra salt in your meals. If you restrict your water intake, your blood gets saltier, and you thus retain even more water. The same benefit as obtained through these diuretics can usually be obtained by salt restriction and extra water consumption. This approach is far safer, since it does not pose risks to the delicate balance of electrolytes in your body. In any event, losing water by whatever means is still irrelevant to the obese dieter. What he or she really needs to lose is fat, along with sloth.

2. The skin

The skin is the largest organ in the body. When it is dehydrated, it starts to look like a prune. Dry skin has more wrinkles to see, and more roughness to feel. Also, the skin needs adequate supplies of water to regulate body temperature through sweating.

3. The gastro-intestinal tract

Good hydration assists in digestion, and in passing of soft stools.

4. The lungs and nasal passages

In dry or cold air, your lungs act as living humidifiers for the surrounding air. The frost you see with each exhaled breath in cold weather is actually just water being lost from your body. The same thing applies to each invisible breath in warm, dry air. The normal mucous lining in the lungs can become very thick and glue-like if the water lost through the lungs is not being matched by water intake.

This can lead to a decrease in your resistance to respiratory infections.

5. The urinary tract

The benefits of good hydration here are many. Maintaining a high volume of urine output helps prevent a host of urinary tract problems, such as stones and infections in the bladder and kidneys. It also keeps the bloodstream washed free of excess waste products from metabolism. Without proper hydration, relative stages of kidney "failure" can occur with serious systematic consequences, including decreased mental alertness, fatigue, blood pressure elevations, fluid retention, and so on.

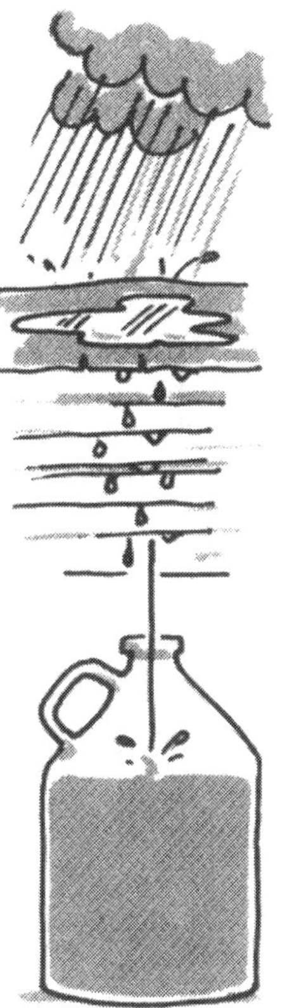

The purest water is distilled, but it has absolutely no taste. The tastiest water is natural spring, or mineral water, but it is probably not running into your tap. Each underground well collects rain and melted snow that has filtered through layers of sand and rocks over years, sometimes several decades... Depending on the nature of the local soil and sand, each spring may have a different mineral content, and thus a different taste. It should be easy for you to find one that appeals to you, and that you will enjoy.

In North America, there has never been any hesitation about buying water, as long as it contained sugar (pop, juices), alcohol (beer, wine), or caffeine (coffee, tea, iced tea). From the point of view of thirst, however, the water alone is all you need. If you view the purchase of your favorite bottled water as a substitute for buying some of these other drinks, you will probably still end up ahead financially, reduce your dental bills, and increase your resistance to stress. Otherwise, enjoy your tap water (filtered if needed).

One of the best diet tips is to keep most of your liquids calorie-free. Otherwise you will drink a lot of empty calories, but not do anything to suppress your appetite for the next meal. In general, avoid clear fruit juices (which are just the fruit without the fiber), and eat the whole fruit instead. On a hot afternoon it would be quite easy to drink several glasses of apple juice, without having any appetite suppression by dinner time. If you tried to eat the dozen whole apples that the juice was extracted from, you couldn't finish them, never mind eat your normal sized dinner.

A word on salt

Sodium is a vital element in our body chemistry; without it we would die. Historically, it was considered so important that workers were given pieces of rock salt as payment. Interestingly enough, this was the basis for our word salary.

Strenuous work or sports in hot weather can increase the body's demands for salt, due to salt loss through sweating. (Ironically, sweat is actually quite low in salt, compared with blood. However, after continued evaporation, a residue of salt is left on the skin (so *that* explains why your dog wants to lick your hand!)

Salt lost in this way needs to be replaced, but handfuls of salt pills can easily become an overdose. You can make a more accurate replacement by adding one teaspoon of salt to a quart of water with lemon juice. Or, if that sounds a little unappetizing, try one of the premixed fruit and electrolyte drinks commonly seen along the sidelines at sports events. But watch out for the sugar in most of them. Sugar is burned off by athletes on the field, but is not needed if you are sitting in an office, so try to stick mainly to water.

Salt is added in large quantities to many prepared foods as a preservative, and as a teaser promoting the craving to have even more salt. (No one eats just one salted peanut or potato chip.)

The average person needs three grams of salt per day, or less than two-thirds of a teaspoon. Apart from the above-mentioned special circumstances, excessive salt need not be added at the table, in cooking, or via high-salt snack foods. Excesses of salt can aggravate high blood pressure, congestive heart failure, and kidney failure. They can also cause fluid retention (often seen during pregnancy, in premenstrual tension, and in cases of heart failure).

A word on "jet lag"

"Jet lag" is the physiological disorientation of all bodily and mental functions that accompanies flights across several time zones (in other words, only on flights in east/west directions).

This phenomenon is particularly annoying to the frequent business traveler, whose ability to make sharp decisions suffers from traveler's fatigue.

To a certain extent, these physiological changes (mediated by our internal diurnal or twelve-hour "clock") are an unavoidable travel nuisance. However, many of the temptations on the flight will actually make the jet lag worse, such as late night movies, cheap (or free) alcoholic beverages, and large meals, especially if served at an unusual hour for your own internal "clock." Overnight flights further interrupt sleeping.

The key to fighting jet lag is to drink water.

In a pressurized aircraft, the ambient humidity during the flight is usually zero in the cargo compartment, because the outside air is dry and freezing (-40 degrees). By heating this cold air up to room temperature, it becomes extremely dry. The only reason there is even 2 percent moisture in the air of the passenger compartment, is, of course, because each passenger is now the plane's humidifier. Body water is donated to the air via the skin (which explains the dry skin and mouth after a flight), and, mainly, through the lungs. Every breath gives up more water, and increases dehydration. In response to this, most people replace this fluid loss with alcohol, which further acts to dehydrate the body. The solution, clearly, is to drink all the bottled water that you can on your flight (at least one to two glasses per hour).

Caveat emptor…

Many dental and medical offices, spas, salons, and massage parlours are now selling supplements. And there is no end of vitamins sold on line, on the air, or by friendly neighbours. But please be careful about these "pyramid" marketing scams. Wild claims are made for success by supplements. Clients are convinced that any symptom can be fixed by this miraculous brand of vitamins and supplements.

In my own practice I find that most people do not need large doses of any one vitamin. I prefer them to get the bulk of their vitamin requirements from a proper, balanced diet. However, due to the depletion of zinc and vitamin C from the body under stress, and the apparent wisdom of taking vitamins C and E to help protect against cancer of the bowel, I usually recommend the daily use of a standard combination of these, such as a "stress" formulated tablet. Remember, if you have any of the many symptoms of vitamin deficiency, you need a diagnosis before treatment, so do consult your doctor.

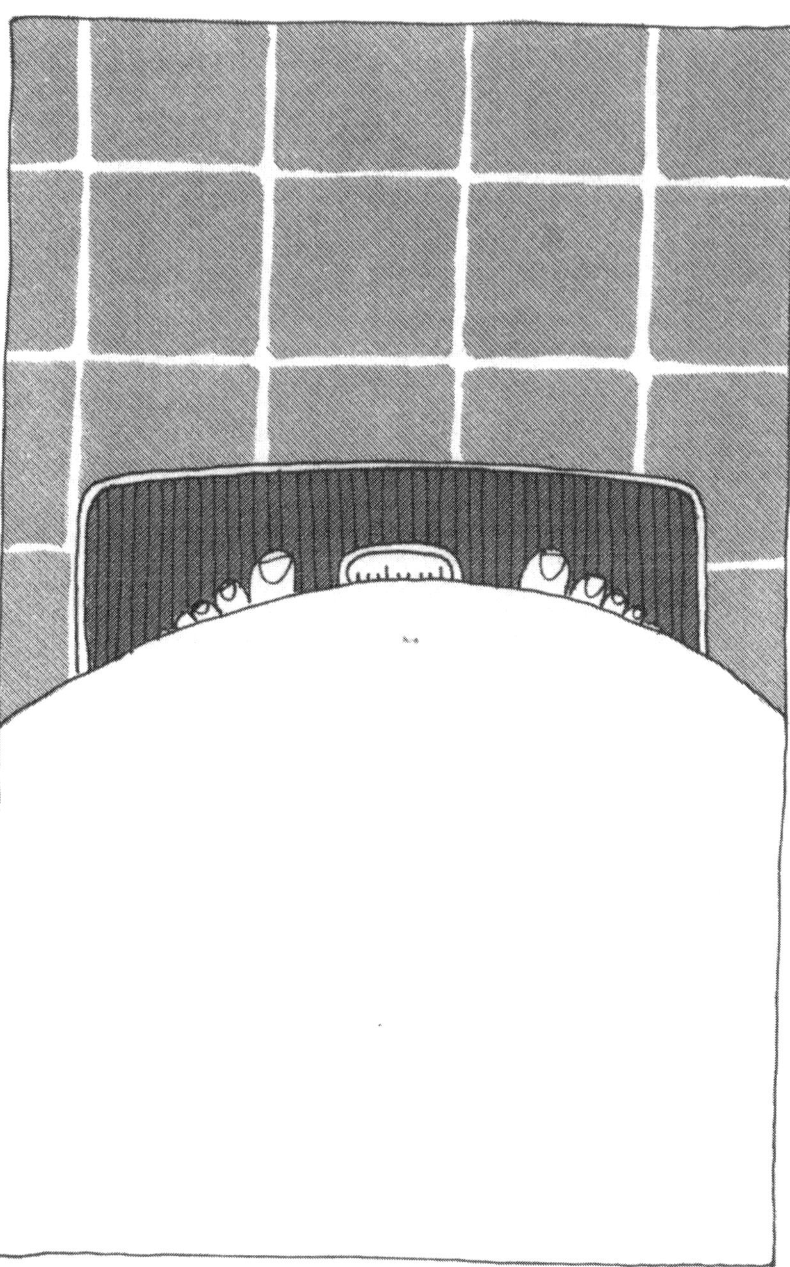

6. Obesity and Stress

Obesity is now a serious health epidemic, one that threatens to make all of us pay the price. The consequences of obesity are deadly serious, and extremely expensive. Consider the costs of coronary artery surgeries, medicines for diabetes, knee and hip replacements, and back surgeries as only the beginning of the burden. Two-thirds of the US (including children) is now overweight or obese; carrying more fat than they need. Not coincidently, the rate of obesity has paralleled the rise in health care costs. Similar trends now sweep the UK, Europe, and most of the Western World. Surprisingly, obesity is now replacing starvation as the main threat to health in the Third World countries, thanks to our exportation of our fast food habits to them. The costs are poised to make private health insurance rates unaffordable, and will soon bankrupt any government programs that try to cover all the costs.

Obesity is not actually a disease at all, but rather a simple lifestyle choice in response to stress. The good news is it can be completely reversed by active personal choice. The bad news is that many people believe obesity is not their fault, so someone else should fix it for them. But in spite of all the money spent on spas, nutritionists, and stomach-bypass surgeons, the problem gets worse every year. Clearly there is no passive solution that can replace active participation.

"What's my "ideal" weight?"

There are many ways of calculating your "ideal weight": one is to start with 100 pounds for the first five feet of a woman's height, then add 5 pounds an inch. For men, start at 120 pounds.

Thus a five-foot-six-inch woman should weigh approximately 130 pounds; a six-foot man should weigh 180 pounds. There may be wide fluctuations for build and frame, and many other ways of calculating ideal weights, such as the BMI or Body Mass Index (see Appendix B). Fitness clubs also use calipers to "pinch" the skin, and assess the fat content.

But the best way to see if you are overweight is really simple. It takes only two pieces of equipment: your bathing suit and a full-length mirror. One look and you will know. Are you featuring a bit of a muffin-top instead of a six-pack? It will be pretty obvious. If you are about right, that will also be apparent. There is no point in losing weight as muscle mass in your limbs, yet retaining fat in your core; all that happens is you'll look like an avocado with four toothpicks stuck in it. If you lose weight, you want your belt size to reduce, not just have your rings and watches fall off.

Obesity is simply an imbalance in arithmetic. In order to be obese, you must take in more calories than you burn off. These excess calories are stored as fat. There are no ifs, ands, or buts; it is a simple, natural law of Arithmetic, which works just as consistently as the law of Gravity.

One of the most common findings associated with obesity is denial. This is the classic "What, me overeat?—You must be JOKING!" defense. I had one patient come in and tell me that he just had "to look at food" to gain weight. All his coworkers at the office could eat large lunches and stay thin. But he had only a small salad and soda water, and gained weight. He honestly believed that his problem was just bad luck and bad metabolism. After long and probing questioning, the patient admitted at last that he does have a problem with absent-minded eating while watching television. His total average daily calorie count was in fact 3,500, while his output was only 1,500 calories. His weight, unsurprisingly (to me, but not to him) was 262 pounds on a five-foot-nine-inch frame: about 100 pounds overweight.

Obese people often deny that they are big eaters, and insist on remembering details of only the very modest lunches—the occasional half grapefruit and the few radish slices that they consume when there are people watching. It is important to remember that "binge eating," even if it occurs only once a month, must be added onto all the other calories that have been taken during the rest of the time period. That is, there is no point in eating a diet that has only eight hundred calories per day from Monday to Friday if, on the weekends, you get into the fast foods and put away five thousand calories in a few minutes. Denying that you ate these extra calories won't make them disappear. Your mind may quickly forget, but your body remembers forever.

Also remember, "picking" or "grazing" can add *thousands* of calories each day, without any conscious awareness of having eaten. This is particularly easy if you nibble on foods low in fiber, which are not very filling to your stomach, or if you drink anything with calories.

In my career, I have treated thousands of cases of obesity. In taking a proper history, it is remarkable how consistently the underlying cause is overlooked. Obese patients are not uninformed. They all know that carrot cake is fattening, and plain carrots are OK. In fact, today's obese adult usually knows a great deal about diets and foods. So why does their obesity resist all attempts to fix it? Here is the plain truth: obesity is ***not*** the problem, it is only the ***result*** of the problem. That's why obesity cannot be fixed unless we address the real cause, which is usually one of the following:

1. Boredom.
2. Excess stress.
3. Lifestyle or peer pressure (cultural).
4. Poor self-image (unhappiness, depression).
5. All of the above.

1. Boredom can lead to obesity

If you are obese, ask yourself a question: Are you bored? Do you find yourself rearranging your spices according to the alphabet (the kitchen equivalent of rearranging the deck chairs on the Titanic)? Would you rather watch a reality show than have your own reality? Would you rather watch people exercise during tv sports instead of doing your own activities?

Ask yourself when you do most of your heavy eating, whether it is binges, picking, or heavy meals at certain times of the day or week. If boredom is a factor here, then make this the time of day that you do something to correct it.

In other words, if you are bored in the evenings and tend to do most of your eating then, this would be an ideal time for you to engage in an enjoyable sport, dance class, or other activity that you find stimulating and can do on a long-term basis.

Exercise is certainly good, but not all exercise fights boredom. While some get into the Zen of repetitive exercises like jogging, many will try it once, get bored, and go back to eating.

If you are eating from boredom, examine your entire lifestyle, from career to relationships and hobbies. If you feel trapped, consider some escape strategies. If your job is boring you, take courses that will lead to different options that better suit your aptitudes. If you are lonesome, consider enrolling in activities that will help you meet people with shared interests. If you are a television or computer addict, consider rationing yourself to an hour per evening in front of the flat screen, and challenge yourself to do something different.

Boredom can be experienced by both sexes, and by all age groups. The solution to boredom in children and teens is usually quite obvious to parents, namely, that some structure or discipline has to be provided each day to give the child a sense of purpose. What we forget is that the same principles can apply to fighting boredom in adults and the elderly. Once boredom takes over, obesity becomes a willing and easy companion. Certainly, if the highlight of your day is treating yourself to a row of Oreos or a bag of chips while you watch other people exercise on tv, then your flat screen will soon become your fat screen.

Patients have told me that they choose to remain in what are essentially very monotonous jobs for the rest of their lives, as they could not afford to make a few dollars less and still keep up the lifestyle they have become accustomed to. However, if they calculate exactly how much money they need to live on, they may find they could get by on less, particularly if they could decrease the stress of having the wrong job, or moving to cheaper real estate markets. Moreover, by trading some money for greater happiness, they may increase their productivity in the long run.

Everyone needs a mission; this is especially helpful if you are bored. If you don't have one during your work day, try to find one in your time off. (See our chapter 4, page 101) Remember, if boredom persists, obesity "cures" will never last for long.

2. Stress as a cause of obesity

Obesity is an abnormal physiological response to stress, as we have seen in Chapter 2. Your body tends to respond to stress by reducing its weight, burning up its stores of fat and sugar with an increased metabolism, triggered by increasing thyroid levels. However, some people have an overwhelming oral urge retained from childhood for gratification. Whenever stress strikes, they panic and shove something into their faces, a throwback to programmed reflexes seen as early as prenatal ultrasounds. My grandfather used to describe this as the "elbow-mouth" reflex: every time you bend your elbow, your mouth opens. In many cases the oral urge involves cigarettes or calories, and often both. Oral oriented people are frequently seen chewing gum, sucking on mints, chewing their nails and smoking—sometimes all at once.

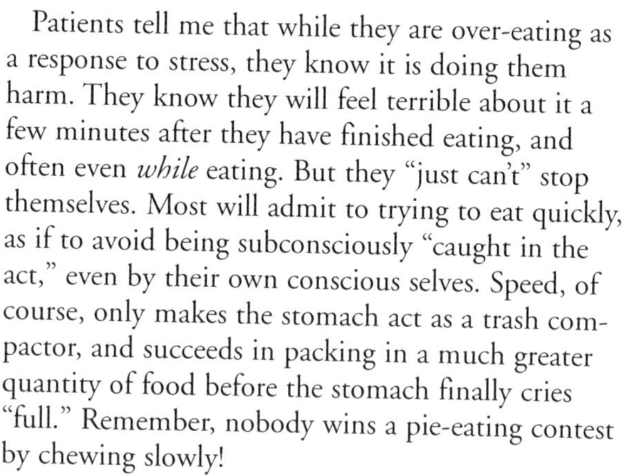

Patients tell me that while they are over-eating as a response to stress, they know it is doing them harm. They know they will feel terrible about it a few minutes after they have finished eating, and often even *while* eating. But they "just can't" stop themselves. Most will admit to trying to eat quickly, as if to avoid being subconsciously "caught in the act," even by their own conscious selves. Speed, of course, only makes the stomach act as a trash compactor, and succeeds in packing in a much greater quantity of food before the stomach finally cries "full." Remember, nobody wins a pie-eating contest by chewing slowly!

Food has a wonderful appeal to the senses of taste and smell, which can bring moments of pure ecstasy to the eater. When you think about it, if you have gone through a very stressful day, the guaranteed ecstasy of a favorite food does seem enticing. Such food can easily be incorporated into your balanced diet. However, under stress, the obese tend to eat beyond the point of satiety, to gratify the mouth even at the expense of straining the stomach. Remember the axiom: Comfort food is rarely comfortable, especially once you are wearing it.

3. Lifestyle and peer pressure: Culture can cause obesity

In many cultures, a fat baby is considered a healthy one. Sometimes this is regional, sometimes it is a "family tradition", and other times it is just because people don't know better. Even in an educated country there can be some stunning pockets of ignorance. This is easily seen on daytime TV. This is where we meet the 120 pound two-year old, and the puzzled parents. The dim-witted mom and dad claim they love their baby, but they "just hate to hear him cry". So they constantly feed sweets into the child, to shut him up. (Sadly, you don't need to have an IQ test to have a baby). As the child gets older, there are additional cultural habits that lead towards obesity: finishing all the food on your plate, and using food as a reward ("stop fighting with your sister in the car, and I'll get you both an ice cream"). Children also imitate their parents; whenever company is invited, fattening food must be made or ordered in. This creates generations of the obese across the map. In southern USA, the obese are overfeeding on fried foods. In the mid-west and north they are eating excesses of cheese, corn and white bread. In Northern Canada, the poison of choice is poutine and donuts. Pockets of obese cultures exist within families, as well as within geographical boundaries. Usually this obesity is associated with a corresponding early death rate from heart disease, diabetes, and cancers, which is what we see increasingly in the US, and now in other countries, such as the UK (Scotland in particular), Europe, and even Asia. Even China is now seeing obesity ramping up, as fast food outlets serve up western sodas and burgers with fries.

Peer pressure begins to take hold as a child grows into the school years, then sets in for life. School is where obesity is institutionalized, with the curriculum that says "yes" to fattening food and drinks, and "no" to any form of regular exercise. After school, obese children congregate in the food court to share their two common interests: sloth and gluttony. The age at which obesity patterns usually commence in North American children is about six, or whenever they start school.

Ideally, every school day should start off with at least thirty minutes of physical activity (formerly known as "fun"). Running, kicking a ball, shooting baskets, or whatever. A proper daily exercise routine at school should consist of at least fifteen minutes of stretching and warm-up, followed by a twenty-minute period of high intensity exercise, and then a five-minute cool-down. The resulting improved concentration and attention span would easily make up for the forty minutes lost out of actual teaching time. It would also instill some lifelong daily habits that would virtually preclude the possibility of sloth in adult years. Some innovative schools are now trying this very successfully, but most resist.

Again, this brings up the importance of peer pressure. If all your friends are participating in sports, you will probably join them. But if they are all indulging in overeating and sedentary habits, you will probably feel pressure to join them in these inactivities. In some schools, obesity is so common that kids make fun of the occasional fit classmate.

As a paradox, once you get thinner, it becomes easier to stay that way. First, your metabolism improves, because your muscle mass will burn off more calories even as you rest or sleep. Also, your toned muscles will remind you of all the exercise you just did, so you will be less likely to splurge on the wrong foods. As an added bonus, the endorphin generated by exercise acts as a natural appetite suppressant, and a mood elevator.

4. Poor self-image as a reason for obesity

Poor self-image is possibly the most significant and common reason for obesity. It is obvious from the way people dress and carry themselves. People with low self-esteem radiate a complete disinterest in their appearance. Their "look" is the loose, sloppy clothing, the slouched posture, and the long, sad face. These are people who seem to have lots of time to spend eating, but no time to stand in front of a mirror. Hair is a mess (or hacked off for easier maintenance), posture is slouched, mouth is downturned, and make-up is nowhere to be seen. Exactly like the "before" scenes in "What Not To Wear" on television. Even at events that might call for decorum, such as going out for dinner or a show, they still show up in their sad-suits, such as stretchy sports shorts, long socks, and a baggy T-shirt. The old image of the "Sunday best" outfits for church has even been subverted, as many people show up in clothes better suited for gardening. When people are this sad, and show such a lack of self-respect, they are unfortunately treated accordingly by others. This only reinforces their poor self-esteem, and drives them toward the only constant pleasure they know, overeating.

One of my patients was a very good looking television star, who had to play the part of an obese person in a movie. The make-up specialists rigged up a "fat suit" that added sixty pounds to her frame. When all made up, her beauty completely disguised, she was surprised to see how differently people treated her. Store clerks were rude, fellow passengers on a bus knocked into her, and no doors were held open for her. She could readily understand why food could easily become a best friend, if people were so unfriendly to her.

To overcome poor self-esteem, one needs a lot of courage, insight, and support from friends or even professional counsellors. If you recognize yourself in this category, stand in front of a full-length mirror, and visualize a complete

"Whether you think you *can* or you *can't*, you're probably *right*."

Henry Ford

If you think of yourself as being fat, you will be fat. If you think of yourself as being friendless and of no use to anyone, you can also fulfill these prophecies. On the other hand, you can think of yourself as a great person, with much to offer. This change of perception will change your attitude, and the external signals that you send to others. In terms of your weight, it will automatically start to fall as you raise your own image. Self-confidence makes the fight against obesity much more likely to succeed for life.

"makeover". Throw out some of your tired outfits, and treat yourself to a new look, even if an inexpensive one. If you are fashion-challenged, enlist the help of a friend, or good shop clerk. If money is the issue, take your new clothing budget from some of your old food budget. While still in front of the mirror, check your posture by backing up against a wall. Force yourself to stand up straight, and smile. Body language is free, and it is amazing what a difference it can make to your self-confidence and happiness.

In spite of all the external factors, a poor self-image can still be overcome. But it can't be changed passively, as the Prescription Drug Cartel has no pill for self-esteem (even though antidepressants are widely over-used in the vain attempt to offer a "cure"). The only solution is an active one; you have to start earning your own respect. Once you signal this self-respect to others by your positive body language and attitude, they will in return treat you with greater respect. Once the self-deprecating phase is past, you will be able to cure the obesity, which in turn further improves your confidence and self-esteem. The constant bombardment with media images emphasizing beauty, thinness, luxury, and wealth represents a sharp contrast for most people. The solution is not to have an "instant" makeover, with plastic surgery or a wardrobe replacement. Find your own inner smile, set goals that are gradual and realistic rather than "all or nothing".

It's your choice

Stress can be managed by various means, including self-hypnosis techniques and positive thinking and imaging. I had one patient who gained a lot of weight after delivering her second child. She ultimately achieved success in losing weight from a five-year-old picture of herself looking slim in a bikini. She placed this picture on the front of her refrigerator. To the right of it was a short note: "It's your choice. You can choose this (with an arrow pointing to the picture), or this (with an arrow pointing to the refrigerator handle)." Her method was highly successful in creating a positive image to fight the siren call of overeating. Undoubtedly you will develop your own favorite techniques that will work for you as well.

The "I just love eating" excuse

This excuse is one that is usually trotted out quite early by the obese person. We all love eating, and most people love good food. The problem occurs when the sense of proportion is warped, and the love of food assumes a much greater value than it should in comparison with other activities—or life itself. If you really love eating, then develop a love of exercising, so you can burn off what you ingest. If you don't have the time or ability to exercise much, then don't eat like a professional athlete, even if you used to be one! Even modest obesity (more than 10 percent above ideal body weight) can be harmful to your health. If you truly love eating, you will be able to eat for many more years if you pace yourself normally, rather than abusing the privilege.

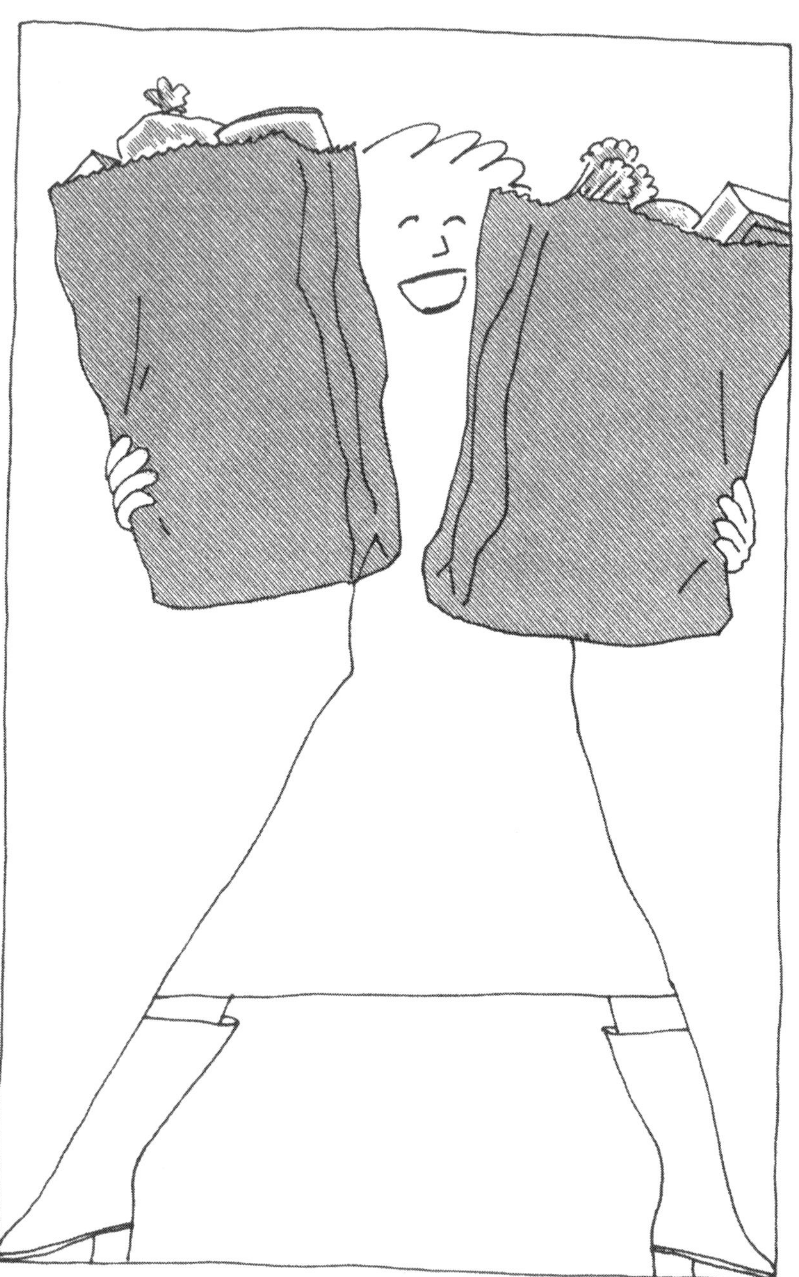

7. The Joy of Stress Obesity Prescription:

Rx: Make your diet a reward, not a punishment

For the obese, food is viewed as friend, and diet has been the enemy. The reality is that the roles here are reversed. We should view the overconsumption of food as a punishment to our body, and view a healthy diet as the reward. This reversal of connotations is the reason why obesity is flourishing in spite of thousands of new books or programs on dieting. Feeling stressed, depressed, or bored? Then food is your ticket to a smile. That diet is just something to endure when you simply have to get ready for a wedding, need to get in shape for your knee replacement surgery, or have to recover from your heart attack. In the meantime, let's party on, and bring on the foods! As a doctor, I always try to help each patient prevent medical consequences before they happen. That's why I emphasize the positive rewards of healthy choices, not only for their long term benefits, but for their immediate improvements as well. In other words, good diet choices will enhance the *quantity* of our lifespans tomorrow, and improve the *quality* of our lives today.

The first step in treating obesity is to correctly diagnose the cause, as we have just seen in the last chapter. Once the real enemy has been identified, you can harness your energy in correcting it.

I approach obesity in a very positive way, namely, encouraging positive elements in the patient's nature. The patient should take stock of his or her good points-such as humor, intelligence, and enjoyment of friends and family-and use creativity to put these to greater use. I had one obese woman, for example, who convinced her obese bridge group to bring along walking shoes instead of brownies. So twice a week they would start off with a half-hour walk through the neighborhood, then deal the cards. They enjoyed trying to walk a little faster and farther each time, and were pleased to note a diminished appetite for sweets during the card games. They used the power of peer pressure in a good way, to replace passive (and absent-minded) eating with active exercise. The whole group felt better about themselves, and were encouraged to change their lifestyle the rest of the week as well.

Rules for losing weight

1. Don't skip meals. If your body is starved for long, it goes into a self-preservation mode, and tries to retain its fat. Keeping to a regular meal schedule reduces the need for snacking, and reduces the temptation for binge eating.
2. Never eat food from its original container. It is impossible to control your portions if you eat mindlessly from a bag, box, or cake-pan. Always serve your food on a plate, so you can keep track of quantities. For purposes of illusion, use small plates. A healthy portion of food can look like a feast on a side dish, or can look lost on a huge dinner plate.
3. Snack well. If you are going to snack, make sure you have good foods, and lots of drinking water at hand. Bite sized pieces of veggies or left-over meals are far better (and less addictive) than sweets and junk foods.
4. Sit down at the table. This forces you to focus on your food, and not on distractions. It is hard to gauge your total intake if you are driving your car, watching television, or standing at the sink.
5. Enjoy your eating experience. Set the table as you would if company was coming. Try a candle or flower for a centerpiece. Turn off your cell phone so you won't text or play games. Use your good dishes and silverware for your regular meals, not just once a year. If you don't know how to cook, give it a try. Even if you are reheating cooked foods, give them some zest. Present the meal garnished and arranged like you would expect in a good restaurant. Turn up the music, and turn down the lights.
6. Take your time. If you have kids, try to have conversations. This can't happen if everyone eats separately, heating their own foods in the microwave. It is supposed to be a "dinner hour", not a "munching minute"!
7. Use your knife to cut smaller portions on the plate. Use

your teeth to chew at least twenty times per bite. Practice putting down your fork regularly during the meal. If you eat slowly, your stomach will feel full with less food.

8. Don't hide what you eat. Even if you live alone, eat as if you had witnesses. Obese people commonly don't eat much when people are watching, they do all their damage when nobody is looking. Thin people are often seen to eat large meals, but that's probably all they eat.
9. Beware of any drinks with calories. Sodas and other sugared drinks are a disaster. They are full of calories, but are not any more filling than the same volume of water. The simple sugars, once into the blood stream, signal the body to make more insulin, which converts these sugars into fat (think cellulite). Also beware of the booze. A glass or two of wine, beer, or an equivalent ounce of spirits can indeed aid digestion, but turns from friend to foe in greater quantities. Not only does alcohol carry its own toxicity in excess, but if it's empty calories are fattening, and not filling. So if you love to eat food, learn to drink lots of water.

10. Find and correct your real problem (see Chapter 6)—the root cause that leads to your obesity.
11. *Develop alternative rewards* for yourself, other than eating. Obesity is not cheap, based on the price of food today. Especially if you learn to cook instead of buy prepared foods,

you can save a lot of money. Once you convert to sensible eating habits, you can pocket the savings, and spend it on an alternative reward. One of these could be a new wardrobe as return to normal sizes. Another could be sporting equipment, such as a bike, roller blades, or running shoes. That daily frappuccino treat could easily cost more than a gym membership, so think twice about your budget.

12. Never shop for food when you are hungry. In the grocery aisle, it is hard to walk past a row of temptations. In the car, it is hard to get all the way home without eating directly from the bag while you are driving. If your stomach is full from a good meal, then food shopping can be far less impulsive.
13. Beware the Binge. The body does not do averages very well at all. So days of good behaviour can be wiped out by an occasional Tsunami wave of binge eating. The same can be said for binge drinking, which can lead to fatal consequences. For that matter, binge exercising after months of slothfulness has lead to more than a few heart attacks. So smooth out your habits, and get the discipline to eat and drink sensibly, and exercise consistently.
14. Take free exercise when you can. If you are on public transport, try getting off at the wrong stop, to get extra daily walking. In an office building, try getting off at the wrong floor, to gain some stair-climbing exercise. If you drive, try parking in the farthest corner of the lot, to give yourself a longer walk.
15. Start today. Don't wait for an upcoming New Year's resolution, somebody's wedding, or your class reunion. And certainly don't wait for your doctor's stern advice after a crisis. The first warning of your next heart attack could be your last breath. So start now! Consult your doctor for further advice.

Justify your fuel intake.

The intake of fuel must match the output. In a car there is no room for a tank full of gas every day if you don't drive much. In the human body, any surplus fuel (food) will be stored as fat. Ski racers will consume thousands more calories than most people, because they are exercising in cold weather for up to eight hours. Many will even start off with an hour or more in the gym before hitting the slopes at first light. They will have stacks of pancakes, lots of protein, and take extra power bars or dark chocolate with them onto the hill. They have a hard time maintaining their weight, no matter what they eat. But if you are at the same resort for a leisurely vacation, think twice before matching their consumption. You won't burn very much of that fuel if you are only taking a few slow runs, then return for cold drinks, a hot tub and a nap.

The *fuel justification* rule is simple: if you want to eat like a lumberjack, you have to chop down trees. If you want to eat like an athlete that exercises hours a day (even if that person was you when you were younger) then you need to have the time to burn it all off. If you ignore this rule, your body will wear the unburned fuel, stored as fat. This is true no matter what diet you are on.

There is more to curing obesity than just the diet

One of the reasons that most published diets fail over the long term is that they require you to have special, personal foods in the house. Such diets may not match standard menu items in a restaurant, or when visiting friends. Another problem with the focus on dieting is that one thinks, reads and talks about food all the time. This means forbidden foods are never far from mind, and exercise is not even on your radar.

If you have success on a diet, of course you should stick with it, as long as it is balanced. However, if you rebound after every diet, then it's time to stop this uni-dimensional focus on food. You need to address the root causes of your obesity (chapter 6), and "sell" yourself some permanent good lifestyle choices. Every patient that I have seen succeed with their weight loss has addressed the whole lifestyle story. And every failure has always had a food-centric focus.

Develop a positive alternative when under stress, and picture it in order to compete with the tempting picture of gluttony. If your choice under stress is between a bag of cookies or going with a friend to the tennis court, you are more likely to choose the exercise. If you have nothing else in mind, the cookies win by default.

Once you get used to exercising control over your stress choices, the self-destructive urges of junk foods will be trumped by the self-reward urges of fun.

Now that we have identified the various causes for overeating, let us consider what to do about it. A good first step is to be aware of the calories you already eat and drink (see the appendix at the end of this book). Remember to be realistic. Don't just record your best day's meals, and forget about the bag of chocolate chips that you ate while reading Facebook. Remember to include binges, even if they are only once a week, as your body will still have to deal with these surges of calories. Binge calories should be averaged into your daily numbers.

Most obese people will be shocked to find they consume several thousand calories per day if they average in the total of all binges (even if they binge only once every few weeks). However, there are, of course, differences in the amounts of calories absorbed by different individuals' digestive tracts from a standard meal. There are also differences in calories burned off while asleep.

The Basic Metabolic Rate (BMR) is the number of calories that you burn off if you slept (or were in a coma) all day. For most people it takes about 800 calories to keep your heart beating and your lungs pumping for 24 hours. People blessed with a higher BMR may be able to bum off fifteen hundred calories per day without exercising, and seem to be able to eat anything and not get fat. Others may burn off only four hundred calories as their BMR, and have more of a problem losing weight. But whatever your BMR, you have to live with it. The only way to increase your metabolism is to increase your exercise each day.

Moderation Is the Key

When you are eating, you should certainly enjoy your food. Eat it slowly, and if you are preparing it, take care to make an attractive presentation. However, once you have finished eating, you should stop dwelling on food. My suggestion for counting calories is simply a guide for the first few weeks, and should not become an obsession. As long as your weight is on a downward trend of at least a pound per week, you need never again refer to the number of calories. However, if you find that you have reached a plateau for more than two weeks, or that your weight is creeping back up, then it becomes imperative to find out what the problem is. At such a time, it would be appropriate to go back to the basics and count your calorie intake (and, of course, your calorie output as exercise).

It is very important for you to still have some of your favorite foods. For example, if you are big on ice cream, which you know you will never find on any diet sheet, then I would suggest you still have some on occasion. Of course, this should be a small-sized version, such as a couple of bites, and not the whole container. Thereafter, it is easier to walk past the ice-cream display without feeling like it is the "forbidden fruit" of temptation. If you simply love chocolate, try a few bites of dark chocolate as a treat. If It has over 70% fat, then it will have much less sugar than milk chocolate, and actually has some anti-oxidant benefits to your health. Remember, I said a couple of bites.

Moderation should not be as radical as it would seem today. You can lose all the weight you need without diet pills, supplements, or stomach surgeries. All you need to learn is normalcy in eating habits, and in lifestyle habits. Food should be one of your enjoyments, but not your only one. Your time is too valuable to waste on just this aspect of your life.

Some Guidelines for Exercising

It is important, when looking at the calorie burn-off guide, to try and pick an activity that is both fun and practical for you. In general, start out with low impact activities, until you are in better shape. Walking is fine, but running on pavement might prove difficult until you are in better shape. If you are carrying excess weight, then impact sports will only multiply the forces going through your feet, legs, and spine. Riding a bicycle, however, is quite safe, since the feet do not touch the ground. Swimming or pool exercises are fine, as gravity is neatly avoided. (Even a hippopotamus can move gracefully under water!) As your cardiac and muscular fitness improves, try introducing yourself to other activities that suit your interests. "Selling" is everything. Pick an activity you can sell to your mind (don't make it boring) and to your body (don't pick a sport that hurts your back or your joints).

Once involved in exercise, take the same precautions a full-time athlete would take, including warm-up and cool-down stretching exercises. Strong core muscles (abdominals, back and side muscles of the torso) are required for such routine matters as standing or sitting upright, avoiding backache, preventing constipation, and for virtually every sport. (See Chapter 5.) However, most sports (except a few such as gymnastics and body building) don't give a full workout to the core muscles. Thus, even marathoners, ski racers, bicyclists, and swimmers will include specific core exercises in their routines. These can include pilates, yoga, tai chi, and boxing, or could simply be a series of crunches and leg lifts added to your routine. From children to the elderly, a daily routine of exercise can be one of life's great rewards. As an added benefit, exercise is a great antidote to the sedentary desk posture of the modern workplace.

Beware of the fast

After months, years, or even decades of losing the daily battle with the refrigerator, most obese people get frustrated and angry at themselves. They want to lose weight, but are in an unrealistic and desperate hurry, and are often vulnerable to weight-loss schemes promising overnight results. The ultimate method would appear to be to *fast*; the very word seems to impart a certain impression of speed to the process.

But is we pause here and reflect on the arithmetic, this is just not possible. To lose one pound per week, you must have an energy shortfall of 3,500 calories; that is, 500 calories per day of decreased food intake or increased exercise expenditure. (See Appendix C.) This pound-per-week rate of loss is not as useless as it at first seems—it means you would lose fifty-two pounds in a year, which is probably better than you did last year.

If you want to increase your rate of weight loss, then go for multiples of this arithmetic. That is, if you cut 1,000 calories from your daily diet, you will lose two pounds a week. Or, eat 500 calories less, and find an hour to burn off an extra 500 calories with cardio exercise.

In the initial week of any diet, an encouraging extra weight loss is seen in the form of water loss. This is because the extra calories that are missing were usually consumed with salt (either in the food, or added at the table). When the salt load is moderated, fluid will be lost (see page 135).

Figure 7.l

Calories used in various activities (per hour)*

	130 LBS. BODY WEIGHT	150 LBS. BODY WEIGHT	250 LBS. BODY WEIGHT
Aerobic dancing	395	490	540
Baseball	250	310	340
Basketball	670	830	910
Bicycling-10 mph	370	460	505
Bowling	240	300	325
Chess	80	100	110
Digging	445	555	610
Eating	80	100	110
Gardening	345	430	470
Housework-general	180	225	235
Lawn mowing-power	225	280	295
Mountain climbing	535	665	730
Rowing-2 mph	270	335	365
Shopping	150	185	205
Sleeping	60	75	80
Tennis	380	470	520
Walking-3 mph	270	336	366
Washing a car	205	255	280
Yoga	205	255	280

*The same rates apply to fractions of an hour's exercise. For example, one-half hour of bowling for a 150-pound person will burn off 150 calories.

Figure 7.2

The calorie content of some favorite foods

Food	Calories
Apple	75
Apple pie	300
Apple pie with ice cream	450
Bacon - 3 slices	120
Banana	100
Beans, green fresh	10
Beer	150
Bread, one slice	60
Butter, one pat	50
Carrots, one-half cup	25
Cashews, one oz.	150
Cheese, one oz.	100
Chicken fried, one serving	300
Coffee or tea, black	0
Cookies, 2 small plain	100
Éclair	275
Grapefruit, one-half	30
Halibut, average serving	100
Ham. Baked one slice	350
Hamburger, 4 oz.	400
Honey, one tablespoon	65
Lettuce, one-quarter head	10
Martini	125
Milk, 8 oz. whole	170

Orange juice, 4 oz.	55
Peanuts, 10	100
Pork chop, one medium	150
Potato, French fries, 30 sticks	465
Potato, boiled, one medium	50
Rib steak, average serving	320
Salad dressing, one tablespoon	100
Salmon, one serving	250
Sugar, one teaspoon	18
Tomato soup, one cup	100
Wine, glass	100

The above list serves to show that your daily calorie intake can be anything that you wish it to be. Avoid high calorie foods, and you are well on the way to success. (For a more extensive calorie listing, see Appendix C at the back of this book.)

It is a shock to find that the number of calories burned off by scrubbing the kitchen floor for an hour (a guaranteed backache) doesn't even equal the number found in a piece of apple pie. This may not seem fair, but it is a fact of life. In order to "earn," or "deserve," a piece of pie and ice cream, you would have to go bicycling for an hour. It is not hard to see how food intake can quite readily get ahead of calorie expenditure. Calories can be very well compacted in foods. For example, one pound of cashews has about 2,400; ten peanuts have 100 calories (and no one eats just ten-be honest!). Just three glasses of pop could add 300 empty calories without diminishing your appetite.

The "Eat Normally" Balance Sheet

"Your Daily Reckoning"

1. Weigh yourself initially, and again at the same time of day at the end of each week. Do not weigh yourself more often. (Otherwise the three to four pounds of daily fluid fluctuation in the body will lead to false confidence or despair.) Use the same scale every time. It may be best to arrange to have the weighing done at your doctor's office. You may not need to see the doctor each time. I have my assistant record the weekly weights of my obese patients, and I see them only if they gain weight. This partial reinforcement works very well.
2. Enter the daily calorie count of everything that you put into your mouth, including drinks, gum, candy, and so on. Right away, this will make you less likely to have absent-minded snacks. Record your daily calorie count for as many days as it takes you to get into a normal eating routine. Keep track of your daily average; for example, you may eat more on weekends than mid-week. If you are good,

developing a normal routine may take only a few weeks initially, and can be restarted whenever you are shocked by a weight gain. You should not need to dwell on the numbers of calories forever.

3. Enter the number of minutes of active exercise each day. This will serve two purposes: it will allow you to roughly calculate the calories burned off, and it will remind you to do some exercise before you call it a day. Remember to consult your doctor to help you choose a level and type of exercise that is safe for your overall condition.

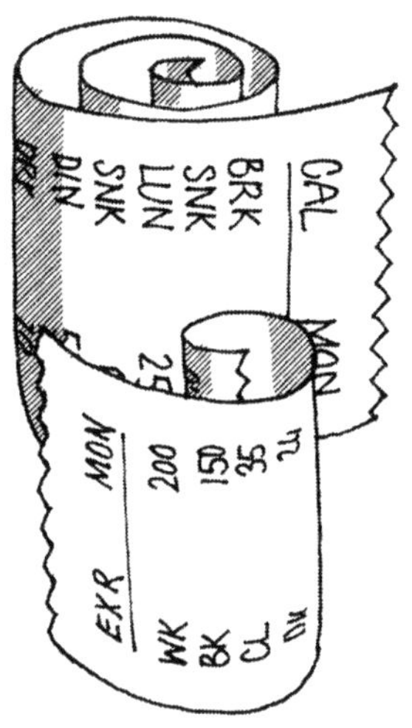

4. Show your written records to your doctor-he or she will be able to see where your problems lie, especially if you fail to lose weight.

The fact that insurance companies have recently enlarged the allowable weights for each height by a few pounds should not be seen as any kind of green light for obesity. Don't let poor food choices make you sick with diabetes, heart disease, cancers, and pains in the knees, hips, and back.

Get out your calculators!

FIRST WEEK:	TOTAL CALORIES CONSUMED (SEE FIGURE 7.2 OR APPENDIX C)		TOTAL CALORIES BURNED OFF (SEE FIGURE 7.1)	
Day 1		cal.		cal.
Day 2		cal.		cal.
Day 3		cal.		cal.
Day 4		cal.		cal.
Day 5		cal.		cal.
Day 6		cal.		cal.
Day 7		cal.		cal.
	Sub-total	cal.	Sub-total	cal.
	÷7=	Cal. intake per day	÷7=	Cal. burn-off per day

CALORIE INTAKE		-		=	
	Average calories consumed per day		Average calories burned off per day		Average net calories intake per day
WEIGHT CHANGE		-		=	
	Starting weight on Day 1		Weight after first week		Weight change in one week

(For additional sheets see Appendix C)

The only two numbers you need to know are: the net average daily calorie intake, and your weight change at the end of each week.

If your weight is declining at a rate of at least one pound per week, then you can leave your net calorie intake as it is. If not, then you have just two options: Reduce calories taken in, or increase calories burned off. There are a number of additional techniques that can help you lose weight. These include hypnosis, as well as acupuncture. While it is beyond the scope of this book to deal with each of these in detail, both have definite merit. I have used acupuncture very successfully on some of my own patients. I have also sent some to a hypnotist with good results. Each technique has its merits, and works differently.

Acupuncture techniques work best for people who tend to suffer "withdrawal" when they change their eating habits. As we have seen, acupuncture produces endorphin from the hypothalamus. This tends to act in exactly the same ways as morphine does from outside the body, which may explain why morphine addicts do not tend to be fat. Endorphin tends to give a sense of well-being and provides an alternative to seeking gratification from food. It has been shown to be a useful treatment for withdrawal in morphine addicts, as the endorphin occupies the same receptor sites in the brain. Acupuncture has also been found to be useful in treating people experiencing withdrawal from smoking, alcohol, or overeating. However, there are a number of other psychological triggers (besides withdrawal) that make people eat; for example, the Pavlovian salivation that comes with the ringing of the lunch-time bell. These are best dealt with through other techniques such as hypnosis. Of course, the best method of all is to be able to help yourself according to the above guidelines. If you need additional support, consult your doctor for help or for referral. You can also consider one of the weight loss clinics in your area, but beware of expenses here.

Diet pills used to work very well, as they used to be amphetamines, or "speed." A whole generation of fat people were commonly given these "uppers", and the side effects were dreadful. After a week of dusting the ceiling, vacuuming the roof of the house, and forgetting to sleep or eat, the obese patient would certainly lose a few pounds. However, there were serious risks of heart attack and other problems, and basically nothing was learned. The patient soon reverted to the same old habits, and, once the pills ran out, up went their weight.

Today, new forms of diet pills are a national addiction, and an expensive illusion. Heavily advertised by the prescription drug cartel to both patients and doctors, these pills are the perfect panacea for the passive. People crave the "instant makeover" results that seem so tempting on television. Pop a pill, and a lifetime of flab vanishes. Of course, it does not work that quickly, and has a long list of dangerous side effects. These are quite daunting when they are read quickly at the end of television ads; and often the side effects are a lot worse than the original problem (for example if the problem was depression, a side effect of suicide is hardly an improvement). The only way diet pills will help in the long term is if they are taken with a proper balance of food intake and exercise output. But wait a minute, you already know that! If you follow the advice above, you will lose weight on your own, and won't need anything from the drug companies.

Conclusion

Carrying a few extra pounds is not a medical problem, as long as you are happy with it. However, when your body fat gets out of control, you should talk to your doctor about addressing it. To lose that extra weight, make sure you plan for fun, and not just for sacrifice. Find new activities that keep you moving to burn calories, and keep you away from temptations. Like alcoholics, you may need to identify "enablers" in your life, and avoid them. If old friends are always serving up the wrong temptations of gluttony and sloth, find new friends to spend time with. You are much more likely to stay healthy if you spend time throwing a frisbee, kicking a ball, or riding a bike. If you would rather be alone, then you can enable your own good behaviours by going for a brisk walk.

Remember that you should fight obesity not simply for the sake of aesthetics. This is a point on which advocacy groups for the preservation of fat people's rights are quite misguided. Granted, they have a good point in criticizing media version of beauty. Cover-girls who are super-thin and have almost no muscle mass are indeed unhealthy role models. In addition, modern photo-shopping can take even more inches off their bodies, leaving normal women with no hope of comparison, without starvation. The tragic results of bulimia and anorexia are indeed very sad. But the encouragement to damage health at the other end of the weight spectrum is similarly misled. Your body's ideal weight can best be found with the full length mirror test, and a visit to your doctor.

Remember, obesity will severely curtail your life, both in quality and in quantity. This is the single most preventable cause of early death and illness that we face. If you take control of your own life, you will save it. If you give that control to the fast-and-fattening food industry, then you will suffer the consequences.

If your own health and lifespan do not inspire you to fix your obesity, then think about those who love you. From whatever source you can draw upon, please take control, starting today. Go back and re-read the above chapter often, and enjoy your new-found control!

8.

Stress and Your Heart

Heart disease— inevitable or preventable?

Heart disease is one of the most complex and hotly debated subjects in the medical profession. Gene mapping may identify the cause of hereditary heart disease in the future. However, the biggest risk factors are mostly within your control.

1. Diabetes mellitus.

Also known as *sugar diabetes.* Diabetes can be associated with heart attacks. This disease has also been described as *premature aging.* This is particularly worrisome due to the current epidemic of self-induced ("type 2") diabetes, starting in young children. However, the bad effects can be greatly helped by good control of diet, exercise, and the proper doses of medications if needed.

2. Hypertension.

Usually silent, with no symptoms at all, high blood pressure can cause hardening of the arteries, including the coronary arteries of the heart. To detect this disease, see your doctor for regular physical examinations. If you do have elevated pressure, then a home unit will help you record a diary of your numbers; these can be valuable to identify the disease. While diet, exercise, and the loss of excess weight can be important, many patients do need to go on medications. There are other reasons to control your pressure, notably to avoid strokes in the brain, and damage to your vision.

3. Hereditary hypercholesterolemia.

In severe cases of this, few males in a given family will reach age forty without having a heart attack. Although the condition is fortunately quite rare, it is always best to check with your family doctor for your serum cholesterol levels. It is even more important if the male members of your family tended to have early heart attacks. In my career, I have seen a few families with high cholesterol levels, where the men did not live past their forties because of heart attacks. With the aid of today's early diagnostics, medicines and cardiac procedures, even these severe cases can be treated or prevented. The best results are obtained if the diagnosis is made before age ten, and appropriate cholesterol reducing measures are taken. It is extremely important to also avoid eating refined sugars and starches cholesterol. (See Chapter 5.)

4. Hyperthyroidism.

Now fortunately quite rare, this overactivity of the thyroid gland can speed up the heart rate, even while you are sleeping. This condition is picked up by routine blood tests, and can usually be well treated by medicines or surgery.

5. Smoking.

Cigarettes are known to cause instant constriction of the blood vessels in the coronary arteries. The many ways in which this outrageous habit harms your heart and the rest of your body are discussed more fully in Chapter 3.

6. Sloth.

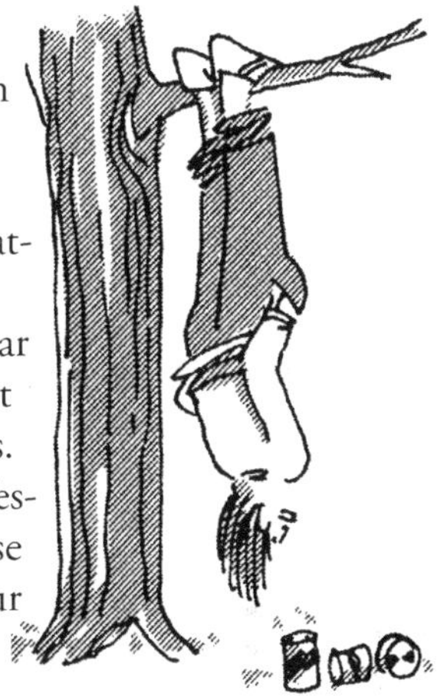

Regular exercise doesn't guarantee protection from heart disease, but evidence suggests it certainly helps. Note the word "regular". Largely slothful habits can be even more dangerous when punctuated by sudden binges of maximal energy. We see this in winter with snow shoveling or pushing a car out of a ditch. We see this in summer when heart rates are tested by heat and exertion during sports. Consult your doctor and a qualified exercise professional for assistance. Make sure you test your pulse whenever you are doing any exertion, to keep your heart rate in a safe zone.

7. Type A behavior.

This will be discussed in the following pages.

The cholesterol controversy: More food for thought

Cholesterol, currently the subject of controversy, has already been discussed in Chapter 5. A high cholesterol intake doesn't necessarily increase the risk of heart disease. One frequently cited example is the study of Boston Irishmen versus their brothers in Ireland. The latter were eating a great deal of cholesterol, whereas the former were eating "diet" foods low in cholesterol. Their respective rates of heart disease were not at all what one might have expected; the Boston brothers had the higher rate of heart attacks. Other groups, such as Navaho Indians and the Masai people in Africa, also eat high cholesterol diets and have very little coronary heart disease. Americans have three times the amount of coronary heart disease today that they had in 1910, but still eat a similar amount of cholesterol. It is thus obvious that there are more factors at play than simple dietary intake, and these are being studied intensively. Other factors that probably play a part include the amount of fiber in the diet; Type A behavior; lack of exercise, overall obesity, diabetes, and, importantly, resistance to stress (see Chapters 3 and 4.). An additional factor is refined (white) sugar, starch, and chemical additives in modern processed foods, which inflames the body's chemistry. This creates a protective response where cholesterol is laid down on the walls of the arteries; this is why one should not only reduce cholesterol intake, but also junk foods. And remember, the main feature of muffins, cookies, and ice creams labeled "cholesterol free" is white sugar.

Type A behavior: Self-induced stress

An understanding of Type A behavior, first described by Dr. Meyer Friedman in his book *Type A Behavior and Your Heart,* has provided a great deal of insight into the most common link among heart attack patients. Quite often, such patients have an "action-emotion" complex. This basically consists of "hurry sickness." Such people are constantly watching the clock, and fighting it every step of the way. They have an excessive competitive drive, with easily aroused hostility.

The Type A person is aggressive, in a chronic struggle to achieve more in less time, even at the expense of offending others. He or she can be very hostile if threatened. Although such a person may seem like a "jerk" in some ways, it is interesting to note that more often than not, his or her activities are socially praised, and rewarded with material goods.

Type A behavior is seen in up to half of all males, and in an increasing number of females in the work force. When given a simple test, such as subtracting 13's from 1,000 in a given time period, Type A people perform as well as Type B, who have all the opposite traits. The difference is that the Type A's treat the test as an emergency. They respond with forty times the amount of cortisol secreted into the bloodstream, three times the amount of blood flow to the muscles, and four times as much adrenalin surging through the blood vessels. As seen in Chapter 2, this means that all the stress responses are activated, including increased cholesterol in the blood, racing of the heartbeat, and so on.

Many successful companies now have stress programs, but usually just for executives. However, even more stress often comes to those in middle management (lots of responsibility, but very little control). Companies would certainly see a good return with investment of stress reduction programs for all levels of their work force. The payback in reducing sick and absentee time and increasing productivity is incredible. The return on investment for prevention is four times the original costs.

Before World War II, women in the United States were found to have a comparatively low level of Type A behavior, primarily because as a group they were not exposed to the working world with its time pressures as much as men. However, this is certainly changing with the modem workplace, where women have equal chances for this behavior.

In a ten-year study. Type A personalities were *three times* as likely to have coronary heart diseases. In predicting who was going to have a heart attack, Type A behavior was found to be more important than other factors, including family history, serum cholesterol levels, and smoking.

In order to learn about the effects of Type A behavior on health, studies were done on rats. Specimens had specific damage done to the brain (the hypothalamus), which caused them to develop Type A behavior. These rats were shown to tolerate Type B rats in the same cage, because of the lack of fear of competition. However, when a Type A rat from this group was placed in a cage with another Type A rat, the two of them fought to the death. A similar effect may be seen with two Type A humans. Often this is evident in a fiercely competitive form of one-upmanship between neighbors, or peers at work. It can also be a disastrous combination in a marriage, unless resolved.

As part of the overall reflex responses to stress seen in the "alarm phase" in Type A rats (see Figure 2.3), it was noted that cholesterol levels in the blood could be dramatically increased irrespective of the amount of dietary cholesterol consumed. The cholesterol question is discussed more fully on page 204.

Not all Type A behavior is dangerous to one's health. The principle flaw from the cardiac point of view is the Type A's inability to recognize a false stress alarm from a real emergency. In other words, it is sensible and life-saving to scream and kick the doors down to escape a burning building. However, being in a slow bank line-up or a traffic jam is not a real emergency; losing your temper here will only serve to build up pressure in your heart, with no way to blow off steam. Where the Type A gets into cardiac trouble is when they constantly sound the false alarm, and burn out the emergency capacity of the heart. In just the same way, if someone cries "wolf", calling 911 for fake alarms, the quality of the rescue response may decline in the case of a real emergency.

Some Type A characteristics

Hurry sickness.

The Type A person overprograms their time, making too many commitments and underestimating potential delays between them, like traffic. This means they are usually late for everything, adding useless layers of stress to their lives. This personality often is inflexible, and not very creative or self-aware. For that matter, the type A does not seem aware of his or her effect on others.

One interesting sidelight is that the key link between Type A behavior and heart disease was first noted not by researchers, but by Dr. Friedman's upholsterer. The upholsterer came into the doctor's cardiology office to recover the chairs, and asked what kind of patients the doctor had. He had noted that the fabric on the chairs was worn out only across the front edges. Not one patient had been sitting back and relaxing in those chairs. "On the edge of the seat" behavior is, or course, typical of Type A individuals.

Number Orientation.

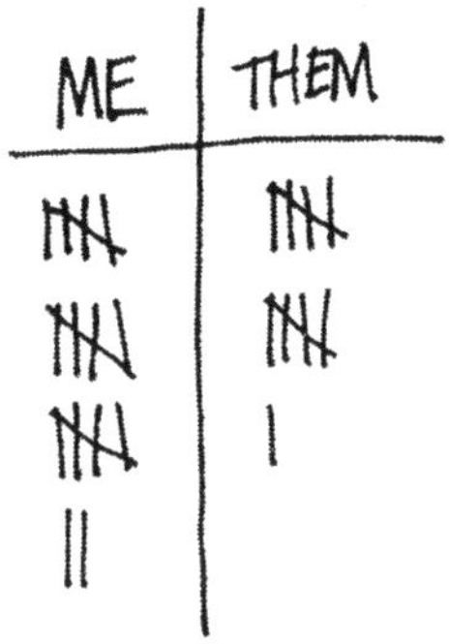

This fixation on numbers begins early in childhood. Video software companies have offered a huge array of games, usually all based on numbers; the winner has the most points, or scores the most hits, or gets to the highest level. In the adult iteration of this, we see the fixation on stock market numbers, or in the quest for more expensive houses and toys.

Score keeping.

Type A personalities tend not to enjoy the journey, unless they are keeping score. Golf is not appreciated for its fresh air and exercise; one must win or the day is spoiled. Instead of enjoying quality turns on the ski hill, they are keeping track of how many vertical feet they have skied. Instead of exploring the byways on a driving holiday, they are trying to see how many miles they can clock per day.

Insecurity.

The Type A person seeks approval from those around him. Not secure enough to keep accomplishments private, the Type A person wants to be noticed when they make a donation, or when they excel at work or at play. If the type A person is overlooked when peers are given an award, he or she is disappointed beyond the few dollars cost of the award, a classic sign of insecurity.

Hostility and aggression.

The Type A person tends to compete to win, and can become hostile if someone else wins. They may have a sense of humour, but usually to laugh at others rather than at himself or herself.

How to tell Type A from Type B behavior

Type A

1. Sharp aggressive style of speech; the end of the sentence is faster.
2. Easily bored; tunes out, only pretending to listen.
3. Always eats, talks, and walks quickly.
4. Impatient with others who dawdle; for example, saying "yes, yes" to speed up someone else's speech, or worse yet, finishing their sentences for them.
5. Polyphasic; for example, eating, shaving, and texting all at the same time. Sometimes doing all this while driving!
6. Selfish. Interested only in conversation about things that relate to him or her; tries to steer conversation his or her way, or tunes out. (After spending a considerable time talking about himself on a TV talk show, a Type A author turned to the host of the program and said, "Well, enough of all this talk about me; let's talk about you. Tell me, what did *you* think about my book?")
7. Feels guilty when relaxing.
8. Not observant and doesn't listen well. Can't remember names of people, or details of rooms. Most likely to be the one to lose keys, sunglasses, pen.
9. Aims for things worth *having*, not things worth *being*.
10. Very challenged by another Type A individual. Sparks can fly. This is particularly bad if two

Type A's are married to each other.

11. Physical signs: very assertive, tense, leans forward, shoulder blades seldom touch the chair (or even the rib cage for that matter).
12. Believes success comes from doing things faster; thus keeps up a very fast pace. Believes that when you are skating on thin ice, the only thing you have going for you is *speed.*
13. Measures success mainly by numbers; for example, more interested in number of points scored than in the quality of the game.

Type B

1. Not characterized by the above traits.
2. Seldom feels any time urgency, but can be just as ambitious.
3. Very easygoing; not hostile.
4. Plays a game for fun, not just to win.
5. Can relax without guilt and work without agitation; in the long run can get just as much work done as a Type A.
6. Is often more efficient. For example, a Type A friend of mine was once watching an old woodcutter neatly stack one piece of wood at a time against his garage. My friend became so agitated at the apparent slow pace that he rushed outside, picked up five logs at once, and with a frenetic expenditure of energy started his own stack of wood. After twenty minutes he collapsed, exhausted, back aching, with his pile of wood in a mess, and only a fraction as large as the old man's. Type B's, it seems, often win because of their steadiness and their economy of movement. (Perhaps this is what the old "Hare and Tortoise" fable was trying to tell us.)

Type A behavior and "the third wave"

In connection with Type A behavior, it is interesting to note Alvin Toffler's classic book *The Third Wave.* According to Toffler, the First Wave of civilization was agricultural, with hand-to-mouth subsistence, and people living wherever there was arable land. The Second Wave was born with the Industrial Revolution, during which the importance of mass production at centralized urban factories was emphasized. Also, at this time, working against the time clock came into being, with the advent of assembly lines and deadlines. With the spirit of free market competition developed the continual race to do more, thus leading to a great increase in Type A behavior.

Individuals who succeeded in acquiring *things* were extolled. Even in the early 1800s America was noted to be Type A both at work and at home, with a willingness to constantly uproot families in order to upgrade job postings. On holidays, Americans used to have the "ugly American" reputation (now no longer monopolized by any one nationality). Type A vacation trips are overly ambitious. Type A's try to visit too many cities, countries, or relatives within a short time frame. They try to impress their peers by the number of countries they have just visited (or are about to visit), how many miles per day they were able to drive, or how fast they could go.

With the diminishing importance of the old class system, life following the Industrial Revolution was, to a great extent, like a land rush or gold rush, in which everyone could make a fortune if only he or she ran fast enough.

This Second Wave behavior has certainly brought North Americans up to the highest standard of living in the world, leaving First Wave countries in the dust (literally).

Since the early 1970's, we have been in what Toffler calls the Third Wave, or the Technological Revolution. People no longer have to commute to central factories to earn a living. This opens opportunities for new kinds of jobs, and in new countries. Many IT workers can communicate on line from their home computer, laptop, or cell phone. People in emerging nations can now compete with those born in wealthier countries; this is known as the "flattening" of the Earth's playing fields. Tech support specialists no longer have to reside in the same country as the customer. They now work virtually, with our calls being answered by skilled IT people in developing nations. The same applies to global sourcing for parts and products.

New stresses are brought to bear in this Third Wave. But there are also many advantages, including the possibility of working from home instead of always commuting.

With the advent of the Industrial Revolution, and the increase of Type A behavior, the stressors that one faced in life went from simple to very complex. Instead of being threatened by the attack of a wild animal, for instance, people were threatened by complex stressors such as insidious noise pollution and time pressures. With our current position in the Third Wave, stressors are now likely to become even better disguised. Thus it is more important than ever to maintain your body in its best possible condition, and develop correct skills and choices to assist you in your defense against stress.

The excessive competition characterizing Type A behavior was often not present in the rural life of yore; subsistence was enough. However, in modern times it seems that each generation of children expects to continue to compete. This includes bettering its lifestyle as compared to that of its parents. Although this is not a hereditary feature, it is certainly one that is fostered by Type A parents, who put excessive emphasis on the acquisition of *things*.

The only way to please a typical Type A parent is for a child to achieve higher grades, clock a faster time in a race, or beat more people in competition. In other words, "Winning is everything" seems to be the credo. But just as those who suffer from the "bigger boat" syndrome are doomed to forever being beaten by one-upmanship, children can eventually become disillusioned with this approach to life, and set their own courses. In my own practice I find that the biggest rifts between teenagers and parents occur in Type A families.

"Rich man, poor man..."

The sense of excessive competition may be worst among the middle classes, who always seem to have to "prove themselves." The rich may have a potential advantage, in financial security. What the wealthy view as bad mannered *"nouveaux riches"* behavior is often just the Type A behavior pattern. In England, the "old rich" are usually Type B in behavior and temperament, having never been involved personally in the race against the time clock.

The wealthy are never in the same "land rush" race as the rest of the population, mainly because they already own all the land. Many owners and bosses of big corporations have Type B tendencies, but the good ones hire Type A employees, to give their companies the balance to succeed. The trick is to keep the Type A person in close check, so that he or she remains in the position of peak stress performance without burning out. (See chart on page 218.)

There are, of course, some disadvantages to wealth. Spike Milligan noted that money won't buy you friends, but you do get a better class of enemy.

Changing from Type A to Type B behavior

1. Recognize you probably won't suffer financially by being Type B. Do not confuse ambition or drive with being Type A only. Any success you have already achieved is likely in *spite* of your Type A behavior. Type B people can still get the job done well. They have just as much ambition, but don't seem to panic while they achieve their goals.
2. Learn to laugh, not just at others, but at yourself. Most Type A humor is made up of a litany of jokes and anecdotes at the expense of others.
3. Expand your horizons with an alternate activity, preferably something that does not involve racing against the stopwatch. If you buy a bicycle, do not buy a computerized speedometer and mileage recorder; just *enjoy* your bike rides.
4. Pace yourself, within your budget. For your heart's sake, learn to let others take over the less important tasks—things that can be delegated. Even though you *can* do something doesn't mean that you *should* do it. Think about what jobs could be better left to someone else, to allow you to get on with more important tasks. This applies to your work, and even more so to your home life. Hiring a student to do some of the gardening could give you peace of mind, plus more quality time with your family.
5. Avoid other Type A's when possible. If you can't avoid them; for example, if you are married to one, then bite your tongue on occasion. Remember, there is a good reason the human head is equipped with two ears and only one mouth: we should listen more than we talk!

Aim more at *complementing* and *helping* your spouse or partner, rather than *outdoing* him or her.

6. Aim for things worth *being*, not worth *having*.
7. Try exercises that force you to slow down; for example, if you jump an amber light, circle the block; go back and do it properly. Try conversing with a slow thinker and not interrupting or finishing sentences for him or her. If you are getting steamed under the collar in a slow bank line, let a couple of people go by—it won't kill you!
8. Try driving for half an hour behind a slow car driven by an anyone wearing a hat. Try really hard to not honk or pass!
9. Try watching anyone do *anything* in the post office without barking at them to speed up.
10. Try watching an entire hour of television and force yourself to not use the "clicker". You can practice your slow breathing techniques through the commercials.

Remember the Cardiology's Two Rules, given to heart attack victims in the Coronary Care Unit:

1. Don't sweat the small stuff.
2. It's all small stuff.

We all face enough stresses from external sources. We don't need to add self-induced stresses to the list. For the sake of your heart, try to moderate some of these Type A behavior choices from your life.

A page from an optimistic Type A daytimer:

	PLANNED DAY	ACTUAL DAY
7:05	Rise and shine; organize clothes.	Slept through four snooze alarms. Wore two different socks, and forgot one cuf-flink.
8:00	Meet for one hour re: ad campaign.	Arrived twenty minutes late.
9:30	Meet client across town.	Underestimated congestion in my own parking garage. Then got stuck behind some slow *imbecile* in the fast lane… made me late.
10:00	Set aside an hour to respond to calls, emails, texts, faxes and snail-mail.	First two call-backs unearthed time-consuming problems. Had to postpone fourteen important items until later today, possibly this evening, or for sure tomorrow.

11:05	Pick up VIPs at airport. Don't be late!	Passed every car on the road to get there on time. Left the car illegally parked. VIPs' plane was late.
11:30	Have VIPs back for boardroom meeting. Look sharp!	Paced in airport for half an hour waiting for VIPs. Then spent forty minutes getting car out of the pound.
12:00	Lunch meeting with important client, to try to close a sale.	Arrived late, did most of the talking, failed to listen to client's concerns, and missed the sale.

Obviously, this Type A person is off to a bad start, having underestimated travel and contingency delays in the interests of cramming too many activities into the morning. Properly used, a time and priority management system can be a most valuable stress aid. You can sync it from your phone to your computer, or even use the old fashioned pen and paper. But you need to account for 168 hours in each week. Don't be too optimistic in your estimations of travel times. You may tell yourself you live only 17 minutes from work, but that might be true only at three in the morning with a police escort. During normal traffic it is closer to an hour! Note your needs for relaxation, hobbies, and sleep, and not just fill everything with work issues. The discipline involved in using such a system pays enormous dividends in efficiency, quality of time, sense of accomplishment (as tasks are ticked off), improved self-image, and less troubled sleep due to avoidance of unresolved or omitted details.

WHUMP!

Conclusion

Do not allow Type A behavior to narrow your coronary arteries, undermine your family life, waste your profits, and shorten your time on earth. Pause, reflect, and reset your priorities. Save your aggressive and explosive tendencies for real emergencies, don't "cry wolf" for false alarms.

It is just as simple to join the (Type) "B Team." You must first recognize that your ambitions, goals, and lifestyle can be better achieved with some Type B traits, and that success does not depend on the frenetic nervous energy of the Type A personality. As a bonus, incorporating some Type B behavior will give you strength instead of weakness in the *health, job, financial*, and *personal* quadrants of your life. As we will see in the next chapter, these are the four areas to consider in predicting a long, healthy, and prosperous life. Read on.

9.
The "Secrets" of Long Life and Prosperity

I have interviewed hundreds of healthy patients over the age of eighty, many over the age of 100. In each case, I asked their secrets for success. The answers were diverse, but a pattern emerged. Surprisingly, the avoidance of stress was not the answer. In fact those we admire in late age are the ones that continue to seek stress; always taking new courses, learning new skills, or maintaining an interest in old hobbies. Those that did really well, and lived well past their nineties, were remarkably balanced in their approach to life. From their stories, I derived a schema of four quadrants of life that we can all learn to balance. Take a look at this chart:

Figure 9.1

My patients who stayed young long into advance years paid attention to the following four quadrants of their lives:

1. *Financial Quadrant.*	**2. *Personal Quadrant.***
Success here means having saleable job skills, adequate money for your goals, and security in case of ill health, recession, or loss of job. It need not involve having millions, but simply living within one's budget.	Success here means a stable support network of true friends (not necessarily large numbers) and family. A happy marriage or life partnership helps enormously.
3. *Health Quadrant.*	**4. *Job Quadrant.***
Success here means being in sound health (both mental and physical) confirmed by your doctor's opinion, not just your own. Correct choices of lifestyle and resistance to stress (see Chapter 4) must be made. While some of this is in your genes, most health problems are from poor lifestyle choices. The good news here is that you can improve your own chances by making better choices.	Success here means having a passion for your work, and looking forward to each week, not just the weekend. If you retire, then find other work or hobbies to absorb your talents. Pride of work is one of the common traits I see in healthy elders.

Success: The key to longevity

As indicated in Figure 9.1, success may be divided into four equal compartments. In order to achieve your maximum enjoyment and span of life, you should address and balance them all. Ignoring any one of these quadrants will give you an "incomplete" chance of living to your full potential.

Following are some true-to-life examples of successes in just one or two quadrants. Note that S indicates success; F indicates failure. Add up the F's for your total. Even one F lowers your chances of making it to old age in style. Let's take a look at some examples.

Reclusive Billionaire Howard Hughes in His Later Years (as played by Leonard DiCapprio in the movie "The Aviator")

REPORT CARD

Financial Quadrant—S.

Storybook success; money beyond anyone's dreams.

Personal Quadrant—F.

He ended up lonely, with no stable base at home. He had to hire people to love him and care for him.

Health Quadrant—F.

His health was terrible. Physically he was wasted, shriveled, frail, and so weak that he needed to be carried everywhere. Mentally, the spots had come off his dice. His obsession with gaining complete privacy, even from germs, was further confirmation of his social disfunction.

Job Quadrant—F.

Enjoyed little admiration from his peers, other than a grudging respect for his success in the financial quadrant. He conducted his business in a ruthless manner, and did not value making friends along the way.

Final Score—3 F's.

Result: A net failure with a predictable decrease in the quality and quantity of life.

Marilyn Monroe in Her Last Years

REPORT CARD

Financial Quadrant—S.

She was one of the highest paid stars in Hollywood.

Personal Quadrant—F

Life of tragedy; search for stability and love.

Health Quadrant—F

Health includes mental well-being as well as physical. Disastrous in Monroe's case; addicted to drugs; mentally unstable.

Job Quadrant—S.

Well respected by peers and public; a tremendous success at both comedy and drama.

Final Score—2 F's.

Result: Two out of four quadrants successful; net result still a predictably decreased quality and quantity of life.

"Mr. Mom"

Profile

While this may be a noble endeavour for some, this particular patient was looking for a way to get out of work. As soon as his wife delivered their first child, he totally stopped his career. The economy and job markets turned sour, and his wife felt trapped and nervous about keeping her salary intact. She needed him to help financially, but he was content to simply stay at home and play video games with the children. While the kids thought he was a super Dad, his lack of overall balance left him vulnerable for his health. In the short term, the health of his marriage would suffer. In the long term, he be unlikely to join the club of long-livers

REPORT CARD

Financial Quadrant—F.

He could have earned a good salary, but he had lost his confidence, his self-esteem, and his "mojo".

Personal Quadrant—S.

A great guy; popular with the kids and neighbors; a loving and warm person.

Health Quadrant—F.

The lack of mental stimulation and the absence of stress from the workplace begin to dull Joe's intellect. His efficiency declined; now it takes him almost all day just to finish simple tasks. He started to gain weight, smoke cigarettes, drink more alcohol, and get less exercise than he used to.

Job Quadrant—F.

What job? Even if he worked at building his resume, or started courses for new skills, he could have felt better about himself.

Final Score—3 F's.

Result: Headed for a shorter good lifespan, with the stress of marital discord on the horizon.

"Joe Fist"

Profile

This patient of mine spent five hours a day pumping weights and amino acids. Although bodybuilding is an outstanding exercise, he carried it to excess, becoming addicted to his exercise and diet. He counted the hours until his boring desk job was done, so he could get to the gym. He was a great physical specimen, but had no time for much of a social life.

REPORT CARD

Financial Quadrant—F

Does not make time to study extra courses, and does not have the priority to get ahead in his career. He works only hard enough to make ends meet.

Personal Quadrant—S.

He is self-confident and seems attractive to others.

Health Quadrant—S.

Joe was the picture of good health. He did not abuse alcohol, didn't smoke, and had good exercise tolerance. His heart rate at rest was excellent, he ate organic foods, and had three square bowel movements per day. However, by focusing only on part of his life, he needlessly sets himself up for later disappointment.

Job Quadrant—F

Joe is an underachiever here, doing work that he describes as "boring", and only marking time as a means to his chosen lifestyle. Most careers and social lives would not leave time for his obsessive five hours of weight training per day.

Final Score—2 F's.

Result: Failure, with predictable decrease in quality and, ultimately, quantity of life.

Wendy Workaholic

Profile

As a student, she was intense. She worked hard on her studies, but spent little time on the "frivolities" of social functions, sports, or developing personal relationships with her peers. She has worked her way up to a responsible position, and loves it because she is good at it. The problem is, she's "hooked" on her work. She's interested in very little else, and can't see the point of starting to learn a new sport or hobby. She can't even tear herself away for a short holiday. If she does, she's on her cell phone or tablet the whole time, and is miserable until she gets back to the office.

REPORT CARD

Financial Quadrant—S.

She is successful in the short term, although very likely headed for burnout if she undervalues the other areas of her life. For now, her finances are good, so this quadrant is going well.

Personal Quadrant—F.

Works long hours; does not have much time to develop and maintain good personal relationships. She does not organize her limited spare time efficiently or at all.

Health Quadrant—F.

Wendy makes her health a very low priority. She doesn't have much time to bother about herself; tends not to get enough exercise, or even take time to eat properly.

Job Quadrant—S.

As recognized by all peers, in awe of her sheer commitment, "could not possibly be doing a better job." However, she probably past her peak efficiency level with *too much* unremitting stress.

Final Score—2 F's.

Result: Wendy is headed for burnout sooner than later. If she could focus her abilities on her personal relationships, she would be better able to recharge her batteries away from work. If she would eat and exercise better, she would be far less vulnerable to simple colds, or to eventual stomach and chest pains. Workaholics not only cheat themselves of a longer life, but deny themselves a better life. If they make it to retirement age, they are lost with all their newfound spare time, due to the lack of other interests.

It is important to realize that the success scale is dynamic. It changes with different stages in your life, so it should be constantly kept in mind. Test yourself often. Remember, Howard Hughes and Marilyn Monroe were successful in their earlier years. A major key to success is balance. If you are an absolute failure in even one quadrant, this will ultimately weaken your successes in the other three, and can reduce your life expectancy in the future and the quality of your life today.

Use the following report card to try to assess yourself. Be flexible enough to invest some effort in areas of failure, if you find any.

Your report card

Life Balance: How am I Doing?

	S	F
1. Financial		
2. Personal		
3. Health		
4. Job (or Education)		
Your Final Score		

If you scored *any* F's, focus on correcting them.

A showdown with poverty: Will you win or lose?

There is no question that poverty increases stress, primarily by decreasing one's control over situations. However, this is not to say it is impossible to experience the "Joy of Stress," though poor. The key is still the same—trying to gain control by organization.

Case history—David F.

Aged forty, unemployed executive, suddenly laid off. After a few weeks of failed job interviews, depression set in. Along with this comes a decrease in self-image, which then leads to a decrease in sales ability—most particularly, the ability to sell himself. He ends up doing odd jobs around the house, and doing a few extra odd jobs for relatives. However, he can't be bothered doing this kind of thing for money, even though he has obvious skills. He could use his carpentry, gardening, electrical, and other general "fix-it" abilities in a productive way to help tide him over, and at least give him some measure of self-confidence and a little spending money.

Instead, he starts smoking, drinking more, vegetating in front of the soap operas during daytime TV, arguing more with his wife, and basically getting worse. This shows the *power of negative thinking*, and demonstrates that disorganization can cause predictable increase in stress.

Case history—John B.

Aged forty, unemployed executive, suddenly laid off, but is a *positive thinker*. Takes stock of what has happened; reassesses his true abilities, strengths, weaknesses, and priorities, including his minimum needs for salary, and his flexibility. Researches job possibilities on line, and organizes his applications. He ends up moving to a new town, and settles for blue-collar work but, with overtime, makes almost what he made before. After a few years, he gets into a better job as a marketing executive for a new company.

John B. is flexible, willing to change locations or lifestyle as required. He is not committed to spending the rest of his days in a ghost town, or in an obsolete profession. While losing a job is incredibly stressful, it need not be a fatal blow to your future. By taking the plunge into something new, he was able to thrive, while others (like David above) failed.

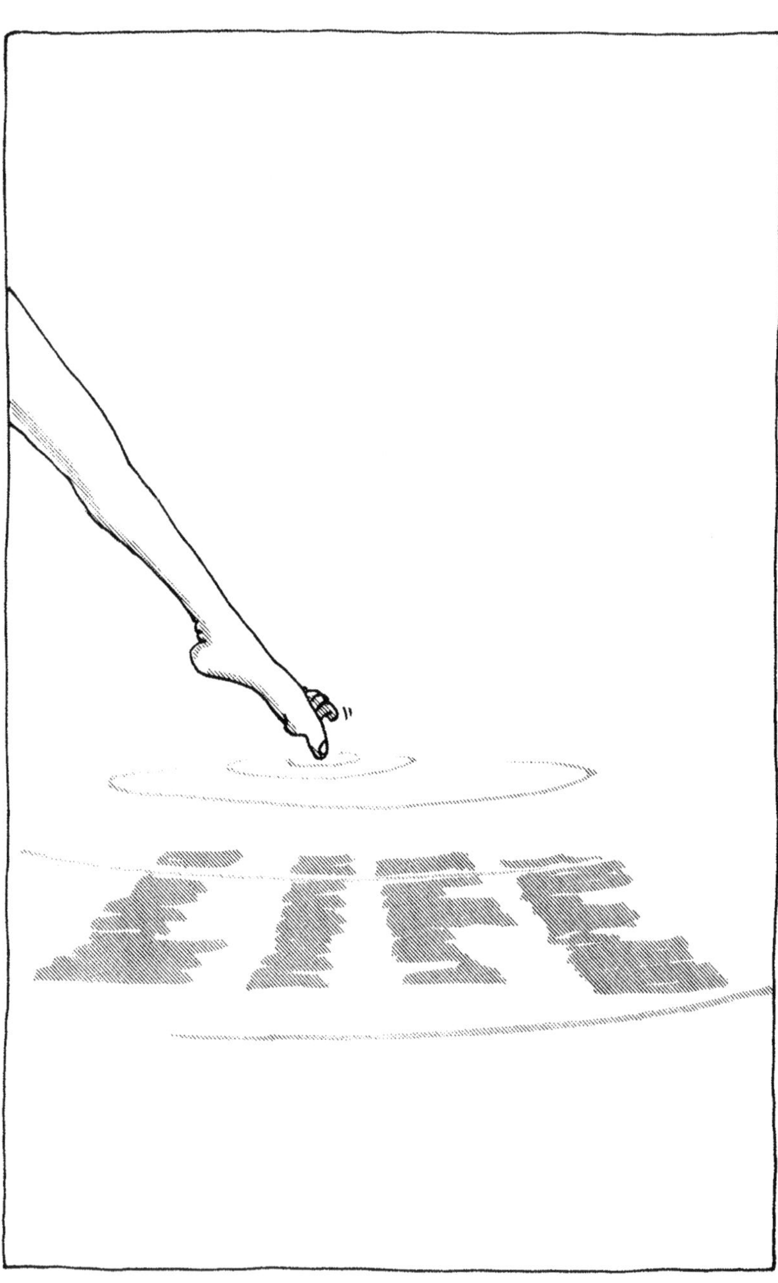

10. Hanson's Three Principles of Stress Management

1. Pamper yourself.
2. Stop stonewalling.
3. Face the truth.

Hanson's First Principle of Stress Management:

1. Pamper yourself

Consider your full time job to be the manager of your own "Department of One". As a good manager, you need to counter negative stresses with a few positive rewards along the way. This does not mean impulsive shopping sprees that break the budget (which then will only add to one's stress levels). Pampering can be done within your budget for time, money, and energy.

In recognition of today's fast-paced stresses, try to

keep these rewards simple and frequent. Long term payback is never timely, and it may never pay back. I have seen couples dedicate their whole lives to a single long-term goal, like early retirement to live on a sail-boat. If this is the only reward for all those stressful years of denial, then it might work out. However, this assumes that they can both retire without shrinkage of their financial savings, without health issues, and without divorce. They would do better to pace themselves: delay the retirement target by a few years, in order to take small vacations along the way.

The "vacation" can now be done as a "staycation" without any travel, and can indeed be done as a mini-vacation for a few hours each week, or even a dedicated half-hour each day. A good example of this is a Spa treatment. The word Spa basically means water therapy, which could be done in your own home. Instead of using your bathtub as the bottom part of your shower, try using it as a bath, especially before bedtime. Use candles and herbal bath salts to enhance the experience. Turn off your cell phone, put on the mood music, and relax totally for a half hour or so. The only real cost here is your own time, and that will be well rewarded by improving your sleep that night, and by rejuvenating your stress responses the next day.

To better select your rewards, consider your needs first. If you spend all day trapped in an office, your pampering might incorporate some fresh air and exercise. It could be a membership in a fitness club, or it might simply mean getting off the wrong stop on the commuter bus or subway, or getting off at the wrong floor in your building to do some free stair-climbing. If you work outside all day, you might find it more rewarding to pamper yourself with something different, like listening to music, or studying something on line.

Some actual case histories will help to illustrate.

1. One patient, whose dream and big reward was to be her own boss at all costs, quit a good job as a sales clerk to open her own clothing boutique. She did it impulsively without having built up enough capital to get through the initial renovations and start-up costs. As a result, she has worked days and evenings, and gone the past four years without being able to afford the needed small rewards of a few days off. Her health, which she took for granted, is now slowing her down with tension headaches. Her relationship with her husband has also suffered. In retrospect, she wishes she postponed her big dream for a few extra years. That way she could have paced herself a little better, and had the resources to pamper herself with more time off.

2. A patient, who was a commissioned salesman, wanted a large deck on the back of his house. To

As we have seen, money can help you pamper yourself. But it is important at any level of income to still be on a budget. I have seen people with very high incomes spend mindlessly, until they end up with too much month at the end of the money. Obviously it can happen to lower income levels as well. One of the lessons of the stressful downturn in our recent economy is that debt can be crushing. If you are under financial pressure right now, it is even more important to pamper yourself, but be smart about the cost-benefit ratio. Set the table for a fine meal at home, instead of at an expensive restaurant; cut back on alcohol consumption (your body will feel better, as well as your wallet); cut back on magazines and newspapers, and get the info on line. Be organized and realistic in your budget, and you will be able to fight back against stress, and still have fun.

save money, he turned down professional help, and tried to do it all himself. Parts of it he had to do again, after he used the wrong mix of cement in the support posts. As a beginner, he took far longer to do the cutting, bolting, and hammering than he imagined. The project took most of his summer, because he insisted on finishing it without calling in help. In the process he spent little time with his wife and children, and was so tired that he lacked energy for his day job. As a consequence, he was losing more in commissions than he was saving in hiring a handyman. Clearly, pampering himself with the big reward (a cheap deck) was not worth the loss of frequent small rewards (enjoying the family).

3. A young couple was renting a modest bungalow, but had a dream of a big house. They overextended themselves to buy it with very little equity, and without accounting for all the additional expenses of maintaining a large home and garden. They worked different shifts, and hardly had time to see each other during waking hours. Because they were "house-poor", they had no money left for baby-sitters or date nights out. They rarely saw their friends, and no longer travelled, even for weekend breaks. Predictably, they came to resent the house, their kids, and even each other. They overspent on their pampering (the huge house) and undervalued their cost (their spare time and energy).

Big rewards can have pretty steep price tags in terms of stress. As a doctor, I have seen too many examples, from heart attacks to ulcers, and from depression to suicide. Pampering yourself should be within your budget for time and for money so it doesn't become punishing. So be creative, pace yourself, and target your pampering to give the best results.

Hanson's Second and Third Principles of Stress Management:

2. Stop stonewalling—Ignore uncontrollable excuses.
3. Face the truth—Focus on what you can control.

With reflex swiftness, people in difficulty "stonewall," or place the blame for their problems on something they can't change. But if you train yourself to look behind this comforting stone wall, you will find the true cause of your problems (often painful to face), which you can control. Sometimes disasters are impossible to avoid, such as an earthquake, drought, warfare, or collapse of the world economy. Of course one must be aware of these issues as context for the big picture, but we should not use these "stone wall" excuses to justify our personal bad habits.

"Stonewalling" is a doubly bad way to handle stress. It allows you to call off the hunt and stop looking for the real culprit; or it may have you losing sleep worrying about things that you can never change.

Let's examine some common problems you might encounter in each of the four quadrants of your life. Note that *in every case* you can defeat the stresses only by facing the *truth* behind each knee-jerk excuse that pops up. Energy and time spent on worrying about the uncontrollable are totally wasted.

When you think of jobs where the public offers lame excuses, traffic cops who catch speeders probably head the list. However, I can tell you that the family doctor gets to hear some really ridiculous excuses when it comes to health issues.

For each of the problems listed below, I have heard patients "stonewall" or blame all of their comfortable, uncontrollable excuses. It is only when I get them to face the *truth* (however unpleasant it might appear) that they can see how to control and solve their own problems.

This makes all the difference between winning and losing your stress battles.

Financial Quadrant

Problem: Too much month left at the end of the money!

Stonewall	***Face the Truth***
"Bad economy, the whole world over."	Yes, the economy has been terrible, but you will need to take a new look at your goals, and your timetables. The days are gone when rising real estate prices make your home into an ATM. So your children may not be able to go to expensive private schools, and they may not be able to afford to live away from home during university. Simplify your lifestyle, even if it means goals have to be moderated or delayed.
"My house has become too expensive to maintain"	If you bought a new home a few years ago, you can expect things to need expensive repairs or replacements over time. It is never easy to repair a roof leak, or to buy a new furnace or air-conditioner, or repaint the exterior. Especially if you are "upside down" in your mortgage, consider renting for now. Consider downsizing if at all possible. The modern home is almost double the size of the ones we grew up in.
"My heating bill is too expensive"	We can control a lot more of our expenses if we turn back the clock. Room temperatures in the winter used to be 5 degrees lower than they are now; people used to wear thicker fabrics or thermal underwear. Now we are used to room temperatures so hot that we can wear summer weight clothes year round.
"The price of gas is killing me."	Try moving to where you work, or work where you live. In most modern cities traffic is equal in both directions across town. People who live on one side cross the whole city to get to the other side; and their counterparts make the same journey on the opposite side of the road. If you can't move closer to work, then consider public transportation instead of the car. In cities that are well served with busses, trains, or subways, you can make do with a lot less driving, and perhaps even getting rid of a car. The money you will save in insurance, depreciation, repairs and car payments will sure buy a lot of bus tickets or even taxi rides. For the odd occasion when you do need to drive, you can rent cars for the weekend, or even rent them for a few hours to run errands. In good weather, a bike or a pair of running shoes can also turn your commuting time into exercise time.

Personal Quadrant

Problem: Marriage/Relationship drifting apart.

Stonewall

"Can't talk about anything controversial with spouse."

Face the Truth

Poor communication; fear of the big "door slamming" arguments. (Before resorting to this kind of theatrics, check out the construction of your front door. Many modem lightweight insulated doors make a most unsatisfactory "biff" sound. This somewhat undermines the effect on the slammee.)

Poor communication is an example of the power of negative thinking. By dwelling on all of the negative reactions to a controversial subject, one can imagine a wide variety of unpleasant conclusions. As a result, couples often go on for decades without ever communicating on key issues. They end up suffering far more than just the few moments of unpleasantness that they were originally afraid to face.

"He never takes me out for dinner."

He eats lunch at restaurants all week so spending more money to eat out for dinner doesn't seem to be a treat. Perhaps taking lunch from home would leave more room in the budget for a restaurant meal in the evening. A regular "date night", even a spontaneous one, can work wonders in keeping the relationship interesting.

"He (she) is a workaholic."

Workaholics usually still work a regular 8-hour day, it just takes them a lot more hours to finish it. Often they are disorganized for the first part of their day, and wait until closing time to really focus. In many cases this is because they are avoiding home duties, where they feel less confident, and chose to stay at work to avoid potential personal conflicts. This is an easy cop-out, as in most professions these traits are seen to be admirable. But from the point of view of the spouse who is left behind, it's no consolation. The absent spouse might just as well be off gambling or drinking every night.

All the "fun has gone."

Your routines might have gone in two different directions. She is not crazy about him watching thirty hours of TV sports every weekend. He is a little tired of hearing her talk about the shopping channels during the week. Try switching off (or recording) programs that just one of you likes, and set aside a few hours to watch a movie together. Or shut off the television, and do something fun out of the home.

Problem: Sex life has become indifferent.

Stonewall

"What else can you expect at my age? "

Face the Truth

Aging is supposed to be a reward, not a punishment. If you have lost interest in your partner, start by seeing your doctor for a checkup. If you are on prescription drugs, your problem could be from their side-effects. If you are overweight, start by losing at least ten pounds, you will be surprised at the positive effect this can have on your libido. If you have deficiencies of hormones as shown on your blood tests, then consider replacement therapies. For the male who suffers from Erectile Deficiency (E.D.), your doctor can recommend investigations and therapies, including drugs like Viagra and Cialis. Remember that stress can cause a lot of anxiety, insomnia, and depression, especially if poor choices have been made. So review your Net Stress Score (page 127) and address any of your problem areas. . Marriage counseling is often helpful here, along with reading such books as The Joy of Sex by Alex Comfort and Human Sexual Inadequacy by Masters and Johnson. Consider the therapeutic benefits of taking an occasional mini-vacation together, even at a bed & breakfast place in your own town. And don't forget to dress as if you feel great about yourself, not like the depressing "before" photos on television's "What Not To Wear".

Problem: Your teenagers have an attitude.

Stonewall	***Face the Truth***

"It's the Generation Gap."

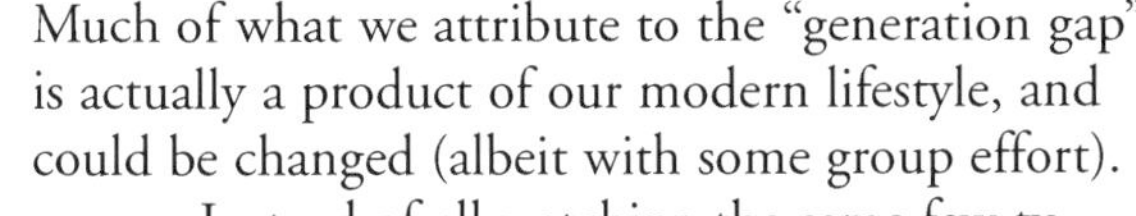

Much of what we attribute to the "generation gap" is actually a product of our modern lifestyle, and could be changed (albeit with some group effort).

Instead of all watching the same few tv shows together, families are now on different screens, plugged into different media. Instead of the "dinner hour" where families converse, meals get "nuked" and self-served at staggered times, and wolfed down without eye contact with anyone else in the family. Talk with your family to work out a solution. Dinner can certainly be improved by a joint effort in its preparation, and by an "unplugged" time-out for cell phones. The mood and the conversation will improve, and become a good stress-reliever for the family.

"I never seem to have any free time with my kids."

If you are like many parents, you may be over programming your kids' activities. Gone are the days of pick-up games with kids of all ages showing up at the field, pool or basketball court. Today we have kids playing no sports at all, unless they are in organized leagues. Home fields sit empty until game day, when teams are driven in from all over town. Kids are sent home if they forgot part of their uniform, and whole teams are sent home if a qualified umpire or ref fails to turn up. Parents no longer have time to play catch, kick a few balls, or shoot a few hoops with their kids. Parents are too busy driving, recording the action on their cameras, and carrying coolers of drinks and orange slices. If it weren't for fist fights in the stands, parents would not get any exercise all weekend! Consider cutting out some of these organized activities, and not training your kids to be "workaholics" before they even start work.

Health Quadrant

Problem: Chest pains.

Stonewall

"It will pass." "Probably something I ate."

Face the Truth

Chest pain (or heaviness) is not something to ignore. This is especially true if the pain occurs with exertion, then stops with rest. For this kind of symptom, please get medical attention at once. Ignore these pains only after your doctor has examined and tested you, and concludes they are not serious.

Problem: Poor exercise tolerance.

Stonewall	***Face the Truth***
"It's just my age."	If you are out of shape now, you probably have been ever since you were six. Your body has no idea what date is listed on your birth certificate. Your body only knows if it has had any exercise lately. Forget about how old you are, and get moving with some regular exercise every day. (Make sure you have medical clearance first!).
"I do play softball."	For all but two minutes per hour, you are leaning on your knees waiting for the ball to come. You could benefit by running around the field a few times as well.
"I do bowl regularly."	The pins get more exercise than you do. Don't think bowling makes you an athlete just because you are wearing a number. It's only your shoe size!
"I play a little touch football on the weekends."	Sounds like a beer commercial, and in fact the calories gained from the post-game beers usually negate the benefits gained in the exercise in the first place. Good to get some exercise, but remember to do something the other days of the week as well.

Problem: Obesity.

Stonewall	***Face the Truth***
"The food is there when I prepare it for my family, so I eat it.	If you can train your dog not to jump up on the counter and eat the family's food, you should be able to train yourself.
"My weight just seems to stay where it is."	You have to eat bags of groceries each week just to keep your weight up there. And, to be sure your weight doesn't go down, you have do burn off as little as possible. Remember, obesity is an arithmetic surplus: the storage of fat that results from consuming more than expending.
"I eat less than all my friends."	That's only when they are watching; on your own you eat like crazy. A quick binge after bed-time can destroy a whole week of good behaviour.
"I only eat to be polite. People often say, 'Eat this; I made it especially for you!'"	This may be sabotage or manipulation by spouse, parents, or peers who resent your success. It can be evidence of jealousy. People, especially if they are overweight, may feel threatened by you being in good shape. For the sake of their comfort, not yours, they want you to be more like them. Stand up for yourself, and politely but firmly decline.
"I have to bake (or buy treats) for the kids."	Let's face it. You bake (or buy) for yourself, and the kids just get what you can't eat.
"I'm big boned."	Big bones won't explain why you stick to a plastic chair. But this stonewall excuse will delude you into thinking your behaviour has nothing to do with your weight problem. Face the truth: you are fat. Only by recognizing self-induced disease can you then self-correct it.

"I eat out at restaurants a lot."

Restaurants don't make you gain weight, even if the food is abundant and part of your expense account. Eating too much makes you gain weight. Practice restraint by turning away the bread basket for a start, and skip the fries and desserts as well.

"It's certainly *not because I overeat."*

It *certainly* is.

"I can't exercise because I'm too heavy, or my back hurts, or my knees hurt."

Try swimming. Even a hippopotamus is graceful under water. You can burn off thousands of calories in a pool, and not cause back or joint pains. As your core muscles and limbs get in better tone, you will be much better at dry-land activities as well.

"It's glandular."

It's not. You take in more fuel than you burn off. Period.

"I have to eat at least three meals a day."

For the obese, skipping a meal is perfectly OK if you are not hungry. But don't dwell on food, and ignore exercise. Start spending time thinking about the calories you are going to burn off, not just about the ones you are going to eat.

"I have to prepare the food for my whole family; that's why I get fat."

You wouldn't have to prepare as much food if you didn't eat it as fast as you made it.

"I get weak if I don't have something in my stomach."

If a brown bear can go all winter without food, you should be able to hang in there for another two hours until dinner. If you really feel you need something in your stomach, try a low-calorie, high-fiber snack. (See Figure 5.2 and Appendix C.) Don't forget that a nice tall glass of water can also fill you up, with no calories.

"It's hereditary."

Your whole family overeats.

"I just have to look at food..."

". . . and then eat it."

"Obesity runs in my family."

Nobody runs in your family.

Problem: Smoking.

Stonewall	***Face the Truth***
"It relaxes me."	So does carbon monoxide if you leave your car running in the garage. Just to complete the analogy, that carbon monoxide is the same poison as the flaming tobacco leaf produces.
"I gain weight if I quit."	Get a pacifier. Many smokers end up with a weight problem as well. The real problem is the oral urge, retained from the thumb-sucking stage of childhood.

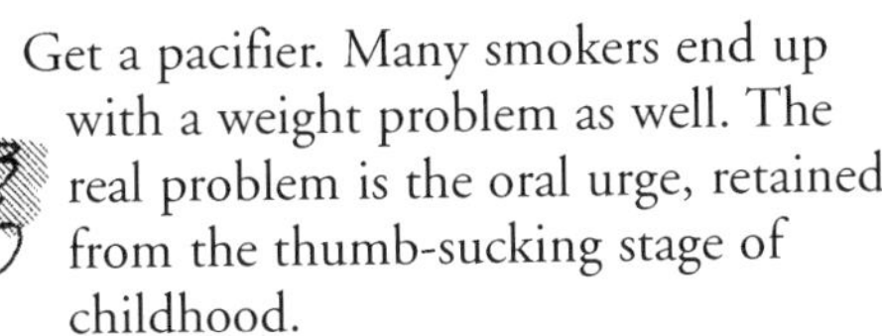

"Nobody can stand me when I'm in withdrawal."	Such behavioral problems can be controlled. See your doctor; try hypnosis or acupuncture, if necessary.
"I can't quit now because they are cutting staff at work."	Then now would be a great time to quit. Not only will you save a lot of money by quitting, your health and energy will greatly improve, and you will be more likely to keep your job, or find success in seeking another one.
"It gives me something to do with my hands at a party."	So does picking your nose. You can't smoke indoors in most places anyway, so get used to it and figure out something to occupy your hands instead of starting fires.
"It makes me look sophisticated and confident to others."	Your sports jacket could set off a smoke alarm by itself. Smokers are now less popular, and more like pariahs. The majority of people now are non-smokers, so you can get used to feeling confident without poisoning yourself.
"It's romantic."	Your breath smells like zoo dust.
"I'll miss the taste of tobacco if I quit."	Try licking an ashtray.

Problem: Excessive drinking.

Stonewall | **Face the Truth**

"Peer pressure."

Have you ever thought of trying new peers? If you continue excessive drinking, the well-known diuretic effect of alcohol on your kidneys might well help you become one of the great "pee-ers" of our time.

"I only average one drink a day."

Beware the law of "averages": if you drink nothing all month, then have 30 shots at a bachelor party, you could very easily turn up dead. At the very least, you will cause damage to your heart, liver, and brain, and leave you even less prepared to face your stresses at the start of the next week.

Problem: Skin wrinkles especially on the face.

Stonewall | **Face the Truth**

"It's just my age."

True, our skin does look older in late age than it did when we were kids. But there are four preventable causes of the aging of the skin that we can address, to help us to save face:

1. Excess Sun.

Devotees of the sun tan start to show damage even in their late teens. Each progressive year of unprotected sun exposure will increase the risks of skin cancer, and will damage the skin's appearance. Wrinkles and furrows are just the start; the skin will also lose elasticity, and likely develop spots and splotches. All of these changes are totally controllable. Stay out of the mid-day sun, or, if you cannot, then wear clothing or creams to block the UV A and B rays. And if you want that tan, go for the fake one. They last just as long as the real tans, and have none of the risks.

2. Excess Alcohol.

Taking excesses of alcohol each day brings about aging of the skin, and for that matter advanced aging of the rest of the body as well. (See Chapter 3.). Most "winos" that I see in the emergency department look at least twice as old as their birthdate would indicate.

3. Excessive Stress.

Severe stress can almost age a person "overnight." Unless that person has been making strong choices to defend themselves (see the Hanson Scale, Chapter 4).

4. Poor Muscle Tone.

Facial muscles will droop and atrophy like any other unused muscles. While we can tone and firm all our big muscles in the gym, we cannot find any station that will tone the small muscles of the face. That's why electrical muscle stimulation of facial muscles can help reverse the atrophy, and take the face to the gym. For more information on this, please see www.face-master.com. (Disclosure: The FaceMaster was co-developed by the author and Rodger Mohme for Suzanne Somers).

Problem: Tension headaches.

Stonewall

"Just too much stress."

Face the Truth

Most tension headaches can be improved with good choices, as seen in Chapter 4. First, identify and correct the root causes, such as poor diet, and poor ergonomics at work. If sensitivity to certain foods is a common link, then avoid them. If you have allergies or blood pressure issues, ask your doctor to evaluate and treat. If the problem is unrelated to these causes, and is purely from tense muscles, then try therapies like relaxation, meditation, massage, hypnosis, and acupuncture. Off-the-counter pills like aspirin or Advil may also be helpful. As a general rule, it is always good to avoid prescription medications for pain or muscle relaxation, due to side effects. While these may have a role, opiates and other strong prescriptions are best reserved for severe pain where the above suggestions have failed.

Job Quadrant

Problem: Bored at work; hate job.

Stonewall

"That's the way everyone feels—that's life."

Face the Truth

Could be a classic Peter Principle case—getting promoted until incompetent; then staying in that position for the rest of his or her career.

Corollary: in any hierarchy, all positions will eventually be filled by people who are incompetent. Solution—know thyself; refuse any promotion that takes you from something you excel at to something you don't do well. Ask for demotion if necessary. In an excellent company, your wishes will be granted; in an incompetent company you may be forced to quit.

If you cannot change your job, start planning your escape. If you need different skills or training, explore courses on line. Some may simply fulfill your hobby interests, others could lead to a whole new job that you like better. If needed, consult a professional career planner.

"Up to my ears at work—but nobody else could do the work as well."

Poor teacher and poor delegator. If you are trying to protect your job by not teaching others to take over, then you may be cutting off your own chances of promotion; after all, how could they replace you?!

Problem: Too much stress from my job.

Stonewall

"I have to stay in this job or else I lose my pension."

Face the Truth

If your job is giving you chest pains, then your pension won't do you much good. Remember the value of preparation, for example freshening your resume, and taking extra courses on line if you have shortcomings for a particular area. Above all, make good choices in response to stress (chapter 4), and give up your bad habits (chapter 5).

Money is no guarantee you will enjoy your retirement. Don't simply contrast your negative feelings about your (wrong) job with the positive feelings you think you will have upon retiring.

You could quit the job you hate today, and start a new career at something you love. Even if your financial intake were a little less, you could work at it for more years, enjoy each *day* in the process, and be more likely to live longer as a bonus.

Conclusion

Now that you have read this book, you should be fully aware of the stresses that pervade your life. You should also know how to assess your defenses, and see if you are vulnerable or "bullet proof". You know what goes on in your body when you are under attack from stress. You also know that your body's reflex reactions by themselves are no longer completely appropriate or adequate, but can be consciously strengthened by the aware defender. The battle lines are drawn; victory is yours for the taking. The costs are negligible; the sacrifices few. The rewards are richer than any lottery, can be drawn upon each day, and accrue the added bonus of a prolonged useful life and greater financial profits in your business.

If you exercise your control competently and make the correct decisions in your response to stress, the odds will be "stacked" heavily in your favor. If you ignore this advice, you may bumble into an easily avoidable ambush, and uselessly squander your gifts of life, health, and reason.

So do not look to the future with a fatalistic shrug. Get involved with the fight for your life, and win. Don't hide from stresses; go out and challenge new ones. Take the thrill from stress, but leave the threat behind. Shore up your defenses, and start your offense right now. See how gratifying the unbeatable combination of a properly maintained body and a well-organized mind can be. Build good karma with your friends and family; don't blow off the importance of relationships. Be justifiably optimistic about your future. Take an active role in your own management; do not be just a passive tourist through life. Shift your paradigm so you continue to think of yourself as young and capable at any age. Put good foods in your stomach, keep your muscles working, and never let your brain stop learning.

Follow Hanson's Three Principles of Stress Management:

1. Pamper yourself.
2. Stop stonewalling.
3. Face the truth.

Best of all, the Hanson method requires only that you seek a life of greater fulfillment, flavor, and fun—for your own sake and for the sake of those who love you.

Now you know THE JOY OF STRESS.

Appendix A

"Know Thyself":

Social style quadrants

As we have seen, good stress management requires an accurate assessment. There are many reasons for this, such as in choosing *realistic goals* (Chapter 4), finding the right sort of *job* for your aptitudes, and in providing a basis for understanding your boss, employees, clients, and most importantly, your spouse and children.

A simple, yet remarkably consistent guideline to the recognition of four basic styles of behavior has been devised for sales people by Larry Wilson, of the Larry Wilson Learning Corp.

While originally devised to teach a salesperson to be versatile, and have *completely different* approaches to each of the four styles, the same versatility can be a great help in daily interpersonal relations. People easily relate to those in their same quadrant, but the trick is to be able to understand and relate to those in the other three quadrants. In the workplace, this leads to better relationships, including sales and motivation with customers and co-workers. In our personal lives, understanding these four quadrants will enhance our communications with those close to us. This is especially helpful considering most rarely marry a spouse from the same quadrant. I have found this system to be an invaluable aid in marital counseling, in helping stressed patients understand why others behave as they do.

These styles are only matters of comfort and preference, and have nothing to do with intelligence, ambition, or success. None of them are right or wrong, they are simply a means of predicting behaviour patterns. Knowing them will greatly improve your understanding of others, and your interpersonal relations at home and at work will benefit.

First let's see where you fit, then assess those around you. There are only two questions to ask:

1. Is this person *responsive*?
2. Is this person *assertive*?

See chart 1 for guidelines for recognition.

Once you have identified your main quadrant (most people have secondary tendencies to at least one other quadrant) then check on chart 2 to find out your predictable "default" patterns.

Check the quadrant of your spouse, children, and parents to see if you can better understand how they approach a problem, and see if you can reduce stress at home by becoming more versatile in your relationships with them.

These same skills can help reduce stress at work; not just by increasing sales, but by being able to better understand how to stimulate an employee to greater productivity, and how to improve relations with your boss and customers.

Finally, in reference to those who may have the wrong job, see chart 3 to see if your social style has predetermined your failure. Use this knowledge to select a more appropriate line of work. (This is particularly helpful to your children when they are at the stage of choosing their own lines of study and career.)

Chart 1a

Quick Recognition Guide

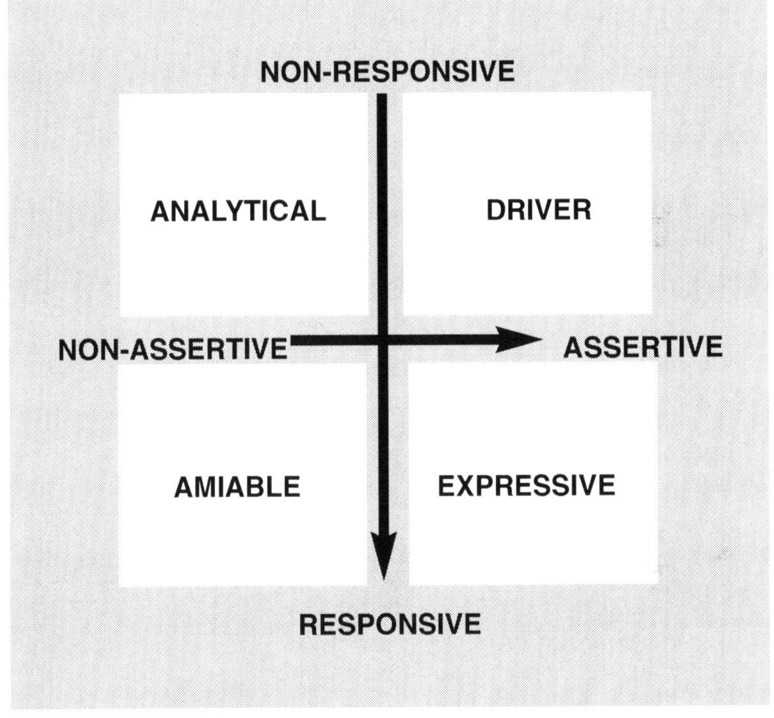

Guideline for Recognition

How Responsive Is The Person?

Non-responsive
Reserved, unresponsive, poker face
Actions cautious or careful
Wants facts and details
Eye contact infrequent while listening
Eyes harsh, severe or serious
Limited personal feelings or small talk

How Assertive Is The Person?

Non-assertive
Few uses of voice to emphasize ideas
Expressions and posture are quiet and submissive
Deliberate, studied, or slow in speech
Indifferent handshake
Asks questions more often than makes statements
Vague, unclear about what is wanted
Tends to lean backwards

Assertive
Emphasizes ideas by tone change
Expressions are aggressive or dominant
Quick, clear or fast paced
Firm handshake
Makes statements more often than asks questions
Lets one know what is wanted
Tends to lean forward to make a point

Responsive
Animated, uses facial expressions
Smiles, nods, frowns
Actions open or eager
Little effort to push for facts
Eye contact frequent while listening
Friendly gaze
Hands free, palms up, open
Friendly gestures
Shares personal feelings
Attentive, responsive, enjoys the relationship

Strengths and Weaknesses

Chart 2	PERCEIVED STRENGTHS	PERCEIVED WEAKNESSES
Driver (Control Specialist)	Determined Tough-minded Decisive Efficient Takes charge	Pushy Severe Dominating Harsh Demanding
Expressive (Social Specialist)	Personable Stimulating Enthusiastic Dramatic Inspiring	Opinionated Manipulating Excitable Reacting Promotional
Amiable (Support Specialist)	Supportive Respectful Willing Dependable Personable	Conforming Retiring Non-committal Undisciplined Emotional
Analytical (Technical Specialist)	Industrious Persistent Serious Vigilant Orderly	Uncommunicative Indecisive Cool Exacting Impersonal

Chart 3	RIGHT TYPE OF JOB	WRONG TYPE OF JOB
Driver	Business or political leader.	Baby photographer.
Expressive	Actor, PR, sales—Anything with a lot of public contact.	Accountant, research scientist, librarian.
Amiable	PR, sales, service, industry	Bill collector, union leader, marine drill sergeant, bouncer.
Analytical	Accountant, stock market analyst, researcher, physicist.	Game show host, entertainment (fun) coordinator on a cruise ship.

Social Style Summary Chart

MASTER CHART USED BY SALES PERSONNEL:	**DRIVER**
STYLE WHEN BACKED "INTO A CORNER"	Autocratic
MEASURES PERSONAL VALUE BY	Results
FOR GROWTH NEEDS TO	Listen
LET THEM SAVE	Time
NEEDS CLIMATE THAT	Allows to build own structure
TAKE TIME TO BE	Efficient
SUPPORT THEIR	Conclusions & Actions
GIVE BENEFITS THAT ANSWER	What
FOR DECISIONS GIVE THEM	Options & Probabilities
SPECIALTY	Control

EXPRESSIVE	AMIABLE	ANALYTICAL
Attacher	Acquiescer	Avoider
Applause	Attention	Activity
Check	Reach	Decide
Effort	Relationships	Face
Inspires to their goals	Provides details	Suggests
Stimulating	Agreeable	Accurate
Dreams & Intuitions	Relationships & Feelings	Principles & Thinking
Who	Why	How
Testimony & Incentives	Guarantees & Assurances	Evidence & Service
Social	Supportive	Technical

Appendix B

Vitamin and Mineral Chart

Fat Soluble Vitamins

Stored in large quantities in the body; supplements rarely tend to be needed.

Vitamin A

Functions: Important to maintain the health of skin and inner linings of the body. Vitamin A is essential for vision. Vitamin A also aids resistance to infection, and is essential for many of the body's chemical functions.

Found In: Carrots, spinach, turnip greens, and other vegetables, palm oil, dairy products, eggs, and so on. High doses of vitamin A are found in liver. However, as inhabitants of the Far North are aware, fish livers and polar bear livers are generally to be avoided. They may contain poisonously high levels of vitamin A.

How Much Do We Need? 5,000 international units (IU) per day for an adult is easily obtained from a sensible diet. Anything in excess of this will be stored in the liver, up to its maximum capacity. After this, excesses of the vitamin will be released into the bloodstream with poisonous and ultimately fatal side effects.

Vitamin D

Functions: Prevents rickets; essential to the absorption of calcium from the intestines, and for normal bone growth and development. (Without sufficient vitamin D, there will be inadequate absorption of calcium from foods, and calcium will be mobilized from the bone into the bloodstream to make up deficiencies.) Abnormal deposits of calcium will be made in some bones. Unless corrected early by a vitamin D supply, victims will be permanently crippled. In adults, vitamin D deficiency produces a softening of the bones, which causes great pain and deformity.

Found In: Fish, egg yolks, butter, cheese, and milk; and in the livers of beef, pork, and lamb. However, most adults obtain all or most of their vitamin D requirement from the action of sunlight on the skin. The fortification of milk with vitamin D has been instrumental in providing adequate sources of this vitamin for North American children. Vitamin D is also obtained through the skin during suntanning; a rare example of something good coming from something bad! Note that only a few minutes a day of sun exposure is helpful for vitamin D production, but it is obviously a bad trade to sunburn, or bake excessively in the dangerous rays of ultraviolet A and B.

How Much Do We Need? First, check with your doctor; blood levels can be taken to see if you are truly deficient. If so, then doses of several thousand units a day are common. If you have normal levels, the about 400 international units (IU) per day for children and pregnant or lactating women. The requirement for children drops to 200 IU after the age of twenty-two.

Vitamin E

Functions: An antioxidant important in preventing destructive attack by oxygen on the essential unsaturated fat in cell membranes, as well as protecting vitamin A in the intestines. It also helps to maintain muscle metabolism. It maintains the health of heart muscle, blood vessels, liver, kidney tubules, brain cells, and so on. Vitamin E deficiency impairs the production of sperm in males, and increases fetal loss during pregnancy in females.

Found In: Vegetable oils, most vegetables, many fruits, eggs, dairy products.

How Much Do We Need? Ten to fifteen international units (IU) per day for adults, but more may be needed when under stress and in certain other situations. People seem to be able to consume mega doses without many side effects. However, taking excesses will eventually lead to significant accumulation in the body, in the fatty tissues. The harmful effects of long-term continuation of high doses are not fully known. It is safest to keep your intake of Vitamin E below 100 IU per day.

Vitamin K

Functions: Needed primarily for blood clotting mechanism, to protect from internal bleeding or bleeding from cuts and wounds.

Found In: Green leafy vegetables, soybeans, many other vegetables, beef liver, green tea, egg yolks, dairy products.

How Much Do We Need? Some 70 to 140 micrograms per day. However, a normal diet typically provides about 400 micrograms per day. Thus supplementation is unnecessary, except in a few unusual cases. Your doctor can advise you as to whether you need extra vitamin K.

Water Soluble Vitamins

Soluble in water; thus excreted in urine daily; constant regular supply needed.

Vitamin B1 (Thiamin)

Functions: Prevention of beriberi, which is characterized by a slow, increasing weakness. B1 is also essential for the functioning of nerve tissue, heart muscles, and energy supplies to the body.

Found In: Natural brown rice, as well as all lean meats, eggs, milk, and seafood. It is also found to a lesser extent in most fruits and vegetables. Historically, in Asia, where rice is a major food in the diet, the very poor have tended to escape beriberi. Unlike the rich, they could not afford the processed "refined" rice, which was depleted of all thiamin (as well as fiber).

How Much Do We Need? Approximately 1.5 mg daily for an adult. Supplements of greater amounts than this are not toxic. Most vitamin supplement pills contain 15 to 20 mg.

Vitamin B2 (Riboflavin)

Functions: Essential for maintenance of the skin, mucous membranes, cornea, nerves.

Found In: Milk and other dairy products, liver, kidneys, fruits, and vegetables. Milk supplies nearly 40 percent of the riboflavin in the Western diet, along with bread and cereals.

How Much Do We Need? 1.3 to 1.7 mg for an adult. Because it is water-soluble, there is no known toxicity with large doses of this vitamin.

Niacin, or Nicotinic Acid (Formerly called Vitamin B3 or B4)

Functions: Prevention of pellagra, which used to be a significant problem resulting from eating an unbalanced diet. Classically pellagra involves dermatitis, diarrhea, dementia, and even death.

Found In: Meats, and to a lesser extent, grains, fruits, and vegetables, along with milk and eggs.

How Much Do We Need? About 20 mg per day for an adult. Doses of nicotinic acid above 500 mg can be harmful. In its niacin amide form, it can be taken in doses up to 4,000 mg without fear. (But consult your doctor; this dose is not usually necessary.)

Vitamin B6 (Pyridoxine)

Functions: Essential for more than sixty enzyme reactions involving key elements of body chemistry including hormone production and nerve conduction. Deficiency causes anemia, weakness, possible urinary stones.

Found In: Liver, fish, brown rice, most vegetables, some fruits such as bananas and grapes. Vitamin B6 is also found in lean meats, fish, butter, eggs, cheese, and milk. Easily destroyed in the processing and milling of cereals, and over-cooking of foods.

How Much Do We Need? About 2.5 mg per day. In doses of up to 10 mg a day, it can help prevent kidney stones, but in larger doses can be toxic.

Vitamin B12 (Cobalmin)

Functions: Prevention of pernicious anemia. Vitamin B12 acts as a crucial component in chemical enzyme reaction for nerve conduction, and synthesis of DNA within the cells.

Found In: Foods of animal origin only. Meats, egg yolks, fish, cheese, and milk contain vitamin B12. There is none in fruit, vegetables, or grains. Thus strict vegetarians may very well need a supplement.

How Much Do We Need? About 6 micrograms per day. If a key element called intrinsic factor is missing in the stomach lining, B12 cannot be absorbed at all by mouth. Pernicious anemia will result unless injections can be given. Check with your doctor to test for your own B12 levels. If they are normal, then there is no need to take supplemental pills or injections.

Folic Acid

Functions: Essential for five different enzyme systems including red blood cell production and nervous system. Helps prevent anemia.

Found In: Liver, wheat bran, spinach, beans, grains. Lesser amounts are found in lean meats, dairy products, and most fresh fruits and vegetables.

How Much Do We Need? About .4 mg per day.

Biotin

Functions: Maintenance of normal nervous tissue, good growth, and so on. Deficiency causes lethargy, depression, sensitivity to touch or pain, and high cholesterol in the blood, along with ECG changes.

Found In: Eggs, cheese, soybeans, meats, cereals, fruits, and vegetables.

How Much Do We Need? About 0.2 mg per day.

Pantothenic Acid

Functions: Part of the enzyme metabolism for regulating energy. Helps prevent impairment of defenses against infection, fatigue, and so on.

Found In: Eggs, meats, wheat bran, peanuts, broccoli, cauliflower, cabbage.

How Much Do We Need? About 10 mg per day. There is no toxicity from overdose for humans.

Vitamin C

Functions: Prevention of scurvy, which used to be widespread, causing illness or death in up to 90 percent of a ship's crew within a couple of months at sea. Vitamin C is essential in a host of chemical reactions within the body, and is needed for creating hormones, healing wounds, keeping cholesterol balanced, and aiding absorption of iron into the bloodstream from the stomach. Commonly used as a supplement in cases of urinary tract infection, to acidify the urine.

Found In: Surprisingly, the greatest amounts are found in black currants, sweet peppers, broccoli, and Brussels sprouts. It is in much greater quantities in these foods than in citrus fruits. In the North American diet, tomatoes are the number one source of vitamin C, because of their high consumption (about 70 pounds per person per year). Citrus fruits do contain medium amounts of vitamin C. Vitamin C is relatively fragile, and can be destroyed to some extent by over-cooking.

How Much Do We Need? In terms of scurvy prevention, the basic requirement is only 60 mg a day. However, Dr. Linus Pauling has suggested that doses up to 2,300 mg are helpful for prevention of colds.

There is considerable scientific debate on this particular point, but it is well known that doses of 1,000 mg are taken without any harmful side effects in adults.

Tremendous claims are made for mega doses of vitamin C. These include: longer life, increased sexual potency, decreased cancer, and decreased heart disease. Such claims are basically unfounded. Self-medication with vitamins can produce serious and even fatal side effects. It is obvious that self-diagnosis and treatment with vitamins alone for such conditions as cancer is a tragic mistake. No amount of vitamin therapy can replace close consultations with your physician in cases of known disease.

However, there has been enough research to show that vitamins C and E can both be depleted during times of stress. Both have also been suggested as helpful in the prevention of cancer of the colon. Thus it seems reasonable to include modest amounts of each in your daily supplement.

Minerals

Calcium

Functions: Formation of bones, maintenance of cell structures, blood clotting.

Found In: Milk products, soups or stews that have parts of the bone left during cooking, gelatin powders, nuts, legumes, some other vegetables.

How Much Do We Need? 800 mg per day. Please ask your doctor for specific blood tests, or Bone Mineral Density testing if you suspect a calcium deficiency. Just because you don't drink milk does not automatically mean you have a problem.

Potassium

Functions: Muscle metabolism, especially cardiac muscle; nerve tissues.

Found In: Meats, dairy products, bananas, overripe tomatoes.

How Much Do We Need? Supplements not needed unless recommended by doctor; for example, when on diuretic therapy.

Zinc

Functions: Essential for over seventy enzyme systems, including synthesis of key protein for growth, sexual maturation, wound healing, maintenance of skin, hair, nails. Deficiency may be seen in cases of acute and chronic stress (where the increased production of corticoids increases its excretion in urine, and decreases blood levels). Deficiency may also be seen in athletes during periods of high exertion, and some cases of very high fiber diet, which binds zinc and prevents it from being absorbed. Deficiencies of zinc cause a low sperm count, poor appetite, weakening of the white blood cells' ability to fight infection, dermatitis, diarrhea, loss of hair, and poor wound healing.

Zinc samples tested by hair analysis are not accurate, because zinc levels in one part of the body do not necessarily reflect what is going on in another part. The results are usually unreliable. I strongly suggest you do not waste your money on such tests. To approach an accurate figure for zinc status in the body, one needs levels from properly sampled hair (new growth), along with blood serum, red blood cells, and for men, semen.

Lack of zinc can also interfere with vitamin A metabolism. Thus, deficiency can cause night blindness. Loss of the senses of taste and smell are also reported. Zinc deficiencies have now been recognized to occur mainly in children who eat little or no meat and dairy products. Strict vegetarians may also be at risk because of the poor absorbability of zinc from the intestines in the presence of cereal grains.

Zinc deficiency has been shown to cause a poor rate of growth in children. This is quite correctable with a zinc supplement.

Found In: Meat, eggs, seafood-especially oysters (which perhaps gives some substance to the legend that oysters have aphrodisiac powers). Lesser amounts of zinc are also found in milk and dairy products. Excesses of zinc, for example, 150 mg per day, can become your enemy, causing copper deficiency that result in anemia.

One reason for zinc's continued attraction to researchers in the field of infertility is that zinc is found in the greatest concentration in the prostate gland. Some infertility cases associated with low zinc in the semen respond very well to zinc therapy, with many cures reported. In the trade, this benefit is colloquially referred to as "zinc for the dink."

In fact, impotence caused by a severe zinc deficiency can be completely corrected by zinc therapy. However, this type of impotence is quite rare. A full investigation of the condition by your doctor is warranted before taking any home remedies. It is important to remember that high doses of zinc may cause a lower blood copper level. Blood cholesterol and triglycerides may also rise. These are certainly most undesirable side effects of excesses of this mineral. Huge doses, such as 6,000 mg, are usually fatal.

How Much Do We Need? About 20 mg per day.

Copper

Functions: Aids utilization of iron; helps prevent anemia. Copper is useful when taking zinc, to aid in the absorption of this mineral.

Found In: Liver, shellfish, nuts, and beans. Up to half your daily requirements can also come from your water supply system, if you have copper piping. Deficiencies of copper are extremely rare.

How Much Do We Need? About 2 mg per day.

Iron

Functions: The key element of hemoglobin, the compound in your blood cells that carries oxygen to the tissues. Iron is also found in muscle tissue. With iron deficiency, anemia quickly follows. Symptoms include fatigue, pallor, and shortness of breath on exercise.

Found In: Virtually any organism that has a blood supply, such as meats, fowl, fish. Also found in beans and peas, enriched grains, shellfish, dried fruits. Iron absorption can be interfered with by high doses of zinc. Vitamin C can enhance this absorption, although vitamin C reduces the absorption of copper. (As you can see, figuring out the doses that are appropriate for you to take is not a job for the home hobbyist!)

How Much Do We Need? About 20 mg per day for menstruating women, and 10 mg for men. These figures are based on the fact that only about 10 percent of the iron will be absorbed. Pregnant and lactating women need more (consult your doctor). Vegetarians must be particularly careful because vegetable iron is much more difficult to absorb than iron from animal sources.

In cases of continued iron deficiency in spite of

taking adequate supplements, it is important that your doctor find out the reason. A chronic low blood loss from a precancerous polyp in the bowel is one of the most frequent causes. Detected early, such lesions are usually harmless. If not detected at all, they can go on to become fatal. One of the important tests done by your physical examination will be a test for occult, or "hidden," blood in your stools.

It is important not to take iron unless you consult your physician, as it can be an extremely dangerous supplement. Please do not leave a bottle of iron pills within reach of children. I have seen one case of death in a two-year-old child from a handful of tablets of his mother's iron supplement, left on the kitchen table. Even after the child's stomach was pumped out, the amount of iron ingested went on to cause death after only a few days in the hospital.

A Note on Amino Acids

There are twenty-two kinds of ammo acids in the body. Nine of these are essential (in other words, must be consumed in your daily diet). The sequence of ammo acids in chain (or ladder) formation determines the type of protein. All nine of the essential amino acids are equally important. But only three are likely to be deficient in most diets-lysine, tryptophan, and methionine. All can be found in a vegetarian diet, as well as in meat. Meat does not have any "special kinds" of protein. Remember that it is important to have a variety of foods. No one food has sufficient quantities of all the essential amino acids.

For example, beans, peas, and other vegetables tend to be high in lysine and tryptophan, but low in methionine. Rice and other grains are low in lysine and high in methionine. Thus a meal of beans and rice would tend to give you complete protein. However, there is really no need to do such in-depth analysis of your food. Simply have something from each of the four food groups in your diet every day. Protein requirements increase during pregnancy, during the growth years of childhood, in post-burn or surgical cases, and during the weight gain phase in body building.

Appendix C

Calorie and Fiber Chart

When you have read this chart, you will see how easy it is to make food choices that greatly increase your intake of calories, yet leave you feeling unsatisfied. This is the calorie count for a typical fast-food meal:

Hamburger	470
French fries (20)	310
Large cola (12 oz.)	154
Ice cream cone (1 scoop)	174
TOTAL	1,108 calories

As you can see, this meal adds up to most of the calories that the diet-conscious person should eat in one day, let alone in one meal! And, because the meal is very low in fiber as well, all of those calories still leave you feeling hungry a few hours later.

Use this chart to choose foods that are consistent with our program of a diet balanced in all six food categories. (See Chapter 5.) Relatively good "bargain" foods that provide high fiber arc in bold-face type.

Food	*Portion*	*Calories*	*Dietary Fiber (grams)*
Apple	**1 medium**	**70**	**4**
Apple pie	1 piece	300	2.7
Applesauce, sweetened	1/2 cup	120	2.7
unsweetened	1/2 cup	55	2.7
Asparagus	**1/2 cup**	**17**	**1.7**
Avocado	1/2 medium	170	2.8
Banana	**1 medium**	**100**	**3**
Beans, baked, canned	**1/2 cup**	**90**	**8**
black	**1/2 cup**	**95**	**9.7**
green	**1/2 cup**	**10**	**2.1**
kidney	**1/2 cup**	**94**	**9.7**
lima	**1/2 cup**	**118**	**3.7**
navy	**1/2 cup**	**80**	**8**
pinto	**1/2 cup**	**78**	**9.4**
white	**1/2 cup**	**80**	**8**
Bean sprouts (mung)	**1/4 cup**	**7**	**0.8**
Beef, rib roast	4 oz.	320	-
steak	4 oz.	422	-
Blackberries, raw	**1/2 cup**	**27**	**4.4**
Bologna	1 slice	130	-
Brazil nuts	**2 nuts**	**48**	**2.5**
Bread, cracked wheat	2 slices	120	3.6
high bran	**2 slices**	**150**	**7.0**
rye (whole grain)	**2 slices**	**108**	**5.8**
white	2 slices	160	1.9
whole wheat	**2 slices**	**140**	**6.5**
Broccoli	**1/2 cup**	**15**	**4**

Food	*Portion*	*Calories*	*Dietary Fiber (grams)*
Brussels sprouts	**1/2 cup**	**24**	**3**
Bulgur, soaked or cooked	**1 cup**	**160**	**9.6**
Butter	1tsp.	36	-
	1tbsp.	100	-
Cabbage, cooked	**1/2 cup**	**11**	**2.8**
raw	**1/2 cup**	**8**	**1.5**
Cantaloupe	1/4 medium	38	1
Carrots	**1/2 cup**	**20**	**3.4**
Cauliflower	**1/2 cup**	**12**	**1.8**
Celery	**1/2 cup**	**10**	**4**
Cereal, All-Bran	**1/3 cup**	**70**	**9**
Bran Buds	**1/3 cup**	**70**	**8**
Bran Chex	2/3 cup	90	6.4
Bran Flakes	2/3 cup	90	4
Bran Muffin Crisp	2/3 cup	130	4
Cracklin' Oat Bran	1/2 cup	120	4
Fiber One	**1/2 cup**	**60**	**12**
Fruit & Fibre	1/2 cup	90	4
Fruitful Bran	3/4 cup	120	4
Nabisco 100% Bran	**1/2 cup**	**70**	**9**
Natural Bran Flakes	2/3 cup	90	5
Puffed Wheat	1 cup	43	3.3
Quaker Oats (long cooking)	1 ounce	110	0.3
Raisin Bran	3/4 cup	110	4
Total	1 cup	110	2
Wheaties	1 ounce	110	2

Food	*Portion*	*Calories*	*Dietary Fiber (grams)*
Cheese, Cheddar, Swiss, or Parmesan, grated	1 tbsp.	28	-
Cottage	1/2 cup	48	-
Cherries, sweet, raw	10	38	1.2
canned in light syrup	1/2 cup	55	1
Chestnuts, roasted	**2 large**	**29**	**1.9**
Chicken, dark meat, no skin	4 oz.	112	- .
dark meat with skin, fried	4 oz.	300	-
White meat, no skin	4 oz.	104	-
white meat, with skin, fried	4 oz.	262	-
Chickpeas	**1/2 cup**	**86**	**6**
Coconut, dried, sweetened	1 tbsp.	46	3.4
unsweetened	1 tbsp.	22	3.4
Cookies, chocolate chip	2 large	240	-
Fibermed ® high fiber cookies	**2**	**120**	**10**
Corn, sweet, on cob	**1 medium**	**70**	**5**
kernels, canned	**1/2 cup**	**64**	**5**
Cornbread	**2 1/2-in. sq.**	**93**	**3.4**
Crackers, graham	2	54	1.4
Ry-Krisp	2	42	1.5
soda (saltine)	2	26	0.2
Triscuit	**2**	**50**	**2**
Wheat Thins	**6**	**58**	**2.2**
Cucumber, raw, unpeeled	10 slices	12	0.7
Dates	**2**	**39**	**1.2**

Food	*Portion*	*Calories*	*Dietary Fiber (grams)*
Eggplant	**1/2 cup**	**17**	**1.5**
Egg, boiled	1	80	-
fried (1 tsp. fat)	1	108	-
Figs, dried	**3**	**120**	**10.5**
fresh	**1**	**30**	**2**
Fish, cod	4 oz.	86	-
flounder	4 oz.	86	-
halibut	4 oz.	100	-
salmon	4 oz.	240	-
sardines, canned	4 oz.	160	-
sole	4 oz.	86	-
tuna (water pack)	1/4 cup	50	-
Grapefruit	1/2 medium	30	0.8
Grapes, green	20	75	1
red or black	20	65	1
Gravy, brown, meat	2 tbsp.	82	-
Greens, cooked (collard, beet, chard, kale)	**1/2 cup**	**20**	**4**
Ham, lean	2 slices	75	-
Hamburger, meat only	4 oz.	180	-
with bun		400	1.9
Hot dog, beef, meat only	1	125	-
with bun	1	262	1.9
Honeydew melon	1/4 medium	42	1.5
Lamb, lean	4oz.	200	-
Lentils, brown, cooked	**1/2 cup**	**108**	**4.1**
red, cooked	**1/2 cup**	**96**	**3.2**

Food	*Portion*	*Calories*	*Dietary Fiber (grams)*
Lettuce, shredded	**1 cup**	**5**	**0.8**
Macaroni and cheese, baked	1 cup	497	2.0
Macaroni, whole wheat	**1 cup**	**200**	**5.7**
Margarine	1 tbsp.	100	-
Milk buttermilk	1 cup	80	-
homogenized	1 cup	161	-
skim	1 cup	84	-
2%	1 cup	130	-
Milk Products cream, whipping	1 cup	869	-
cream, table	1 cup	493	-
ice cream	1 scoop	174	-
ice milk	1 scoop	137	-
sour cream	1 cup	328	-
yogurt (low fat)	1 cup	128	-
Muffins, bran, no raisins or dates	**1**	**78**	**2.3**
English, whole wheat	**1**	**125**	**3.7**
homemade, bran, wholewheat	**1**	**68**	**2.3**
Mushrooms, raw	**4**	**4**	**1.4**
sautéed	4	45	1.4
Noodles, egg	**1/2 cup**	**98**	**3.0**
whole wheat egg	**1 cup**	**200**	**5.7**
Olives, green or black	6	42	1.2
Onions, cooked	**1/2 cup**	**22**	**1.5**
green	**1/2 cup**	**22**	**1.6**
Orange	**1**	**70**	**2.4**

Food	Portion	Calories	Dietary Fiber (grams)
Peach, canned in syrup	2 halves	70	1.4
raw	**1**	**38**	**2.3**
Peanut butter	1 tbsp.	86	1.1
Peanuts, dry roasted	**10**	**100**	**2.2**
Peas, black-eyed	**1/2 cup**	**74**	**8**
green	**1/2 cup**	**60**	**9.1**
split	**1/2 cup**	**63**	**6.7**
peas and carrots, frozen	**5 oz.**	**40**	**6.2**
Pear, raw	**1 medium**	**70**	**2.4**
Pepper, green	**2 tbsp.**	**4**	**0.3**
Pineapple, canned	1/2 cup	74	0.8
fresh	1/2 cup	41	0.8
Plums	**2**	**38**	**2**
Popcorn (no oil or butter added)	**1 cup**	**20**	**1**
Pork, bacon	3 slices	120	-
boneless, lean	4 oz.	242	-
Potatoes, baked in skin	**1 medium**	**91**	**5**
boiled in skin	**1 medium**	**80**	**3.5**
French fried	10 pieces	155	3
mashed	**1/2 cup**	**85**	**3**
sweet, baked or boiled	**1 small**	**146**	**4**
Prunes	3	122	1.9
Raisins, seedless	1 tbsp.	29	1
Raspberries	**1/2 cup**	**20**	**4.6**
Rhubarb, cooked with sugar	1/2 cup	169	2.9

Food	*Portion*	*Calories*	*Dietary Fiber (grams)*
Rice, brown	**1/2 cup**	**83**	**5.5**
instant	1/2 cup	79	0.7
white	1/2 cup	79	2.1
Rutabaga (yellow turnip)	**1/2 cup**	**40**	**3.2**
Salad oil	1 tbsp.	100	-
Salami	1 slice	130	-
Sauerkraut (canned)	**2/3 cup**	**15**	**3.1**
Seafood			
Clams, canned	1/2 cup	52	-
crabmeat	1/2 cup	84	-
scallops	1/2 cup	160	-
shrimp	1/2 cup	91	-
Soft drinks			
Club soda	6 oz.	0	-
Cola	6 oz.	72	-
Orange	6 oz.	82	-
Root beer	6 oz.	82	-
7-Up	6 oz.	72	-
Tonic water	6 oz.	54	-
Spaghetti, whole wheat	**1 cup**	**200**	**5.6**
Spinach, raw	**1 cup**	**8**	**3.5**
cooked	**1/2 cup**	**26**	**7**
Squash, summer	**1/2 cup**	**8**	**2**
winter	**1/2 cup**	**50**	**3.5**
zucchini	**1/2 cup**	**7**	**3**
Strawberries, raw, no sugar	**1 cup**	**45**	**3**

Food	*Portion*	*Calories*	*Dietary Fiber (grams)*
Tomato, catsup	1 tbsp.	18	0.2
sauce	1/2 cup	20	0.5
Tomatoes, canned	1/2 cup	21	1
raw	**1 small**	**22**	**1.4**
Tortillas	2 6-inch	140	4
Turkey, roasted	1 slice	80	-
Walnuts, chopped	1 tbsp.	49	1.1
Watermelon	**1 slice**	**68**	**2.8**
Yams, cooked or baked in skin	**1 medium**	**156**	**6.8**

Get out your calculators!

SECOND WEEK:	TOTAL CALORIES CONSUMED (SEE FIGURE 7.2 OR APPENDIX C)		TOTAL CALORIES BURNED OFF (SEE FIGURE 7.1)	
Day 1		cal.		cal.
Day 2		cal.		cal.
Day 3		cal.		cal.
Day 4		cal.		cal.
Day 5		cal.		cal.
Day 6		cal.		cal.
Day 7		cal.		cal.
Sub-total		cal.	Sub-total	cal.
÷7=		Cal. intake per day	÷7=	Cal. burn-off per day

CALORIE INTAKE	Average calories consumed per day	-	Average calories burned off per day	=	Average net calories intake per day
WEIGHT CHANGE	Starting weight on Day 1	-	Weight after first week	=	Weight change in one week

Get out your calculators!

THIRD WEEK:	TOTAL CALORIES CONSUMED (SEE FIGURE 7.2 OR APPENDIX C)		TOTAL CALORIES BURNED OFF (SEE FIGURE 7.1)	
Day 1		cal.		cal.
Day 2		cal.		cal.
Day 3		cal.		cal.
Day 4		cal.		cal.
Day 5		cal.		cal.
Day 6		cal.		cal.
Day 7		cal.		cal.
Sub-total		cal.	Sub-total	cal.
÷7=		Cal. intake per day	÷7=	Cal. burn-off per day

CALORIE INTAKE	Average calories consumed per day	-	Average calories burned off per day	=	Average net calories intake per day
WEIGHT CHANGE	Starting weight on Day 1	-	Weight after first week	=	Weight change in one week

Get out your calculators!

FOURTH WEEK:	TOTAL CALORIES CONSUMED (SEE FIGURE 7.2 OR APPENDIX C)		TOTAL CALORIES BURNED OFF (SEE FIGURE 7.1)	
Day 1		cal.		cal.
Day 2		cal.		cal.
Day 3		cal.		cal.
Day 4		cal.		cal.
Day 5		cal.		cal.
Day 6		cal.		cal.
Day 7		cal.		cal.
Sub-total		cal.	Sub-total	cal.
÷7=		Cal. intake per day	÷7=	Cal. burn-off per day

CALORIE INTAKE	Average calories consumed per day	–	Average calories burned off per day	=	Average net calories intake per day
WEIGHT CHANGE	Starting weight on Day 1	–	Weight after first week	=	Weight change in one week

Get out your calculators!

FIFTH WEEK:	TOTAL CALORIES CONSUMED (SEE FIGURE 7.2 OR APPENDIX C)		TOTAL CALORIES BURNED OFF (SEE FIGURE 7.1)	
Day 1		cal.		cal.
Day 2		cal.		cal.
Day 3		cal.		cal.
Day 4		cal.		cal.
Day 5		cal.		cal.
Day 6		cal.		cal.
Day 7		cal.		cal.
	Sub-total	cal.	Sub-total	cal.
	÷7=	Cal. intake per day	÷7=	Cal. burn-off per day

CALORIE INTAKE	Average calories consumed per day	–	Average calories burned off per day	= Average net calories intake per day
WEIGHT CHANGE	Starting weight on Day 1	–	Weight after first week	= Weight change in one week

Appendix D

Body Mass Index Table

Body mass index (BMI) is a measure of body fat based on height and weight that applies to both **adult** men and women.

To use the table, find the appropriate height in the left-hand column labeled Height. Move across to a given weight (in pounds). The number at the top of the column is the BMI at that height and weight. Pounds have been rounded off.

BMI categories:

- Underweight = <18.5
- Normal weight = 18.5-24.9
- Overweight = 25-29.9
- Obesity = BMI of 30 or greater

PLEASE note that this is only a rough guide. Most professional athletes will fail this test, showing up as overweight or obese, when they simply have large muscles and very little fat. The ultimate test of obesity requires only two things: a full length mirror, and your bathing suit. One look at your reflection and you will know! If you have the time to work out your muscles and can maintain a trim torso, then the BMI is not relevant. If you look like an avocado with four tooth-picks stuck in it, then you will need to lose weight, even if your BMI rating is "normal". Please use the following chart as a guide, to understand the frame of reference that insurance companies use.

BMI	19	20	21	22	23	24	25	26
Height (inches)	BODY WEIGHT (POUNDS)							
58	91	96	100	105	110	115	119	124
59	94	99	104	109	114	119	124	128
60	97	102	107	112	118	123	128	133
61	100	106	111	116	122	127	132	137
62	104	109	115	120	126	131	136	142
63	107	113	118	124	130	135	141	146
64	110	116	122	128	134	140	145	151
65	114	120	126	132	138	144	150	156
66	118	124	130	136	142	148	155	161
67	121	127	134	140	146	153	159	166
68	125	131	138	144	151	158	164	171
69	128	135	142	149	155	162	169	176
70	132	139	146	153	160	167	174	181
71	136	143	150	157	165	172	179	186
72	140	147	154	162	169	177	184	191
73	144	151	159	166	174	182	189	197
74	148	155	163	171	179	186	194	202
75	152	160	168	176	184	192	200	208
76	156	164	172	180	189	197	205	213

27	28	29	30	31	32	33	34	35
BODY WEIGHT (POUNDS)								
129	134	138	143	148	153	158	162	167
133	138	143	148	153	158	163	168	173
138	143	148	153	158	163	168	174	179
143	148	153	158	164	169	174	180	185
147	153	158	164	169	175	180	186	191
152	158	163	169	175	180	186	191	197
157	163	169	174	180	186	192	197	204
162	168	174	180	186	192	198	204	210
167	173	179	186	192	198	204	210	216
172	178	185	191	198	204	211	217	223
177	184	190	197	203	210	216	223	230
182	189	196	203	209	216	223	230	236
188	195	202	209	216	222	229	236	243
193	200	208	215	222	229	236	243	250
199	206	213	221	228	235	242	250	258
204	212	219	227	235	242	250	257	265
210	218	225	233	241	249	256	264	272
216	224	232	240	248	256	264	272	279
221	230	238	246	254	263	271	279	287

Read the speed.

Reading the "tachometer" of your body during exercise is a matter of life and death to your heart. If you have already seen your doctor for a stress EKG, you will likely already know your maximum safe heart rate during exercise; but for those who have not had such tests, here is a good working approximation. First start with the number 220. Next, subtract your age to see your maximum ***possible*** heart rate. Multiply this number by .75. This gives your maximum ***SAFE*** heart rate during exercise. Take note of this number, and remember it forever.

Now, practice feeling your pulse at the wrist, as shown below. Remember, the key is to press firmly with your middle finger against the edge of the bone as shown, and press lightly with the index finger. Now measure your pulse (while sitting) for a full 60 seconds, and record it here: ____. Now record it for a minute while standing: ____. Next, walk on the spot for three minutes by the clock, the more vigorously the better. Now record your 60 second pulse rate immediately after exercise: ____.

As you see, it is easier to record your pulse when resting, and it becomes easier to lose count during a full minute of exercise. If you have no trouble counting your pulse, the full minute count is the most accurate. If you tend to lose track of the count, measure off six seconds on your watch, and count the pulse: ____. Now add a zero to find your rate per minute: ____. As you will likely find, this last number might be a little off your sixty second count, but it will still give you a sense of when to call for time out. The most important thing to remember is check your pulse at all times when it could be too high. This includes not only sporting activities, but walks on hot days, shoveling snow, pushing a car out of a ditch, sitting in a whirlpool or sauna, climbing long flights of stairs, or severe emotional upset (such as anger, rage, etc.). (To see my video demonstration of checking your pulse, please go to www.stressipedia.com, and enter "pulse" in the search box.)

In Pain? Keep Up The Pressure

Practice your acupressure. As seen below, apply the crease of your right thumb to the skin fold between the base of the left thumb and index finger. Roll the right thumb down into the meaty part of the muscle, and oppose it with the right index finger. Now relax the left hand and firmly squeeze the muscles between the right index finger and thumb. Do this for at least sixty seconds then stop. You may already feel a greater sense of pain relief (if you started this exercise with any aches), and will likely feel a greater sense of control over your body. There are no side effects, and you can do this while waiting your turn to speak, or any time you feel a headache coming on.

If you can find a volunteer at hand, either at home or at work, try the thumb-tip shoulder massage as shown below.

First seat your volunteer in front of you, facing away from you. Now find the acupressure point in question, halfway from the bony prominence at the base of the neck to the bony corner of the shoulder (see below). Now gently press with the thumb deep into the muscle, increasing the pressure until your thumbnail is white. Be firm, but sensitive to the underlying muscle tension. Think of a four-story building, and take the elevator down one floor at a time. After about ten seconds, your thumbs will feel the underlying shoulder muscles ease up. Push the thumbs down to the "third" floor, again waiting ten seconds or so until the muscles ease. Again down to the second and first "floors" respectively. Do NOT go suddenly from the fourth floor to the basement, or you will only hurt the patient, and cause the muscles to seize up. Once you take the pressure off, the shoulder should feel instantly better, and you may have found a friend for life. However, fair is fair, and it is now time for you and your volunteer to change places.

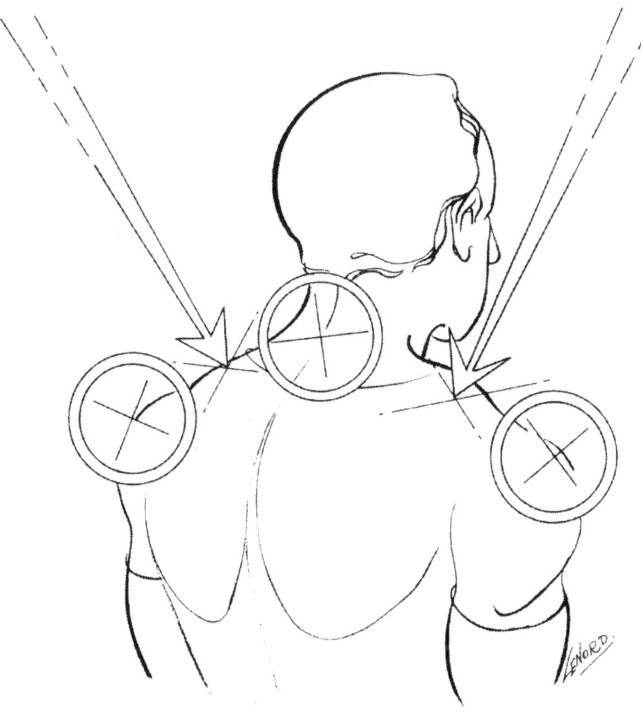

Bibliography and Recommended Reading

The idea of a bibliography is to refer the reader to other books on related topics. But in the age of the internet, the quickest way to search is on line.

The first place I send my patients (and you, the reader) is to our site: www.stressipedia.com. There you will find my regular blogs and other materials I have selected in response to practical questions from my patients. You can drill down to recommended links, including lists, animations, or vids for clarification. That way you can use your cell phone from the grocery aisle or gym to refresh your memory!

For most other info, just use www.google.com, or www.wikipedia.com. But please do not diagnose your own illnesses from these sources, or you will only add to your stress levels!

About the Author

Peter G. Hanson, M.D.

Dr. Peter Hanson has a unique background, one that gives him outstanding qualifications on the subject of stress.

Born in Vancouver, British Columbia, Canada, he developed qualities of public speaking at an early stage. By the age of 14, he was working in live television, performing regular comedy monologues to fill in the gap between the afternoon movie and the daily news.

But despite his comedic talents, Dr. Hanson had serious career objectives. At the age of 24 he graduated from the University of Toronto Medical School. A year later, he was appointed team doctor for the Toronto Argonauts Football club, becoming the youngest team doctor in professional sports. In this position, he learned a great deal of the effects of stress on human performance.

Further establishing his medical credentials, Dr. Hanson worked as an Emergency Room physician in a busy suburban Toronto hospital for three years. His office practice in family medicine grew to over 4,000 active patients from newborns to centenarians. He has delivered over 1,000 babies, and made over 5,000 house calls. This gave him a truly unique window on stress and its effect on health from cradle to grave.

When *The Joy of Stress* was released in 1985, it broke all records for a self-published book at the time. The book rose to number one in the country, and stayed on the national best-sellers list for a then-record 69 weeks. Since then, it has been published in over a dozen languages, most recently Chinese and Arabic, and has sold well over a million copies.

Dr. Hanson has used his aptitudes for entertainment well, doing key-note speeches to hundreds of live audiences, from Fortune 500 corporations to business associations, as well as the general public. In promoting his books around the world, he has appeared on hundreds of live television shows in Europe, the US, Canada, and Australia, and New Zealand. He has had a nationally syndicated radio feature that ran daily in Canada for over five years.

Dr. Hanson also practiced sports medicine in Denver, Colorado, using medical acupuncture. His first patient here was the Bronco's football star John Elway, whose throwing arm he treated. He continued to treat professional, Olympic, and college athletes from all over the country as well as local weekend warriors of all ages. He has also served as one of the team medical consultants for the Colorado Avalanche and the Los Angeles Kings of the NHL.

Dr. Hanson has faced stress, literally, by addressing the effects of stress on our faces. Teaming up with Suzanne Somers and Rodger Mohme, one of Apple's leading engineers, he has developed the FaceMaster, a home unit that tones the underlying muscles of the face. He and Suzanne have often appeared on television, marketing this amazing machine. (available at www.facemaster.com)

Mohme and Hanson then joined creative forces to co-found www.stressipedia.com. This was inspired by comments from Dr. Hanson's current patients, who find alarming and catastrophic consequences of almost any symptom when they search on line. By answering questions from his real patients in family and sports medicine, Hanson can take the stress out of the information trail. Far better than giving each patient a "core dump" of verbal lists, stressipedia.com allows the information to be called up on their cell phones in the grocery store or at the gym.

Dr. Hanson continues to practice family medicine and sports medicine in downtown Toronto. He also continues to perform in front of live audiences as a professional speaker. He can be reached at his web site: www.stressipedia.com.

Made in the USA
San Bernardino, CA
26 February 2017